'David Leser has for years been one of Australia's finest long-form journalists, and here he takes on one of the most important subjects of our time. What begins as an examination of the global #MeToo movement turns into a poignant, sometimes personal and often horrifying deep dive into past and present masculinity and "the mess of human relations" that's left in its wake. In grappling with these monumental themes, Leser is at one point advised by writer Helen Garner to "just humbly approach the mountain and go up it". *Women, Men & the Whole Damn Thing* does reach a summit in this ever-fluid, ongoing debate, and the view it offers forces you to rethink almost everything you thought you knew about female/male relationships, and plants a flag of hope for the future.'

MATTHEW CONDON, author of *Three Crooked Kings*

'Brilliantly argued, fiercely lucid, there won't be a more vital book this decade. Nor one to be more widely read, argued with, felt— and *comprehended*. Leser captures our need to wake up finally to the most ancient harming of all: men's conditioned and often dangerously aggressive attitudes towards women—and themselves. Pushing boundaries or leaping them, *Women, Men & the Whole Damn Thing* illuminates changes every bit as urgent as rescuing the planet—which is utterly interdependent with them.

STEPHANIE DOWRICK, author of *Intimacy and Solitude* and *Seeking the Sacred*

'David isn't an ideologue finding evidence to support a conclusion he's already arrived at. As ever he's a fearless searcher after the truth in a complex situation. He's horrified as he unearths the grim statistics of male violence and mistreatment of women, but at the same time concerned that #MeToo can tip over into lynch mob mentality, condemning lesser crimes with the same ferocity as greater ones. But his final verdict is unequivocal. #MeToo is a necessary clarion call that male/female relationships need urgent restructuring, not just for the good of women, but to benefit us all.'

DAVID WILLIAMSON, playwright

'As we agonise over the breadth and complexity of the volcanic eruption captured by the #MeToo movement, David Leser has given us a gift—the gift of deeply considered thinking. This book is a triumph of storytelling, painstaking research, personal vulnerability and nuance. I did not really believe anyone could do justice to the size and scope of this topic, and David has proved me mightily wrong. As I pored over every page I variously felt enraged, sorrowful, entertained, respectful and, at the last, hopeful.'

AUDETTE EXEL, Founder of the Adara Group, former Telstra NSW Business Woman of the Year and Australian Philanthropist of the Year.

'Curiosity, courage and candour are David Leser's great strengths as a journalist. Here, he sets out to understand the explosion of female fury that is the #MeToo movement and ends up asking himself some tough questions. A wistful one too: should he have asked the beautiful stranger on the French train to have a drink with him?'

JANE CADZOW, journalist

Women, Men, AND THE WHOLE + DAMN THING

FEMINISM, MISOGYNY, AND WHERE WE GO FROM HERE

DAVID LESER

PEGASUS BOOKS

NEW YORK LONDON

WOMEN, MEN, AND THE WHOLE DAMN THING

Pegasus Books, Ltd.
148 West 37th Street, 13th Floor
New York, NY 10018

First Pegasus Books cloth edition January 2021

Library of Congress Cataloging-in-Publication Data is available.

ISBN: 978-1-64313-628-8

10 9 8 7 6 5 4 3 2 1

Printed in the United States of America
Distributed by Simon & Schuster
www.pegasusbooks.com

Contents

Preface

I am a straight, white, middle-class male who has breathed the untroubled air of privilege all my life.

This, some will argue—have already argued—makes me spectacularly ill-equipped for the task that lies ahead, which is nothing less than trying to understand the eruptions of female anger and distress that have shaken the world since October 2017, following the *New York Times'* and the *New Yorker* magazine's shocking revelations of alleged sexual abuse by movie mogul Harvey Weinstein.

Certainly, my own daughter Hannah begged me not to wade into this debate when the opportunity first presented itself in the form of a magazine article a few weeks after the Weinstein scandal had blazed across America. It was late 2017 and Katrina Strickland, the new editor of *Good Weekend* magazine, called to see if I was interested in writing again for the publication. I was, I said, depending on the story.

When we met a few days later to discuss ideas, I kept returning to the news reports filled with the uproar and the seeding of the new social protest movement known as #MeToo.

'There's only one story I'd really be interested in doing at the moment,' I said, 'And this is it.'

Like almost everyone I knew, I was gripped by what had been unfolding in America. Every day a new name, another industry, another once-darkened corridor of power held up to the blinding light of disgrace.

Names had been falling everywhere, human skyscrapers of celebrity crashing to the earth, and it felt like a 9/11 moment: we knew the world had changed irrevocably—or was in the process of changing irrevocably; we just couldn't grasp quite how, or to what extent.

I actually had no idea how I would approach the story, or, in fact, whether I should. Hannah felt—understandably, I can see in retrospect—that I didn't truly appreciate what was unfolding, that I had no real moral imagination for the depth of female fury breaking out across the world. That wasn't to say she saw me as a male reactionary, only that she saw me for what I was, and am: a man blessed by all the favours a good life confers.

'Dad, we don't want to hear from you right now,' she said as we sat on my balcony overlooking the palm-fringed rooftops of Sydney. 'Not unless you're being totally supportive.'

It was our second conversation on the subject in two weeks. The first had roused her indignation. I'd said something along the lines of: 'I worry about where this is heading, what's it going to do for male–female relationships? How are men and women going to relate now in the workplace? What will be the new rules for courtship? What if men are falsely accused?'

For Hannah, a 24-year-old photographer and student of international relations possessed of a fierce commitment to gender equality, these were not the most pressing issues. Women were finally speaking out en masse—roaring, in fact—and men just needed to stop and listen.

'This is not about you,' she told me. 'And it's not about how the nuances will affect men. This is about women, millions of us, deciding to voice what's happened to us and to say enough is enough.'

'But it's not a black-and-white issue,' I countered. 'This is about the mess of human relations and how they're played out in real-life situations. Not all men are like this.' And, of course, wasn't that just the most predictable salvo to fire from the male trenches?

'Look, I know not all men are like that,' she retorted. 'And I know that you love exploring the grey areas of life. I'm also fascinated with the grey areas. But right now it's time for men to shut up and listen to us. And not just listen to us—defend us, stand behind us and stand beside us.'

Then, with the unflinching candour that is one of the most precious gifts in my life, she described her first sexual experiences and explained how it was only now, in the wake of the #MeToo movement, that she had come to see the extent to which she'd been mistreated, and to understand how these formative moments had, in turn, come to inform her early troubled relationships with men.

Our conversation that day did much to inspire this book. It was important to me to show my daughter there were men prepared to listen and learn as women around the world revealed their anger and heartache.

My intention in writing this book, however, was never, and is not, to speak for women about their mistreatment, or to claim to understand—as women understand only too well—how male contempt expresses itself across all walks of life. It is, rather, an attempt to investigate as a writer and a man how murderous male hatred and disrespect rages across the world against billions of women and girls, of all colours, creeds, classes and ages.

How to find the right words to frame this horror? How to understand why men do what they do to women with their guns, their hands, their cocks, their taunts, their hate-filled diatribes, their threats and acts of violence? How to comprehend this malign force that seems to seep from the male psyche and infect us all? Not from all men, of course—and does that need to be said? But from enough men, surely, to compel all men to want to look at the nature of men.

That is the central hope, the *appeal*, embedded in this book: that other men might join me in this investigation and ruthless self-interrogation—and, in doing so, become part of the change that is so urgently required.

Introduction

Not everything that is faced can be changed; but nothing can be changed until it is faced.

JAMES BALDWIN, *NEW YORK TIMES BOOK REVIEW*

A few years ago, my social entrepreneur friend Jeremy Meltzer delivered a TED talk in Melbourne titled 'Where is Men's Roar?'.

He began by asking his audience to raise their hands if they had a sister. 'Now leave your hand up and raise the other hand if you also have a daughter. Great, keep both of them up, and if you have a mum raise your knee.' The audience was a sea of upstretched hands and knees.

Meltzer then went on to cite United Nations statistics on the global pandemic of violence against women, describing it as 'the most systematic and pervasive human rights abuse in the world'.

'What the hell is going on?' he asked. 'Any one of these women could be our sister, mother or daughter. So where are the men? Where is men's roar? Not for the football, but for what really matters? [Because] this is the greatest moral challenge of our times.'

Meltzer was calling on men to become accountable, to examine what it was in our conditioning that we were blind to, or had normalised, or both. Nothing short of a 'revolution in the masculine', he said, was going to return us to a healthy masculinity.

That talk—in both its title and substance—scorched itself into my brain, and this was five years before the moral alarm bells of #MeToo began sounding across the world, first in Hollywood with the forensic takedown of Harvey Weinstein, then with an oh-God-not-you-too cast of stellar names drawn from across American arts and entertainment, politics, business and sports.

When millions of women worldwide began to share stories of mistreatment via the Twitter hashtag #MeToo, in what was being described as a 'watershed', a 'tipping point,' a 'karmic earthquake', I felt the tremors too. And not just because of the stories tumbling forth—they were bad enough—but because of the realisation of how much I didn't know that I now felt an urgent need to explore, first of all in the pages of *Good Weekend*. I wanted to survey the universal crimes against women, and the spectrum of abuse to which they were all too often subject. Stories of violence and coercion. Stories of rape, mutilation and silencing. Stories from the workplace: of gender pay gaps and institutionalised enabling, where confidentiality clauses, both in employment contracts and legal settlements, were designed to shut women up. Stories of men refusing to take no for an answer; of women being pressured into having sex and/or being made to feel guilty if they didn't comply. Stories of horrifying emotional and psychological violence, where men used their children as weapons of punishment. Stories of shame and sadness and crippling loss of confidence and ambition, of the light inside precious human hearts being extinguished.

I wanted to investigate the historical causes of this rampant aggression, but also the effects that this violence had had on men themselves—the once sweet innocent boys who had become severed from their emotions in order to conform to the unforgiving world of male teenage culture. Men who had become so removed from their natural compassion that they were left isolated and vulnerable, and all too often prone to violent and abusive behaviour.

In my original article, I posed far more questions than I had answers to; no answer seemed up to the assignment of addressing the enormity of this subject. How, in the midst of this global bonfire of harassment and abuse allegations, were we supposed to also examine the mechanisms—and the insistent call—of human desire, and the way this had always informed our behaviour? How did evolutionary psychology play into the differences between men and women, if at all? To what extent did the masculine libido, and its various pathologies, drive our culture, politics and economy?

When did a clumsy move cross over into a form of harassment? What actually constituted harassment? Was it a wolf-whistle, a fondle, a lewd comment? What about a pass at a colleague after work—was that just poor training, or bad intentions, or was this how couples often came together, through some combination of risk-taking and bumbling awkwardness?

And when the sun went down, how did we corral our nocturnal sexual appetites, our private kinks and chinks? And where the hell did these kinks and chinks come from anyway? (Probably from that border country where the forbidden and erotic meet.)

Would we be advised to follow Sweden's recent proposed changes to sexual assault laws, so that victims only needed to prove an explicit consent had not been granted in order to prosecute? Did it matter if, sometimes, the guiltless went down, because in any war there would always be 'collateral' damage? What happened when a touch on the arm of a colleague at work, or a friendly 'x' on the end of a text message, was interpreted differently by each party?

How did men find the courage to challenge other men—sometimes our close friends—when conversations crossed the line? Where exactly was that line, given that so often men's talk was shrouded in humour?

How were we supposed to view some of our favourite creative works? Did middle-aged people like me need to reassess the pleasure we'd once derived from, say, Woody Allen and Roman Polanski films and Philip Roth novels, because we could see with fresh eyes their misogynistic tendencies, youthful obsessions or, as the case may be, their perversions?

Then there was the not insignificant matter of pornography. How did we hold back the tide of teenage boys and their use of smartphones and unlimited access to the objectification of women? How did we challenge teenage boys not to think of themselves as 'heroes', 'legends' and 'top dogs' when they'd had numerous sexual partners, while girls doing the same thing were called 'sluts', 'skanks', 'hos', 'whores' and 'bitches'?

And it was not just boys and men. How did we stop young women measuring their worth solely through male eyes? How did we stop mothers from internalising—and thereby perpetuating—the patriarchy in the way they raised and talked to their sons and daughters? Or the way they buried themselves in work, exiling themselves from their families, just as absentee fathers had done for so long? Or the way they—according to some women I know—undermined other women at work; or, more subtly, the way they bolstered men's fragile egos, because they knew only too well what could happen if a man collapsed into shame—he could hurt himself or someone else.

Many of these questions I posed, but could not answer, in my original article, 'Women, men and the whole damn thing', but in the days and weeks following publication on 10 February 2018, I received a response unlike anything I'd ever experienced in nearly 40 years of journalism: hundreds of emails, texts, tweets, Facebook comments, phone calls, letters, all taking up various aspects of the story.

I had messages from ex-police officers, school principals, teachers, international students, Gestalt therapists, men's networks, men's rights activists, women's refuges, mothers of teenage boys, fathers of teenage boys, musicians, writers, journalists, PhD researchers, academics, feminist academics, feminist philosophers, angry spurned wives, angry spurned husbands, mental health workers and a woman who merely wanted me to know she'd emailed my story to Donald Trump. One correspondent wanted to tell me about the *fa'afafine*, the thousands of boys raised as girls on Samoa who, rather than being labelled homosexuals, transgender or transvestites, were considered a 'third gender' in this tolerant society.

The Press Council of Australia received—and ultimately rejected—a complaint that I'd used foul language 'at least three times' in my article. I'd spelt out the word 'cunt' and pondered how it was that the most offensive word in the English language was a reference to the most sacred part of a woman's body.

'Listen, mate,' a new lesbian acquaintance told me at a party when I'd shared these musings with her, 'I've been with hundreds of cunts in my life and none of them was sacred.'

Of all the letters I received, however, the one that truly unseated me—and probably contributed most to the belief that I should try to write this book—was from a woman whose anguished, wild defiance leapt across my screen late one afternoon from somewhere in Australia.

They were the words of a woman's quiet desperation and will probably be all too familiar to many women. I am grateful for her permission to reprint part of it here, albeit with her husband's name changed to protect both their identities:

I woke up this morning on the couch cause my husband verbally abused me again last night and the idea of sharing a bed with that pig makes me physically sick.

I woke up feeling slightly more powerful cause I got to choose where I slept.

It was my SILENT protest. 'See, Frank, you can't control every part of my life. I'm not gonna sleep next to you tonight. I'm on the couch.'

I can't say out loud that his behaviour is abusive and disgusting. He hurts me more . . .

I have never sent back food.

I have never called the manager to complain.

I have never rung a radio talkback.

I have never sent a letter to my local politician.

I've never said NO.

I've never said STOP.

I've never said, 'Leave me alone.'

I've never told my husband: ENOUGH.

I HAVE NEVER SAID I DESERVE BETTER.

I always thought it was my fault.

I was too fat.

I was too ugly.

Too slow.

Too lazy.

Too dumb.

Not strong enough.

Not pretty enough.

Not good enough.

But then. This morning on the couch . . . I read your article.

It explained.

I understood.

I realised.

It's not me.

#

Perhaps you remember that sun-kissed day in September 1997 when practically all of Britain seemed to weep for the loss of Diana, a sea of flowers—some 60 million blooms in all—stretching across parts of London in floral tribute to their adored princess.

British psychotherapist Adam Phillips observed later that this was no overreaction from a normally stoic citizenry; it was more a recognition of 'how much grief people were [already] bearing', how much they had already suffered in their lives.

We appear to be living through such a moment now—one that is more universal in its reach. Every day, every hour, there is another incident, remembered episode, confounding new dimension to this epic drama of the sexes. Surrounded as I am by more than 80 books (yes, I've counted) on history, religion, politics, psychology and gender relations, buckling under the relentless influx of emails, Facebook alerts and tweets, wading through interviews, filtering, sifting, sorting one shocking experience from another, the noise has become deafening and the sorrow, at times, difficult to bear.

Women have always carried this sorrow, of course. They've been living inside their own bodies all their lives. But now it's my turn—not to experience anything remotely like this, but to imagine what it might be like to live in this world without protective coating. As instructed by my wise-beyond-years daughter, I'm listening to this collective rage and sadness, and I'm wondering how on earth we got to this place . . . or have we always been here? Why it is that so many men inflict this hurt on others and themselves? What causes the threads of empathy to break, if the empathy was ever there in the first place? And what part might I play in all this? Because, surely, it's not enough to say, as so many men are quick to do, that they share nothing in common with abusive men, that they would never hurt or harass a woman. What is it that we've all absorbed through our conditioning, and how do our behaviour patterns reinforce the worst views of women?

As Jack Holland wrote in *Misogyny: The World's Oldest Prejudice*, 'What we call history is merely the tale that patriarchy wants to tell, and misogyny its ideology, a system of beliefs and ideas, the aim of which is to explain the domination of men over women.'

#

It's April 2018. A news alert appears on my laptop screen, listing the charges against the six men accused of raping, mutilating and killing an eight-year-old girl in the Indian state of Jammu and Kashmir. That, in turn, leads me to a story about women and girls taking up self-defence classes in Delhi, which then sends me into the uproar in Ireland over the acquittal of two rugby players accused of rape, then on to updates on the Stockholm Forum on Gender Equality, a long article about the legacy of childhood trauma from rape, and a report on the misogynistic tendencies of Alek Minassian, whose deadly rampage in Toronto—he deliberately drove a rental van onto a busy footpath—left ten people dead and another fourteen injured. The majority of the victims were women.

'The incel rebellion has begun,' Minassian posted on Facebook, using the term coined for 'involuntary celibates'—those men furious about the lack of sex 'granted' to them, and homicidal in their loathing of women because of it.

I need some fresh air after reading this, so I check my mailbox and find a letter bristling with indignation over the injustice and unfairness of the #MeToo movement. It's from a man representing a group called Addressing Discrimination Against Men (ADAM) and he wants me to know how men such as himself are often stitched up by scheming women.

'[I] have had strange women play footsies, press themselves against me, sit on my lap, flash their breasts, spread their legs deliberately in my direction, and walk about naked or scantily clad (when I was a salesman),' he writes. He then details how his fellow ADAM members have been similarly traumatised by feminine manipulations.

'I did not think,' he says, 'that there were any new depths left to plumb in the endless saga of false allegations and the ruin of innocent men. But I was wrong. A book entitled *How to Destroy a Man Now* is available on Amazon and apparently features on the website of the MeToo campaign. I have read the first few pages and am shaking with outrage . . .'

Everywhere anguish and fury, and as I try to grapple with all the ramifications that spring from this moment in history—questions of power, desire, consent, the presumption of innocence, vigilante justice, the conflating of mild transgressions with the worst kinds of abuse, religion, history, culture and so much more—I am urged on in myriad ways by colleagues, friends and strangers alike.

'David, if you're going to do this book you have to read *The Second Sex*, *The Feminine Mystique* and *The Female Eunuch*, plus *Down Girl: The Logic of Misogyny*, *Half the Sky*, *Fight Like a Girl, Boys Will Be Boys, The War on Women* and *Mating in Captivity.* Don't forget *The Creation of Patriarchy, Sex at Dawn, Anatomy of Love, Stiffed, Backlash, The Beauty Myth, Vagina: A New Biography* and *Pussy: A Reclamation.* And that's before you tackle the subject of men—because you *are* tackling the subject of men, aren't you? Then you must read *Playing the Man, The Descent of Man, The Myth of Male Power, Boy Crisis, Raising Boys, Angry White Men, Testosterone Rex.* (This last was a suggestion from my beloved mother, who tells me: 'It's all about the brain, darling, and apparently, there's less difference than we thought between men and women.')

'By the way who's your readership going to be?' I am asked. 'Men or women? Because, if it's men, how are you going to get them to read your book? *You have to make them read your book.* And are you taking a global or national perspective? You can't just write about Australia. You have to look at the Irish abortion referendum; the femicide rates in Guatemala and El Salvador; the rape of German women by Middle Eastern refugees; the backlash against women in Italy; the rise of strongmen like Trump, Putin, Erdogan, Duterte; child brides in Malaysia; the Taliban's murderous assaults on woman and girls in Afghanistan; the rise of the #MeToo movement in China (#WoYeShi), Japan (#WatashiMo), Vietnam (#TôiCũngVậy), and the new movement in Russia launched by doulas aimed at combatting abuse of women in hospitals (#violence_in_obstetrics).

'And you'll be talking to hotel workers in Chicago, right? What about fruit pickers in Minnesota and high-class escorts in Brussels? This is not just about rich, mainly white Hollywood actors, you know. Maybe you should also think about going to Iceland, because that's where gender equality has really asserted itself. On your way home, you should detour via Rwanda to see how the collective grief from genocide has helped shape a society and economy driven by women. But don't forget America, because that's where this whole thing started. You'll need to track the way #NotOk led to #MeToo (or was it the other way around?) then to #TimesUp, #BelieveWomen, #HerToo, #YouOkSis, #WhatWereYouWearing, #IDidThat, #IHave, #IWill, #BlackLivesMatter, #MarchForOurLives . . .

'I mean, how wide is your aperture going to be? Will you be dealing with university campus assaults, sexual assault in the Church, gay hate crimes, domestic violence, bullying? What about the law courts? False accusations? Trial by Twitter? Masculinity in popular culture? Childhood development? The suffragettes, intersectionality, race, labour rights, the corrosive core of power structures?

'Obviously you're going to explore gender pay gaps too, yes? And corporate board diversity? What about issues of consent, childhood trauma, familial trauma, historical trauma ('the clusterfuck of trauma', as Australian writer Meera Atkinson puts it in her book *Traumata*), sex trafficking, child brides, pornography, video games, virtual reality sex tours, sexual abuse in medicine, the neuroplasticity of the brain, the biochemistry of love?

'Will you look into the origins of patriarchy and the evidence for matriarchal societies? What about religion, history, anthropology, biology and evolutionary psychology? Because there's a big debate between the social constructivists and the evolutionary psychologists—*you know, we're more like bonobos than gorillas*—and I trust you're not going to make this too personal, because it's not about you, and you've got to be even-handed and speak to men's rights activists. *What do you mean you're not going to talk to them? What kind of journalist are you?*

'And how about engaging men and boys in discussions around feminism; and exploring toxic masculinity, toxic feminism, gender identity, gender fluidity, midwifery, moon cycles, menarche, menopause and the Mother Goddess in history. You're bringing all that into it, too, I hope?

'Speaking of gender identity, what about investigating the transgender movement, because there are trans-exclusionary radical feminists (TERFs) denying the validity of other people's self-affirmed genders and sexes.

'By the way, are you listening to *The Guilty Feminist* podcast, and have you seen that film on the history of the vibrator? What's it called? That's right, *Hysteria*. What about the YouTube clip "It's Not About the Nail"? It's funny and you'll need some jokes in your book because, goodness knows, this subject needs some levity.'

In other words, anyone who knows anything about being human—which is all of us—has a view on how this #MeToo movement, in all its fast-moving, far-reaching implications, applies to our own lives.

Because, unless you've been miraculously spared, all of us—women and men—carry the sorrows of our existence. We've been abandoned in love, rejected, lied to, betrayed, humiliated, silenced, ignored. We grew up fatherless, motherless, or both. There was abuse when we were young—a grandfather, grandmother, father, mother, stepfather, stepmother, uncle, brother, friend, priest, teacher, scoutmaster.

We lived with superstition, guilt, cruelty, despair, no inkling of self-love. Our fathers were cold, withdrawn, often violent. Our mothers were cold, withdrawn, often violent. Our mothers and fathers failed to protect us, or suffocated, spoilt and indulged us. We were never breast-fed. We never bonded properly. No gentle touch, intimacy, safety.

We've never had our cravings for friendship and companionship met. The affliction of loneliness. Separation anxiety. Tragedies, freak accidents. Our bodies were brutalised and humiliated. Our hearts were cracked open, then cracked apart. We grew up poor, had few friends, broke the law, joined a gang, went to prison.

We lost our jobs, our children, our home. Our parents fought over us. The legal system screwed us. We were never given lessons on how to behave, talk to a girl, share our feelings. We never felt confident with boys. Not beautiful enough. Breasts too small. Breasts too large. We never felt confident with girls. Not manly enough. Too small in all the places that counted. Too much pressure to conform, dress, act the right way, comply with what we never should have complied with. All the things that can go wrong with being on this earth.

And now that the earth has moved, we are able to see more clearly the hidden bones and muscles of all these neglected, damaged places, and it's a terrifying—and humbling—thing to try to bear witness to what feels like the collective wound of the world.

1

Of all the wild animals

It was all around me from the beginning, the weight of female suffering, with its biblical justification and vanishing acts.

JEFFREY EUGENIDES, *MIDDLESEX*

As a young Jewish boy, I never understood why it was that all the girls and their mothers and grandmothers were forced to pray separately from us boys and men in that grand old synagogue on Elizabeth Street in Sydney.

I remember sitting downstairs with my father on Saturday mornings, looking away from the rabbi, up towards the gallery where the dark-eyed daughters of the faith were assembled, hoping to catch a toss of their locks, a furtive gaze, an arch of the back, anything that would both affirm and quell the commotion inside my young heart.

Alongside the courting cues were the Hebrew prayers we were supposed to recite, but which I never understood properly because

I couldn't speak the language. I could memorise the music and incantations, but I wonder now if I sang the traditional morning prayer: 'Blessed are you, Lord, our God, ruler of the universe who has not created me a woman'? Probably not, because that was supposed to be invoked on waking, and short of wishing for Margot Adams to hold my hand at Bondi Beach, I'd never uttered any prayers on waking.

What about Deuteronomy 22:20 which asserted that if a man could find no proof of his wife's virginity on their wedding night, she 'shall be brought to the door of her father's house and there the men of her town shall stone her to death'?

There was also Leviticus, the third book of the Old Testament, where it stipulated that 'when a woman has a discharge, and the discharge in her body is blood, she shall be in her menstrual impurity for seven days, and whoever touches her shall be unclean until the evening'. Leviticus goes on to declare that anything upon which a woman lies or sits during her menstrual cycle is rendered unclean; that if you touch any of these objects you will need to wash your clothes and bathe yourself, presumably with some kind of disinfectant; and, furthermore, that if you go so far as to have sexual intercourse with her during this time, you will be contaminated for seven days. (In 77 AD Pliny asserted in *Natural History*, the first authoritative book about the natural world, that meat turned bad when touched by a menstruating woman.)

Not to be outdone by Leviticus, Ecclesiastes, one of the canonical so-called 'wisdom books' of the Old Testament, declares: 'And I find something more bitter than death: the woman whose heart is snares and nets, and whose hands are fetters. He who pleases God escapes her, but the sinner is taken by her.'

It also says, in what is perhaps the perfect summation of misogyny peddled by the Old Testament: 'From a garment cometh a moth, and from women wickedness.'

Did I examine any of these devotions back in my callow youth? Not for a second. Did I ever ask, subsequently, who it was that decided a menstruating woman could not enter a 'House of God' lest she defile it? Or that a woman's sexual agency and desire meant her heart was made of 'snares and nets', requiring her to be put under control or, worse, sentenced to death? Or that, by implication, from my grandmother's, mother's, sister's, female friends' hearts sprung 'wickedness'?

No I did not, but I'm asking now. And the answer is the men who coveted and feared her, revered and reviled her, in equal measure. Who was this mystery creature—Woman—who could bleed in rhythm to the moon, create and sustain life, manufacture milk, turn a man half mad with desire, receive endless rapture, calm the seas (according to Catalan mythology), protect cities (Athena in the Greek pantheon), ensure bountiful harvests (Demeter in ancient Greece, Isis in ancient Egypt), exact retribution (Nemesis)?

My Jewish forefathers elevated women in certain areas, but where and when it counted, they were misogynists, all the way down to their desert sandals, starting with the Book of Genesis, where God fashioned Eve from the rib of Adam and then gave Adam mastery over her through naming rights: 'She shall be called Woman because she was taken out of Man,' it is written in Genesis 2:23, before going on to declare in the following chapter that a wife's desire 'shall be for your husband and he shall rule over you' (3:16).

There are plenty of other rich morsels to consider in this first book of the Hebrew Bible, including the permission granted a man to marry as often as he desires, while also maintaining as many concubines as he wishes. (Wise King Solomon had 700 of the former, 300 of the latter, although this didn't occur without fatal consequences for his kingdom.) Needless to say, no such permissions were granted a woman.

And while a husband could divorce his wife if he chose, no such prerogative was available to a woman. If her husband died, she could be forced to marry her brother-in-law and, either unmarried or married, be permitted to leave home only with the consent of either her father or husband.

Woe betide her if she was a virgin who'd been raped, as she could be forced to marry her attacker, the only caveat being that her attacker might be required to pay the woman's father 50 shekels of silver.

On the matter of crude monetary worth, the Book of Leviticus states that a boy between the ages of one month and five years old was worth five shekels of silver, while a girl the same age was worth three. There we have it, not just the original gender pay gap, but the caste system that would ultimately come to define the religious moral order of western civilisation, one that the Church Fathers would reinforce with vigour.

Tertullian, the second-century Latin Christian author regarded as the founder of western theology, described the vagina as a 'temple built over a sewer' and 'the Devil's gateway'. Thomas Aquinas, one of the most influential Christian philosophers in history, declared a woman to be an 'incomplete man' and an 'incidental being'.

In her landmark history of feminism *The Second Sex*, Simone de Beauvoir quoted St Augustine, arguably the third most influential figure in Christianity after Jesus Christ and St Paul, proclaiming a woman to be 'a beast who is neither firm nor stable'. De Beauvoir also mentioned St John Chrysostom, the fifth-century Archbishop of Constantinople who observed that 'of all the wild animals, none can be found as harmful as woman'.

'Woman has always been if not man's slave, at least his vassal,' de Beauvoir wrote in the 1940s.

Lawmakers, priests, philosophers, writers and scholars have gone to great lengths to prove that women's subordinate condition was willed in heaven.

Religions forged by men reflect this will for domination: they found ammunition in the legends of Eve and Pandora. They have put philosophy and theology in their service, as seen in the previously cited words of Aristotle and St Thomas.

Aristotle, one of the towering figures of ancient Greece, wrote: 'The female is female by virtue of a certain *lack* of qualities. We should regard women's nature as suffering from natural defectiveness.' He also claimed women had fewer teeth than men, drawing the following riposte from British philosopher Bertrand Russell more than 2000 years later: 'Aristotle would never have made this mistake if he had allowed his wife to open her mouth once in a while.'

Now perhaps all this is familiar to you, or perhaps, like me, you're coming to these startling details a little late in life because, to paraphrase Confucius, real knowledge is finding out the depths of one's own ignorance.

I hadn't heard of the 'cutting days', when girls scream in agony as their legs are forced open and first their clitorises then their labia are excised with razors, obliterating any future sexual pleasure so that they may be rendered faithful and submissive.

'The scissor went down between my legs and the man cut off my inner labia and clitoris,' the Somali-born author Ayaan Hirsi Ali recalled in her bestselling memoir *Infidel*. She was five years old at the time.

I heard it, like a butcher snipping the fat off a piece of meat. A piercing pain shot up between my legs, indescribably, and I howled. Then came the sewing: the long, blunt needle clumsily pushed into my bleeding outer labia, my loud and anguished protests, my grandmother's words of comfort and encouragement. 'It's just this once in your life, Ayaan. Be brave, he's almost finished.' When the sewing was finished, the man cut the thread off with his teeth.'

I hadn't encountered any of the estimated three million women and girls who've been sold into sex slavery to be raped, auctioned, raped again, drugged, beaten and threatened into sexual servitude in what is the fastest-growing criminal activity in the world.

In *Half the Sky: How to Change the World*, writers Nicholas Kristof and Sheryl WuDunn documented with terrifying clarity the global epidemic of violence against women.

In India, a 'bride burning'—to punish a woman for an inadequate dowry or to eliminate her so a man can remarry—takes place approximately once every two hours.

In the twin cities of Islamabad and Rawalpindi, Pakistan, five thousand women and girls have been doused in kerosene and set alight by family members or in-laws—or, perhaps worse, been seared with acid—for perceived disobedience just in the last nine years (2000 to 2009).

The authors also cited a demographic study which revealed that 39,000 baby girls died annually in China because parents declined to give them the same medical care and attention that boys received—and that was just in the first year of life.

The writers then turned their attention to a seventeen-year-old Kurdish girl in northern Iraq, Du'a Khalil Aswad, who was accused—without proof—of sleeping with a Sunni Arab boy with whom she'd fallen in love. The young woman was dragged into the street by eight men as a large crowd gathered around her.

At least one thousand men joined in the assault. So many men in the crowd shot video clips with their cell phones that on the web you can find a half-dozen versions of what happened next.

Du'a was thrown to the ground, and her black skirt was ripped off to humiliate her. She tried to get up, but they kicked her around as if she were a soccer ball. Frantic, she tried to fend off the blows, to get up, to cover herself, to find a sympathetic face in the crowd. Then they gathered rocks and concrete blocks and dropped them on her. It took thirty minutes for Du'a to die.

#

Gloria Steinem, the pioneering American feminist, once said, 'The truth will set you free, but first it will piss you off.'

Women have been pissed off for centuries, and for a lot of men this is hard to hear. Hard to hear the brutal truths about male violence. Hard to think about the nature of men, particularly if you believe you're one of the good guys, or one of those men who feel undermined by economic and political forces beyond your control. Far easier, of course, to blame others—radical feminists, refugees, politicians, affirmative action, the law courts—for the cataclysmic loss of utility and purpose that's been caused by political, economic and social structures shifting under our feet.

A few of my male friends—not many, I hasten to add—are prone to this kind of thinking. They tell me they're bored rigid by feminist talk. They hear sanctimonious whining and/or militancy at every turn, rather than a reason to investigate, even in cursory fashion, the catalogue of suffering that might inform women's fury and distress. They see powerful women not just equal before the law, but running countries, industries, corporations, presiding over courtrooms, sitting on boards, heading up police departments, universities, aid organisations, writing opinion columns, broadcasting . . . They see the barricades as having fallen. What could possibly be the problem?

The problem is that more than a century of feminist activism has not prevented a gross gender imbalance in most walks of life, nor has it prevented millions of women suffering at the hands of men. We know this now from all the distress signals pouring out of social media, although this has been with us long before October 2017, when the trumpets of the #MeToo movement first began blaring.

'We've been saying for 50 years that violence against women is the greatest violence on the planet today,' Tony Award–winning American playwright Eve Ensler told me during a Skype interview from New York. 'We're talking about one billion women who will be raped or beaten in their lifetime—and that's just reported by the World Health Organization and the United Nations.

'That's not including sexually harassed or undermined . . . we can go down the list. In fact, I think you'd be at odds to find a woman on this planet who hasn't been sexually harassed in one form or another. We're talking about something of epidemic proportions—like nothing else I can think of on the planet.'

In 1996, Ensler's *The Vagina Monologues*—a 90-minute distillation of more than 200 women exploring their femaleness—was performed for the first time, and by 1998 had been showcased from Islamabad to London, Oklahoma to Jerusalem.

In 2001, in New York's Madison Square Garden, actor Jane Fonda simulated giving birth on stage, while fellow actor Glenn

Close repeatedly shouted the word 'cunt' to 18,000 women, followed by the collective orgasmic moaning of the Vulva Choir.

'Twenty years ago,' Ensler says, 'no one said the word *vagina*. You couldn't say it anywhere. I always make a joke that you can put plutonium on the front pages of newspapers, or Scud missiles, or radiation, or death, but if you say vagina everyone goes into hysterics. That tells us everything we need to know about the world. The place where most of us come from . . . the majority of human beings on the planet have passed through the vagina.'

Ensler spent years traversing the global landscape of female suffering and her discoveries are highly instructive when trying to grasp what is happening today. Stories of mutilation, of date rape, gang rape, incest and shame; of women with black eyes and broken bones; of women humiliated and violated and left mute and homeless in their own bodies.

In the Mexican city of Ciudad Juárez, just over the US border, Eve Ensler learnt of 400 women who had disappeared over the previous decade, 370 of them murdered, ravaged and disfigured. 'These women,' she was to later write, 'had become as disposable as empty Coca-Cola cans. Sometimes their bones turned up next to old bottles in parking lots. Sometimes they were blamed for being mutilated and tortured because of what they'd been wearing. They were rapidly becoming an endangered species.'

During the Bosnian war of the early 1990s, she visited the 'rape camps' where Serbian paramilitary units herded up to 50,000 mostly Muslim women into enclosures and preyed on them around the clock. Often they were only released when they were pregnant, or their bellies were torn open first. Public rapes. Rape as an instrument of terror. Rape in the service of ethnic cleansing. Rape of mothers, daughters, sisters, aunts, girls as young as twelve. Sons ordered to rape their mothers, fathers their daughters. Women with their vaginas destroyed, as Ensler captured so chillingly in one of her monologues, 'My Vagina Was My Village':

> My vagina. A live wet water village. They invaded it. Butchered it and burnt it down. I do not touch now. Do not visit. I live someplace else now. I don't know where that is.

Yes, I know this is hard to read, but stay with me, because I think this hatred for, and violence against, women is the framework for understanding how rampaging male aggression obliterates women and girls, both close to home and far from our shores. And how it also obliterates other men—weaker men, more feminine men, gay men, different men, transgender men and, of course, children in all their divine innocence.

We see its gruesome manifestations in sex trafficking, bride and widow burning, forced marriages, female feticide and the hurling of sulphuric acid into the faces of women and girls in Asia—usually by men who've been spurned.

We see it in sharia law, the Islamic legal code, where the testimony of two women is the equivalent of one man's and where a daughter inherits half as much as her brother.

We see it in the staggering figures for female genital mutilation; according to World Health Organization estimates, up to 130 million women and girls worldwide have been subjected to total or partial removal of their clitorises.

We see it in India, where in 2016, according to the National Crime Records Bureau, the rape of female minors increased by 82 per cent over the previous year, and where, in April 2018, eight-year-old Asifa Bano was drugged and raped over three days in a Hindu temple by up to seven men, including four policemen, before being burnt, strangled and then bludgeoned with a rock.

We see this in honour killings—although we should call these for what they are: premeditated murders. According to the United Nations, some 5000 women throughout the Middle East, South Asia and North Africa are killed each year for adultery, or merely for behaving in ways that male family members find morally indefensible.

We see it in rural Ethiopia, where the kidnapping and raping of girls is a time-honoured tradition. A BBC report found that 60 per cent of Ethiopian women have suffered sexual violence. We see it too in eastern Congo—the world capital of rape—where, Nicholas Kristof and Sheryl WuDunn explain, the most 'cost-effective' way for militias to terrorise the civilian population is to use sticks, knives or bayonets to rape their victims, or to fire guns into women's vaginas. (In early 2018, Philippines president Rodrigo Duterte told soldiers confronting female communist fighters: 'There's a new order coming from the mayor. "We will not kill you. We will just shoot you in the vagina."')

We see it here in Australia, where in 2001 the Australian Institute of Criminology reported that more than 1.2 million adult women had experienced an incident of sexual violence since the age of fifteen, and where more than one woman is killed by a current or former partner every week. And that doesn't include all the women on the run from violent partners, or former partners, hoping to find refuge for themselves and their children.

Nor does it include strangers with lethal intent.

Is it already six years ago, now, that 29-year-old Jill Meagher, an ABC staffer, was raped and strangled to death while walking home from a bar in Brunswick in Melbourne? Is it just three days ago—as I write this—that 22-year-old Melbourne comedian Eurydice Dixon was raped and murdered in Carlton North, her body dumped in Princes Park, after walking home from a late-night gig? 'I'm almost home safe,' she messaged her partner, Tony Magnuson, shortly before her life was taken.

Her death prompted vigils around the country and sparked an immediate social media outcry—not just because of the horrific and senseless ending of this young woman's life, but because Victorian police responded clumsily with a message for other women that read to many as code for victim blaming: 'Make sure you have situational awareness,' they said. 'Be aware of your own personal security.'

One woman countered on Facebook:

You know what would be great? If an instance of a young man murdering a woman was seen as the opportunity to talk about what's going wrong with our boys and men. That we keep seeing them 'snap' and take their frustration and damage and dysfunction out on women and girls. That they harm them. That they rape them. That they kill them.

The questions we should be asking are not 'how can girls make themselves safer?' Or 'why do women take these risks (walking home)?' Or 'when will women be more aware of their surroundings and take some responsibility?' That is all bullshit.

The questions we SHOULD be asking are 'how are our boys connecting to other people? Are they showing respect for the girls and women in their lives? Do they seem withdrawn and hostile? Are you ever worried about their ability to regulate anger, control their temper, admit when they're in pain? Should my son be getting professional support from a counsellor or psychologist? Is my brother dangerous? Is my father stable? What options are available to me if I think any of the men in my life pose a risk to someone else, or themselves?'

That's what a society that cares about violence against women would be asking right now. How do men get to this point? Where in their boyhood do they start to view girls as less than them? What is fuelling this endless and toxic hatred of women?

It was a view endorsed by Victorian premier Daniel Andrews who, in a series of tweets on 15 June 2018, wrote that violence against women would not change until men changed. Elaborating later on ABC Radio, he said it was time to reflect on the 'appalling attitudes' held by many men towards women.

'I, for one, am a bit sick and tired of the focus that all too often is brought on the behaviour of the woman when it comes to an incident like this. This tragedy presents us with an important opportunity—and an obligation—to call out very bad behaviour which comes from, almost inevitably, bad attitudes.'

'Bad attitudes', which, in the first 24 weeks of 2018, had already claimed 31 Australian women's lives, almost all of them at the hands of men. (Actually, make that 34 women in the first 27 weeks of 2018. Amanda Harris, a childcare worker and mother of three, was stabbed and set on fire, allegedly by her male partner. That was 48 hours after Sydney financial planner John Edwards murdered his two teenage children in their home, and less than a week after the body of missing Queensland teenager Larissa Beilby was found in a barrel in the back of an abandoned ute. A 34-year-old man was accused of her murder, and 'misconduct' with her corpse. All this within four weeks of the slaying of 28-year-old Chinese woman and Australian resident Qi Yu in Sydney, and Eurydice Dixon's murder in Melbourne.) The day after writing the above, a 48-year-old mother and her two children—an eight-year-old boy and a fifteen-year-old girl—were murdered in their home in Perth. That made eight Australians killed in their homes in eleven days, four of them children.

And yet we have Mark Latham, once an intellectual light in the Australian Labor Party and strong contender for the prime ministership (yes, I know that's hard to believe) issuing Twitter tirades at female journalists like Jane Gilmore because she had the temerity to suggest after Eurydice Dixon's death that all men, not *some* men, should look at the problems swirling through masculine culture and assume some measure of personal responsibility for addressing it. (Gilmore tweeted her suggestion after Eurydice's memorial site was desecrated with a painting of a 25-metre penis.) Mark Latham had previously descended into the squalid lowlands of human unkindness in 2016 by leading—along with his 'hate buddy' radio broadcaster Alan Jones—a vicious campaign against Rosie Batty, whose son Luke had been killed by his father two years earlier at cricket practice.

Latham has aimed his poisoned arrows at many prominent women, as has Alan Jones, who sunk below his own low-lying Plimsoll line in 2012 when he suggested that Julia Gillard, Australia's first woman prime minister, be placed in a 'chaff bag' and taken out to sea. He later declared that Gillard's beloved father had died of shame because she was a 'liar'.

These attitudes are everywhere, and in places you might never expect. During the course of researching my original article, I was horrified to learn that in Byron Bay, where my former wife and I raised our two daughters during the early noughties, the rape and abuse of teenage girls was purportedly not uncommon. Verbal and physical assault—young men urinating on girls, calling them 'whores', 'fat cunts', 'bitches' and 'sluts'—was also prevalent.

'I don't think what happens [there] is unique,' Ivy D'Orsogna, who grew up in the same town and is making a web series on the subject, told me. 'There is definitely a feeling of xenophobia among a lot of the young guys—*this is our town*—and this sense of entitlement extends to the bodies of young women. There were prosecuted cases, but there were so many things that happened where boys were never charged or held accountable.'

Now Sydney-based, the 25-year-old recounted to me that, in one incident, an underage girl was put 'on the spit' by five teenage boys and penetrated with penises and other objects while they filmed it on their iPhones.

'Many [teenage] girls I know who grew up there experienced sexual assault in one form or another,' she said. 'For a while guys were also pissing on girls, or pissing in cups and throwing them on girls. They were just like dogs pissing on their territory. "You're ours and we can do what we like with you."'

Anyone who has studied the history of anti-Semitism knows that the virus was transmitted early, with some of the most destructive ideas about Jews built into the sacred Christian texts. That's how the Jewish people were turned into historical scapegoats—because humanity was already contaminated by prejudice. So, too, with women. We might never have read St Augustine, or heard of St John Chrysostom, or studied Aristotle, but their ideas have lived on, miring men in such harmful thinking about women as to enable them to behave as the very 'beasts' and 'wild animals' they've accused women of being.

2

Desire and hatred

Behold yon simp'ring dame . . .
Down from the waist they are centaurs, though women
all above.

WILLIAM SHAKESPEARE, KING LEAR

In America, a woman is beaten every nine seconds and a rape is reported every 6.2 seconds. (Yes, you read those figures correctly.) In Australia, according to Our Watch—a federal and state government–supported not-for-profit organisation devoted to raising awareness about violence against women and children—the figures are just as bleak.

Beyond the 1.2 million women in Australia who have experienced sexual violence since the age of fifteen, one in four women has suffered physical or sexual violence at the hands of an intimate partner. Women are three times more likely than men to experience violence from an intimate partner, five times more likely than men to require medical attention or hospitalisation, and five times more likely to report fearing for their lives.

The women most at risk, according to the Australian Institute of Health and Welfare, are Aboriginal and Torres Strait Islander women, young women, pregnant women and women with disabilities.

I know one woman right now—a dear friend who is planning to leave the state with her children in the dead of night because her former husband has turned into a ticking time bomb. There's been no physical violence. Not yet. But the fear has her by the throat.

'My situation with Brian [not his real name] is full of psychological violence and aggression, all of it a vile expression of his deep hatred towards me because he can't control my choices and decisions,' she tells me.

'The relationship is characterised by him punishing me for having the children he didn't want and, since my leaving him, punishing me for separating him from his children. To some people, that's an understandable grief, noble even, but when you understand it properly as having nothing to do with the children, and everything to do with maintaining agency over me, it's clear what is really going on.'

The family courts are filled with such cases—men not necessarily resorting to physical violence, but asserting control through a menacing mix of psychological and emotional intimidation. And then, as with Brian, parading themselves before the courts as both victims of an accursed system and crusaders for men's rights.

In his stunning book *Misogyny: The World's Oldest Prejudice*, the late Irish journalist and novelist Jack Holland acknowledged that trying to trace the history of any hatred was no simple task.

At the root of a particular form of hatred, whether it be class or racial hatred, religious or ethnic hatred, one usually finds a conflict. But on the depressing list of hatreds that human beings feel for each other, none other than misogyny involves the profound need and desires that most men have for women, and most women for men. Hatred co-exists with desire in a peculiar way. This is what makes misogyny so complex: it involves a man's conflict with himself. Indeed, for the most part, the conflict is not even recognised.

I happened to be reading Jack Holland's book in May 2018, at the very time the Irish people were voting to overturn one of the most restrictive bans on abortion in the world, one that had criminalised abortion even in the event of rape or incest, and had caused women to leave their country in their tens of thousands in order to secure safe terminations.

One of the catalysts for this historic vote had been the fate of 31-year-old dentist Savita Halappanavar, whose repeated failed requests in 2012 for a termination had resulted in her dying from septicaemia in a Galway hospital.

Before reading Holland's book, I'd also devoured Sue Lloyd-Roberts and Sarah Morris's book *The War on Women*, in which they'd outlined Ireland's obsession with so-called 'fallen women' and the network of religiously run 'laundries' these women had been condemned to for more than 200 years, up until 1996. Named after Mary Magdalene, Christ's so-called 'apostle of apostles', these laundries were established by the Church to institutionalise women who challenged Irish Catholic concepts of morality—prostitutes, unmarried mothers, women who'd been raped (sometimes by priests) and girls considered too attractive for their own good and, therefore, in need of 'protection'. In 2017, a mass grave containing the remains of up to 800 babies and children was discovered in Tuam, in County Galway. Many had died from infections, malnutrition and neglect after their mothers had been isolated between 1925 and 1960.

Of all the horrors these authors discovered, the one that shocked them most was the practice known as symphysiotomy, first introduced in Ireland in 1944 by doctors wary of performing caesarean sections. A number of their more secular-minded colleagues were recommending women be sterilised after their third caesarean section, but Catholic doctors feared this could be used as a ruse for contraception. They devised a fresh approach.

'If a woman's pelvis was too small to allow for a normal birth, then the accepted procedure should be to break the pelvic bone,' the authors explain. They quote one such woman, Norma Clarke, telling documentary makers Anne Daly and Ronan Tynan: 'I saw the doctor go over and get a hacksaw . . . He started to cut through my bone. The blood spurted out like a fountain. It went everywhere. The nurses were being physically sick. The doctor was angry because the blood splashed his glasses.'

In 2012, almost 100 survivors of this hideous procedure converged on Dublin to describe their horrors and to demand compensation. 'Many women arrived in wheelchairs and complained of difficulty in walking, chronic back pain and incontinence,' Lloyd-Roberts and Morris write.

'Put five of us in a room,' one survivor remarked, 'and you'll get different stories but the same ending. We are all cripples.'

Across the border in Northern Ireland, Jack Holland lived with the stark paradoxes of the Catholic Church's attitude towards women. Here the exalted form of the Virgin Mary; over there, scrawled on the walls of fetid back alleyways and public toilets stinking of urine and faeces, the word 'cunt'.

It was a place where the word . . . expressed the worst form
of contempt one person could feel for another. If you loathed
or despised a person, "cunt" said it all . . . Nothing was worse

than being treated like a "cunt" or nothing so stupid as a "stupid cunt."

Belfast, Northern Ireland, the city where I grew up, had its own peculiar hatreds. Its sectarian animosities over the years have made it a byword for violence and bloodshed. But there was one thing on which the warring communities of Catholics and Protestants could agree: the contemptible status of cunt.

(And let's not forget other words that have long been used by men to describe their age-old disrespect: 'hole', 'gash', 'slash', 'slit', 'snatch'. Even the word 'pudendum', or woman's vulva, originates from the Latin word *pudere*, meaning to be ashamed of, and 'vagina' derives from the seventeenth-century word meaning 'sheath' or 'scabbard'—presumably where a man puts his sword— while the provenance of hysteria is the Greek word for womb: *hyster*. Perhaps none of this should be surprising, however, given all the female body parts named after men, including the Bartholin's glands, in honour of seventeenth-century Danish anatomist Caspar Bartholin the Younger; the pouch of Douglas, named after seventeenth-century Scottish anatomist James Douglas; and the G Spot, attributed to German gynaecologist Ernst Gräfenberg and his studies of women's erogenous zones.)

Holland noted Belfast's similarity to other poor, industrialised parts of Britain where routine contempt for women was expressed through wife-beating, a practice all too familiar in countries like Australia and New Zealand, after the now-obsolete 'six o'clock swill', when early pub-closing often delivered men home to their wives in drunken rages.

'Men would step in to defend a dog from being kicked around by another man,' Holland wrote, 'but felt no obligation to do the same when faced with brutality being inflicted on a wife by her husband. Ironically, this was because of the "sacred" status of the relationship between man and wife, which barred intervention.'

Holland observed that when violence flared in the late 1960s in Northern Ireland, the mentality of hatred towards women expressed itself in a much more public fashion:

Catholic girls who dated British soldiers were dragged into the street, bound and held down (often by other women), while the men hacked and shaved off their hair, before pouring hot tar over them and sprinkling them with feathers. They were then tied to a lamp post to be gaped at by the nervous onlookers, with a sign hung around their necks on which was scrawled another sexual insult: 'whore'.

Perhaps we were imitating the French, to whom the English-speaking nations usually defer in matters sexual, having seen those news pictures as France was liberated of what befell women found guilty of going out with German soldiers. But we were also following the inner logic of our own powerful feelings, the same rage which we articulated with monosyllabic conclusion in the word 'cunt'.

A man will often rage against the object of his desires, especially if he can't control her. He will blame the enchantress for inspiring his lust; and on the turn of a dime, she will go from being the source of his deepest cravings to the source of his darkest intent.

The traditional patriarchal religions have much to answer for here. Although Jesus Christ was considered a revolutionary in his attitude towards women—'He that is without sin among you, let him first cast a stone at her,' he famously told a crowd of Pharisees baying for the blood of an adulteress—by the second century AD, women were being linked to the devil by the Christian theologian Tertullian. By the third and fourth centuries, they were being cast as the source of all bodily temptation and sins of the flesh.

The exception, of course, was Mary, mother of Jesus, the Jewish peasant woman from Nazareth who in 431 AD was suddenly declared the virgin Mother of God by the highest council of the Catholic Church.

'The most venerated woman in the world,' Holland wrote, 'could only be venerated on the grounds that she did not share with other women something so fundamental to their nature as the experience of sex. A woman was being exalted, yet at the cost of holding in contempt her sexuality.'

Women would hereafter find themselves divided into two categories: the pure and the tainted, the nurturing and the corrupted, the revered and the repellent, the Madonna and the whore—a dichotomy which Sigmund Freud would have much to say about in the early twentieth century. Men loved the virgin, but they desired the whore.

This reductionism—and demonisation—would reach its horrific apogee from the late fourteenth to the late seventeenth centuries, when women were accused of witchcraft and murdered en masse throughout Europe. The figures are still debated, but possibly millions were hanged, beheaded or burnt at the stake—healers, herbalists, poetesses, midwives and anyone displaying signs of sexual independence. Many were tortured and their heads shaved before being killed, on account of their supposedly having consorted with the devil.

With the enthusiastic support of the not-so-innocent Pope Innocent VIII (1484–92), inquisitors were given licence to torture women as part of a desperate search for evidence of Satan. It was a gruesome centuries-old experiment to make visible the invisible—a fulfilment, if you like, of Charles Baudelaire's later maxim: 'The finest trick of the devil is to persuade you he doesn't exist.'

One of the forms of torture, described by Naomi Wolf in her celebrated 2012 book *Vagina: A New Biography*, was a device known as 'the Pear of Anguish'—a pear-shaped iron object that expanded inside the victim as the torturer turned the screws. Women's vaginas were the target of these searches for the 'witch's' or 'devil's' mark.

'I cannot stress enough,' Wolf wrote, 'how many of our current anxieties about the vagina and about female sexual pleasure were introduced to society at this time and descend to us even now in forms recognisably dating to this period.'

All too often, desire for a woman has lived side by side with pure hatred, bringing to mind the experience of Port Macquarie woman Dr Angela Jay, who in 2016 was stabbed eleven times by an ex-boyfriend before being doused with petrol. Or contempt, as in the case of Saxon Mullins, who, at the age of eighteen, alleged that she was anally raped in a Kings Cross alleyway by 21-year-old Luke Lazarus, whom she'd met only a few minutes earlier. (Lazarus was convicted and then eventually acquitted of the charges, despite a jury and two judges finding Mullins had not consented to sex.)

'I never knew what panic attacks felt like until my incident,' Mullins told the ABC's Louise Milligan on *Four Corners*, when she spoke publicly for the first time five years after the event. 'I never knew what it felt like to be utterly helpless . . . I thought that once I left the alleyway, all the pain would go away. But it didn't leave me for weeks . . . I know a part of me died that day. The part that trusted others. The part that saw the good in everyone. The part that held my innocence.'

> Luke Lazarus (in text message to a friend that same day): *I honestly have zero recollection of calling you, was a sick night. Took a chick's virginity, lol.*

Friend: *Bahahahah. Nice popping those cherries. Tight?*
Lazarus: *So tight. It's a pretty gross story. Tell ya later.*

When I watched that program I felt sick, although not quite as sick as I felt early in my journalistic career when I'd reported on the Anita Cobby murder trial in Sydney. It was 1987 and the evidence of what those men did to that nurse—her rape, torture and slaying—was so shocking that it took me years to erase from my mind.

Fifteen years later, I'd sat in court and stared into the merciless coal-black eyes of Bilal Skaf, the 21-year-old who led the gang rapes of Sydney women and girls in the lead-up to the 2000 Olympics. One of his young victims had later described to me how the men had dragged her by her hair into Gosling Park, in south-west Sydney's Greenacre, and repeatedly raped her at gunpoint.

'I tried to kill myself [afterwards],' she told me. 'I . . . just felt worthless. I felt dirty. I thought, "Who is going to want me now?" I was in year ten at the time and I was going extremely well, and then everything fell apart. You could never imagine that one event could change your life so dramatically. I used to just sit in my room and cry and cry and cry, and not come out.'

This is part of the global horror story we are now trying to come to terms with. Never mind where you find yourself in the world, this is, as Jack Holland observed finally,

the hatred of women [which] has thrived on many different levels, from the loftiest philosophical plane in the works of Greek thinkers, who helped frame how Western society views the world, to the back streets of nineteenth-century London and the highways of modern Los Angeles, where serial killers have left in their wake a train of the tortured and mutilated corpses of women.

From the Christian ascetics of the third century AD, to the Taliban rulers of Afghanistan in the late 1990s, it has directed its rage at women and tried to suppress their sexuality.

At least once, during the witch hunts of the late Middle Ages, it has launched what amounted to a sexual pogrom, burning hundreds of thousands—some historians say millions—of women at the stake throughout Europe.

It has been expressed by some of the greatest and most renowned artists that civilisation has produced, and celebrated in the lowest, most vulgar works of modern pornography. The history of misogyny is indeed the story of a hatred unique as it is enduring, uniting Aristotle with Jack the Ripper, King Lear with James Bond.

And, of course, there's Islam, too, which I have mostly tried to avoid until now, mainly because I am no expert on the faith (nor Judaism or Christianity, for that matter), but also because I know how easy it is—especially in these shrill, poisonous times—to unfairly judge the faith of 1.5 billion people by the actions of a relative few extremists.

We recoil in horror and fear from murderous jihadi movements like al-Qaeda, Islamic State, Boko Haram, al-Shabaab and Jemaah Islamiyah, and, unless more measured minds prevail, we think, 'This is Islam.'

We see an Iranian woman in a chador, a Saudi woman in a burqa, a Bangladeshi woman in a niqab, an Indonesian woman in a jilbab, and we assume that we are seeing only the veils of oppression, without knowing which country discourages its wearing, which country makes it mandatory, where it's a statement of fashion or self-assertion or where it's a symbol of totalitarian rule.

We read stories like that of Malala Yousafzai, the extraordinary young Pakistani Nobel Laureate who, in 2012, at the age of fifteen, was shot in the head by a masked Taliban gunman for daring to advocate for female education, and, again, we think *Muslim*.

There are so many stories that stoke these flames. As I write, the Saudi female human rights activist Israa al-Ghomgham faces a public beheading because she called (peacefully) for an end to discrimination against the country's Shia citizens. (Saudi Arabia is a majority Sunni country.)

We know that in 2017 an Indonesian woman was publicly lashed in Aceh province after being caught in private with a man who was not her husband. The Friday prayer services had to be interrupted because her agonising cries were so loud.

In 2016, in eastern Algeria, 34-year-old Amira Merabet was burnt alive for refusing a man's advances.

We know that women are routinely murdered in Afghanistan, with the perpetrators invariably granted immunity from prosecution, and with the Taliban now resurgent in much of the country, beware an unleashing of more horror stories from their 'Committee for the Promotion of Virtue and the Prevention of Vice'.

We saw a few years ago the way Islamic State militants turned thousands of women and children into sex slaves after capturing large swathes of Iraq and Syria, and we're aware of the number of Iraqi female activists who've been slain, or have gone missing, for daring to challenge their society's increasingly conservative views on women, including cosmetic surgeon Dr Rafeef al-Yasiri (known as the 'Barbie of Iraq'), found dead in her home in August 2018, believed poisoned; and model Tara Fares, assassinated the following month in broad daylight by two men on a motorbike as she was driving her white Porsche through the streets of Baghdad. Two months before her murder, Fares had posted to her 2.8 million Instagram followers: 'I'm not afraid of the one who denies the existence of God, but I'm really afraid of the one who kills and chops off heads to prove the existence of God.'

It's very tempting, therefore, to adopt the views of someone like Somali-born author Ayaan Hirsi Ali, who turned her back on Islam after a lifetime of institutionalised violence against women. Ali herself was circumcised at the age of five and forced to flee an arranged marriage at the age of 23. She had been taught explicitly, first in Somalia then in Saudi Arabia, that a woman could be beaten by her husband if she disobeyed him; that she would be required to be sexually available to him at all times— except when menstruating; and that she was always responsible for his sexual arousal, thus the requirement that she be covered at all times.

Her legion of critics (Muslim and non-Muslim) have accused her of Islamophobic 'hate speech' and of projecting her own considerable traumas onto a faith that is practised by more than 20 per cent of the world's population. They point out, too, that she fails to distinguish between Islam as it is practised in, say, Kurdistan, Turkey, Morocco or Indonesia, as opposed to Saudi Arabia, South Sudan or Pakistan.

Suffice to say that gender roles in the Muslim world are often contradictory, and forever baffling. In Iran, a woman can be a judge but not necessarily have her testimony accepted in court. In Jordan, we can see more political female representation today than in countries like Hungary, Ukraine or Brazil, and yet the number of honour killings continues to rise.

We can marvel, too, at brave female Kurdish fighters who comprise 40 per cent of Kurdish militia deployed across the Middle East—by comparison, only 14 per cent of the US military service is female—and yet wonder how it is that in rural Kurdistan genital mutilation and child marriage are still time-honoured practices.

Is this religion or culture? And when we attempt to understand women in the Muslim world, are we talking about faith, or a political ideology that has appropriated the faith?

I don't know, for example, whether all those black-eyed virgins in paradise—yes, the same ones who inhabit the dreams of male suicide bombers—are a literal reading of the Koran, or a gross misinterpretation, particularly of the word *houri*. If you read Arabic, you might think one thing; if you understand Aramaic, you might think another.

I can't quite work out, either, where the ban on women driving in Saudi Arabia came from, given that Mohammed, the sixth-century prophet and founder of Islam, allowed his own wives to drive camels. Does that say more about Islam, or about the House of Saud and the doctrines of Wahhabism? (The ban was lifted by royal decree in June 2018, although Saudi women still suffer under a crushing tyranny, requiring—among other things—the consent of a male guardian to study, travel, work, marry and obtain certain documents. Witness the case in January 2019 when eighteen-year-old Saudi woman Rahaf Mohammed al-Qunun barricaded herself in a Bangkok airport hotel room after fleeing her family because she feared being killed by them. She was given asylum almost immediately in Canada.)

'Often we blame a region's religion when the oppression instead may be rooted in culture,' write Nicholas Kristof and Sheryl WuDunn in *Half the Sky*.

At the same time the Muslim world is overpopulated with misogynists quoting Mohammed to justify their actions, a phenomenon which inevitably leads to the question: Is Islam misogynistic? It is a question Kristof and WuDunn have tried to answer:

One answer is historical, and it is no. When Muhammad introduced Islam in the seventh century, it was a step forward for women. Islamic law banned the previously common practice of female infanticide, and it limited polygamy to four wives who were supposed to be treated equally.

Muslim women routinely owned property, with rights protected by the law, while women in European countries often did not have the equivalent property rights. All in all, Muhammad comes across in the Koran and the traditions associated with him as much more respectful of women than early Christian leaders.

Another answer, also historical, is yes: Islam is, if not misogynist, then certainly graded in favour of men, if judged by the sura—or chapter—in the Koran that says: 'Men have authority over women because God has made the one superior to the other.'

The answer is the same if judged by the standards of conservative Islam which have been snap-frozen in seventh-century Arabia, despite recent piecemeal reforms from the Saudi royal family. In 2002, for example, Saudi Arabia's notorious religious police prevented schoolgirls fleeing a burning building in Mecca because they were not wearing their traditional Islamic headscarves and black robes. Fifteen pupils died, most of them crushed in the stampede.

Is that the Saudi royal family or Sunni Islam? Once again, it's tempting to conflate the two. 'The Koran explicitly endorses some gender discrimination,' Kristof and WuDunn observed, notwithstanding many reformist-minded Muslims pushing for greater gender equality and, in the case of countries like Morocco, vigorously promoting the mystical traditions of Sufism to combat extremist ideologies. '[Morocco's] King Muhammad also reformed family law, giving women more rights in divorce and marriage, and he supported the pathbreaking appointment of fifty women imams, or preachers.'

Islam, they concluded, was not inherently misogynistic, but as long as 'smart, bold women . . . disproportionately ended up in prison, or in coffins, in some Muslim nations, then those countries were undermining their own hopes for development'.

But whether it's religion or rap, God-fearing societies or godless, it's not hard to see how craving and loathing have come to co-mingle in the breast of man. An idea gets planted—*woman is less than . . . she is there to serve . . . she is a wild beast . . . the source of all temptation*—and that idea, that *morality tale*, takes root deep in the soil of history; propagating its seed, then reproducing itself over centuries, new seeds sprouting but still fouled with the same disease.

What was it Iggy Pop, the so-called 'Godfather of Punk', said at the height of his drug-addled, terrorising career? 'I hate women. I mean, why do I even have to have a reason for that? . . . My terms are simply phoning them up, telling them to be at such and such a place at such and such a time, in good physical condition, to be fucked. And then leave, goddamnit.'

3

When God was a woman

All intelligent thoughts have already been thought.
What is necessary is only to try to think them again.

JOHANN WOLFGANG VON GOETHE, *MAXIMS AND REFLECTIONS*

I'm not an anthropologist, archaeologist, historian, biologist, psychologist, mythologist, theologian or religious scholar. I'm a journalist trying to do what so many before me have attempted, some more successfully than others: to make sense, in some small way, of history—or *her-story*; of the story of relations between the sexes, and how we arrived at this knife-edge moment.

I'm under no illusion that I've got the answers, but I'm trying to rethink everything again—or maybe think things for the very first time—because I'm realising now how little I've understood of where our values, ethics, morals, attitudes and conduct might have sprung from.

Winston Churchill famously said that history was written by the victors, and ever since my Hebrew forefathers decreed in the Book of Genesis that woman should be subordinate to man, history's pages have been largely written by men. Political history, economic history, religious history, art history . . .

There was a time, however, before the great creation legend of Genesis and the myths of ancient Greece, when societies all through the Middle East, Asia and Europe were said to have venerated the feminine. Goddesses, priestesses, healers, physicians, lawmakers, even warriors.

True, written records are sparse or non-existent; therefore, some of this remains highly speculative. But enough scholars have studied murals, statues, figurines, inscriptions, archaeological digs, clay tablets and papyri to conclude that, long before people began praying to the Judaeo-Christian god Yahweh/Jehovah, they were praying to female deities—as far back as 7000 BC, possibly stretching into the Upper Palaeolithic Age, from 25,000 BC, when vagina symbols were carved into cave walls.

One of those scholars was Merlin Stone, American author, sculptor and professor of art history, who spent a decade travelling the world, visiting libraries, museums, universities and excavation sites, poring over myths, poems and legends, examining ancient sculptures and figurines, in order to write what became her defining 1976 work, *When God Was a Woman* (first published in Britain as *The Paradise Papers*). Stone described in detail how female religions were subjected to centuries of persecution and suppression by the proponents of newer religions—i.e. Judaism, Christianity and Islam—which held to a masculine version of the Creator.

However, prior to Abraham, Isaac and Jacob, prior to Christ being declared the Son of God and to Mohammed emerging as Allah's prophet, prior to the notion that a masculine god had created the universe and produced Man in his own divine image—and, yes, prior to the great origin myth in which Eve was born from Adam's rib and then cast as the cause of humankind's downfall on account of her shameful sexuality—female deities were regarded in many parts of the world as the creators of existence. She was the Great Goddess, the Mother Goddess, the Divine Ancestress, the Queen of Heaven and, depending on where she was revered, she went by various names: Isis in Egypt, Astarte in Canaan, Inanna in Sumer, Ishtar in Babylon, Sarasvati in India, Brigit in Celtic Ireland, Nu Wa in China. As Merlin Stone wrote:

> In India, the Goddess Sarasvati was honoured as the inventor of the original alphabet (also knowledge and music), while in Celtic Ireland the Goddess Brigit was esteemed as the supreme deity of language. In Mesopotamia . . . the Goddess Ninlil was revered for having provided Her people with an understanding of planting and harvesting methods.
>
> In nearly all areas of the world, female deities were extolled as healers, dispensers of curative herbs, roots, plants and other medical aids, casting the priestesses who attended the shrines into the role of physicians of those who worshipped there.

In ancient Mesopotamia, the vulva of Inanna, the Sumerian goddess, was considered a sacred site. Sumerians sang hymns to her 'lap of honey'. In the city of Nimrud—30 kilometres south of Mosul, where the murderous Islamic State was to take control in 2014 before being ousted three years later—the goddess Ishtar was worshipped as the inventor of agriculture and the first to establish laws of justice. Women also served as judges and magistrates.

Throughout Canaan (today's Israel), prior to the Hebrew invasion around 1300 to 1250 BC, the worship of female deities was widespread, and, along with it, a female kinship system that valued female independence, including sexual autonomy.

Agrarian societies honoured the goddess, as menstrual cycles were interconnected with the lunar-based agricultural cycles. The earth was Gaia, the ancestral Mother of Life—inherent to all of nature. She *was* nature, until the rise of patriarchal religions began declaring goddess worship and female sexuality akin to sorcery.

The study of ancient Sumerian texts also posits the theory that women were engaged 'in the business activities of the temple, held real estate in their own names, lent money and generally engaged in various economic activities'.

Stone quoted the Greek historian Diodorus Siculus, who recorded his travels across North Africa and the Near East 49 years before the birth of Christ. Women in Ethiopia, Diodorus noted, carried arms, practised communal marriage and raised their children collectively. In ancient Libya, their independence went further.

> All authority was vested in the woman who discharged every kind of public duty. The men looked after domestic affairs . . . and did as they were told by their wives. They were not allowed to undertake war service or to exercise any functions of government, or to fill any public office, such as might have given them more spirit to set themselves up against the women. The children were handed over immediately after birth to the men, who reared them on milk and other food suitable to their age.

Several centuries before Diodorus, the classical Greek historian Herodotus chronicled the state of affairs in Egypt: 'Women go in the marketplace, transact affairs and occupy themselves with business,' he wrote, 'while the husbands stay home and weave.' Inheritance passed through the female line and, according to French theologian and archaeologist Roland de Vaux, 'the wife was often the head of the family, with all the rights such a position entailed'.

All this began to change, Stone posits, from around 2400 BC, when a succession of Indo-European or Aryan invasions brought with them the worship of a warrior, or supreme father, Dyaus Pitar (literally 'God Father', who would later become known as Zeus in Greece, and as Jupiter in Rome). Women began to lose their rights to property, their sexual freedom, their influence on public life. Matrilineal kinship and customs of descent were replaced by patrilineal clans imposing their traditions—usually violently—on those they conquered.

In 2000 BC in Sumer, the earliest known civilisation in southern Mesopotamia, when a man was found guilty of raping a woman, he was sentenced to death. By the time the Assyrians began codifying their laws between 1450 and 1250 BC, and the Hebrews theirs between 1250 and 1000 BC, a raped woman could be put to death if she was already married or betrothed and had not cried out for help. A father was also entitled to force his daughter to marry her rapist, while a woman who failed to bleed on her wedding night was sentenced to death by stoning or burning.

In his monumental study *The Greek Myths*, British classicist Robert Graves declared that, prior to these Indo-European invasions,

> the whole of Neolithic Europe [10,000 BC to 3000 BC] had a remarkably homogenous system of religious ideas, based on worship of the many-titled Mother-goddess.
>
> Ancient Europe had no gods. The Great Goddess was regarded as immortal, changeless and omnipotent; and the concept of fatherhood had not been introduced into religious thought. She took lovers, but for pleasure, not to provide her

children with a father. Men feared, adored and obeyed the matriarch.

From this, a female theocracy, together with matrilineal traditions, proved the rule until, first, the Hellenic invasions, then the Achaean and Dorian invasions around 1100 BC, began to erode the place of women, eventually transforming them into men's chattels. Part of men's upgraded status, according to Graves, only came from the growing realisation—first captured in the Hittite myths dating back to 1600 BC—that women's magical capacity to give birth was not the result of the wind or the rivers impregnating them, as previously thought; it was men. 'Once the relevance of coition to child-bearing had been officially admitted . . . man's religious status gradually improved.'

By the time Greek democracy was founded in the fifth century BC, Solon, the great lawmaker of Athens, had decreed that any woman found not to be a virgin on her wedding night could be sold into slavery. (He also legalised the first state brothels.) In a precursor to many conservative Muslim societies, Solon also declared that rape victims were responsible for their own ruin.

Ancient Rome was hardly an improvement on this, although it was here that women mounted possibly the first female public protest movement in history. In 195 BC, hundreds of upper-class Roman women gathered in the Forum to protest the *Lex Oppia*, a law that sought to restrict their travel, ownership of gold and the wearing of dresses with purple trim. Their fiercest opponent was Cato, the conservative Roman senator and historian who delivered what Jack Holland described as a 'misogynistic tour de force', one that was recorded in Titus Livy's *Early History of Rome*. Cato's speech could have come straight from US vice-president

Mike Pence's hymn sheet or the dystopian horrors of Margaret Atwood's *The Handmaid's Tale*:

> If every married man had been concerned to ensure that his own wife looked up to him and respected his rightful position as her husband, we should not have half this trouble with women en masse. Instead, women have become so powerful that our independence has been lost in our own homes and is now being trampled and stamped underfoot in public. We have failed to retrain them as individuals, and now they have combined to reduce us to our present panic . . .
>
> Woman is a violent and uncontrolled animal, and it is no good giving her the reins and expecting her not to kick over the traces. No, you have got to keep the reins firmly in your own hands . . . Suppose you allow them to acquire or to extort one right after another, and in the end to achieve complete equality with men, do you think you will find them bearable? Nonsense. Once they have achieved equality, they will be your masters.

Cato failed to persuade his colleagues. The Senate overturned the *Lex Oppia*, but the thrust of Cato's argument has been employed ever since to deny women everything from the right to vote to access to birth control.

The next major protest from women came 153 years later, in 42 BC, when Hortensia, the daughter of the Roman orator Quintus Hortensius and herself a great orator, protested against the brutal triumvirate of Marc Antony, Marcus Lepidus and Octavian (later the emperor Augustus).

On behalf of upper-class women, Hortensia spoke out against the imposition of a heavy tax. She asked: 'Why should we pay taxes when we have no part in the honours, the commands, the statecraft for which you contend against each other with such harmful results?'

Similar words would not be uttered until a woman's march on the English parliament in 1642, and then with the rise of the suffragette movement in the late nineteenth and early twentieth centuries, with women like Edith Cowan and Vida Goldstein in Australia, Jane Arthur and Emmeline Pankhurst in Britain, and Susan Anthony and Alice Stone Blackwell in the United States, campaigning for women's rights.

In Rome, women's protests led to the kind of conservative backlash currently assailing Trump's America, although with far more deadly consequences. Once Octavian became Emperor Augustus in 27 BC, he drafted a series of laws known as *Lex Julia*, which attempted to restore traditional Roman values. Ancient laws that had permitted fathers to kill their daughters and husbands their wives if caught in sexual relations outside marriage were reinstituted. Adultery became a public offence, but only for women.

And all this before the rise of Christianity, which would absorb—and expand upon—the misogyny embedded in Greek philosophy and Old Testament teachings, and that would insinuate itself into the western psyche for thousands of years.

'This symbolic devaluing of women in relation to the divine,' Gerda Lerner wrote in *The Creation of Patriarchy*, 'becomes one of the founding metaphors of Western civilisation . . . [where] the subordination of women comes to be seen as "natural".'

\#

Before the advent of agriculture around 8000 BC, and certainly well before the rise of the ancient Greeks and the patriarchal faiths, it is plausible that women had as much access to food, protection, social support and sexual freedom as men.

Christopher Ryan and Cacilda Jethá argued in their controversial book *Sex at Dawn* that the true story of female sexuality had long been 'silenced by religious authorities, pathologised by physicians, studiously ignored by scientists, and covered up by moralising therapists'.

A great deal of research, from primatology, anthropology, anatomy and psychology points to the same fundamental conclusion: human beings and our hominid ancestors have spent almost all of the past few million years or so in small, intimate bands in which most adults had several sexual relationships at any given time.

This approach to sexuality probably persisted until the rise of agriculture and private property no more than ten thousand years ago. In addition to voluminous scientific evidence, many explorers, missionaries and anthropologists support this view, having penned accounts rich with tales of orgiastic rituals, unflinching mate sharing, and an open sexuality unencumbered by guilt or shame.

This, of course, flies in the face of the standard narrative of human sexuality that has been largely transmitted to us through Charles Darwin's theories of natural selection and sex selection, buttressed by evolutionary psychologists who argue that men and women have radically conflicting—and largely genetically determined—reproductive agendas. According to this narrative, men are designed to spread their seed as far and wide as possible, while also ensuring the certainty of their paternity, whereas women are designed to achieve security, both emotional and material. Social constructivists, however, posit a rich diversity of emotions, beliefs and preferences based on wildly different cultures throughout history.

Who's right? I don't know. Probably both, although I'm leaning slightly towards culture over biology. And even if I'm wrong—which I could well be—would it alter the case for gender equality?

In his international bestseller *Sapiens: A Brief History of Humankind*, Yuval Noah Harari argued that societies throughout history assigned a host of attributes to women and men which, for the most part, lacked any firm biological basis.

> For instance, in democratic Athens of the fifth century BC, an individual possessing a womb had no independent legal status and was forbidden to participate in popular assemblies or to be a judge.
>
> In present-day Athens, women vote, are elected to public office, make speeches, design everything from jewellery to buildings to software and go to university. Their wombs do not keep them from doing any of these things as successfully as men do.

How then to distinguish what is biologically determined from what people try to justify through their biological myths? Harari asked.

> A good rule of thumb is 'biology enables, culture forbids'. Biology is willing to tolerate a very wide spectrum of possibilities. It's culture that obliges people to realise some possibilities while forbidding others.
>
> Biology enables women to have children—some cultures oblige women to realise this possibility. Biology enables men to enjoy sex with one another—some cultures forbid them to realise this possibility.

From a biological perspective, therefore, nothing is unnatural if it occurs anywhere in nature; only the moral significance we ascribe to the act renders it 'unnatural'.

Australian comedian Hannah Gadsby gave riveting voice to this in her internationally acclaimed one-woman show, *Nanette*, in which she excavated the loneliness of growing up in the deeply conservative Bible Belt of Tasmania in the 1990s.

Although surrounded by people she loved and trusted, almost all of them believed homosexuality to be a sin. By the time Gadsby was prepared to identify herself as gay, she'd become homophobic herself. Like tens of millions of people throughout history, she'd internalised the shame and self-hatred that comes from repressing one's true self.

Harari explored this further in *Sapiens* by maintaining that our concepts of 'natural' and 'unnatural' are taken not from biology but from Christian theology (although he might have added Islamic jurisprudence, given that in countries like Iran, Saudi Arabia, Sudan, Yemen and parts of Nigeria and Somalia homosexuality is still punishable by death). He argued that the theological meaning of 'natural' refers to 'the intentions of the God who created nature' and that to use limbs and organs contrary to God's intention is, therefore, 'unnatural'.

Mouths, for example, appeared because the earliest multi-cellular organisms needed a way to take nutrients into their bodies. We still use our mouths for that purpose, but we also use them to kiss, speak and, if we are Rambo, to pull the pin out of hand grenades. Are any of these uses unnatural simply because our worm-like ancestors 600 million years ago didn't do those things with their mouths?

On the matter of physical strength—often proffered as a reason for man's historic domination of woman—Harari maintained this holds true only 'on average' and only with respect to certain types of strength. Women were, in fact, generally more robust in the face of disease, hunger and fatigue than men; while also, in many instances, able to run faster and lift heftier weights than men. They'd also been historically excluded from jobs requiring little or no physical effort (such as the priesthood, law and politics) while still engaged in arduous manual labour.

Another theory that supports masculine dominance over women is that men have evolved to be far more aggressive than women, far more prepared to engage in physical violence, thus the history of warfare being a masculine enterprise.

Harari attempted to turn this on its head, too, by suggesting that in order to prosecute a war, you needed stamina, but not necessarily physical strength or aggression. Rather than being 'pub brawls', wars were highly complex projects requiring an extraordinary mix of 'organisation, co-operation and appeasement.'

> The ability to maintain peace at home, acquire allies abroad, and understand what goes through the minds of other people (particularly your enemies) is usually the key to victory. Hence an aggressive brute is often the worst choice to run a war.

(Yes, but not to fight the war, surely.)

The third biological explanation that Harari took apart—and arguably the most common—was that men and women developed different survival and reproductive strategies through millions of years of evolution. Men sought to outperform and defeat other men for the prospect of impregnating fertile women. The more aggressive and competitive the man, the better the chances of his genes surviving to the next generation.

Women, on the other hand—so the theory goes—needed to carry a child for nine demanding months, then nurture that child for years. She needed help. She needed a man, therefore, she complied with whatever conditions the man imposed.

Harari believed this approach was also belied by biological evidence because it relied on the assumption, firstly, that women's 'dependence on external' help put them at the mercy of men, rather than tying them to close-knit networks of other women; and, secondly, that male competitiveness always resulted in the same thing: male social dominance. He cited elephants and bonobo chimpanzees as examples of species where the dynamics between 'dependent females and competitive males' results in a *matriarchal* society. In both bonobo and elephant societies, strong networks of cooperative females controlled the group, pushing to the sidelines 'the self-centred and uncooperative males.' 'If this is possible among bonobos and elephants,' Harari wrote, 'why not among *Homo sapiens*?'

Yuval Noah Harari and the authors of *Sex at Dawn*, Christopher Ryan and Cacilda Jethá, pointed to the beginning of agricultural settlement 10,000 years ago as the time when women's ability to survive began to radically alter.

Nomadic foragers had few, if any, personal possessions, and gave little or no thought to ownership of the land and waters they depended on for their survival. Once our ancestors began settling in agricultural communities, however, social realities began to shift deeply and permanently. Ryan and Jethá observed:

> Suddenly it became crucially important to know where your field ended and your neighbour's began. Remember the Tenth Commandment: 'Thou shalt not covet thy neighbour's house, thou shalt not covet thy neighbour's wife, nor his manservant, nor his maidservant, nor his ox, nor his ass . . .'

Clearly, the biggest loser (aside from slaves perhaps) in the agricultural revolution was the human female, who went from occupying a central, respected role in foraging societies to becoming another possession for a man to earn and defend, along with his house, slaves and livestock.

This is not to glorify the 'noble savage', but rather to suggest that in many hunter-gatherer societies a 'fierce egalitarianism' might well have been a major pattern of social governance. In these societies sex was a shared resource, much like the provision of food, child care and group protection.

Ryan and Jethá's *Sex at Dawn* is rich with anthropological examples of 'primitive' societies that believed in what scientists call 'partible paternity', whereby the foetus was regarded as having been formed from accumulated semen. They list a number of South American societies—from Venezuela to Bolivia—where different notions of conception and foetal development apparently held sway.

This understanding of how semen forms a child leads to some mighty interesting conclusions regarding 'responsible' sexual behaviour. Like mothers everywhere, a woman from these societies is eager to give her child every possible advantage in life.

To this end, she'll typically seek out sex with an assortment of men. She'll solicit 'contributions' from the best hunters, the best storytellers, the funniest, the kindest, the best-looking, the strongest, and so on—in the hopes her child will literally absorb the essence of each.

The authors offer a variety of examples of human sexuality that stand in direct contradiction of what we regard today as 'normal'.

Among the Mohave people of the Colorado River region of America, women were famous for their licentious behaviour.

The Lusi of Papua New Guinea believed that foetal development depended on multiple acts of intercourse, often with different partners. The Aché people of eastern Paraguay identified four types of father, according to American anthropologist Kim Hill: the one who inserted it, the one who mixed it, the one who spilt it, and the one who provided the child's 'essence'.

Anthropologist Thomas Greg found that among the Mehinaku people of central Brazil, the sharing of multiple partners 'contributes to village cohesion' by 'consolidating relationships between persons of different clans' and 'promoting enduring relationships based on mutual affection'.

In the far-eastern foothills of the Himalayas, the Mosuo have always placed women at the centre of their Buddhist society, in which multiple lovers are common, children are born out of wedlock and women own and inherit property.

The authors paint a compelling picture of an alternative universe where, rather than men attempting to control female libido through an inventory of diabolical methods—'female genital mutilation, head-to-toe chadors, medieval witch burnings, chastity belts, suffocating corsets, burying women up to their necks in desert sands and stoning them to death', never mind just plain insults and disparagement—that women in many parts of the world have at various times, in various places, been free to be generous and, therefore, free from guilt with their sexuality.

Which begs a number of questions. What if our standard narrative is wrong? What if man's automatic impulse to control woman's sexuality has never been an intrinsic feature of human nature, but rather a reworking of the social order that arose from agriculture? What if there is an abundance of evidence in the animal kingdom for female promiscuity, 'from fruit flies to humpback whales', as Cordelia Fine asserted in her 2017 book *Testosterone Rex*? (Fine identified 39 species in which female promiscuity has resulted in greater reproductive success, including sandpipers, lionesses, savanna baboons and langur monkeys.)

What if the need for certainty of paternity only became important once permanent agricultural settlements required people to cultivate, defend and populate the land? What if cultural beliefs have always affected the scientific process, and women's sexual libido had always been as high as men's, or higher, or just different, and that what we're seeing now is the cumulative response to an ancient crusade waged over centuries against female sexuality?

4

Sex, lies and videotape

A woman, a spaniel, and a walnut tree
The more they're beaten the better they be.

JOHN TAYLOR (1578–1653)

New York City, 26 May 2018. My flight arrives at JFK airport on a steamy Saturday evening, 24 hours after Harvey Weinstein has had his mugshot and fingerprints taken in a police station, and is then led in handcuffs through a gauntlet of photographers and shouting onlookers into a TriBeCa courthouse to be charged with rape—first degree and third degree on one charge; a first-degree criminal sex act on another. Weinstein professes his innocence.

I watch the news the next morning in a state of physical shock. There, on the screen, is the once almighty Hollywood titan, pale and dazed, being virtually frogmarched towards his Place de la Révolution—a modern adaptation of the last French king, Louis XVI, being escorted to the guillotine.

Weinstein's walk of shame is a stunning moment in the revolution that—in one sense—had begun a little more than seven months earlier, in October 2017, with a tweet by American actor Alyssa Milano, encouraging women to use #MeToo as a hashtag on their Twitter feeds if they'd been sexually harassed or assaulted.

The response became, of course, an unprecedented global movement, but to say this was the beginning of the revolution is a bit like saying hurricanes are caused only by the warming of ocean waters, without mentioning the earth's eastward rotation, or the way water vapour releases heat before it is converted into wind energy. (Yes, I think I've murdered that simile.)

The beginning of the reckoning had been building for years— make that centuries—although there were a few key episodes in recent decades that were to eventually cause Hurricane Harvey to blow. These were, if you like, the warm-up acts.

In 1991, Anita Hill, a liberal black attorney and academic, accused conservative black judge Clarence Thomas, a nominee for the United States Supreme Court, of sexually harassing her when she worked for him at the Department of Education and the Equal Employment Opportunity Commission (EEOC).

Thomas denied the charges, while his supporters accused Hill not only of lying, but of vengeful and delusional behaviour. Hill's detractors suggested—much to the outrage of millions of women—that she'd been spurned by Thomas. They also asked, in effect: 'Why wait ten years to report the allegations? And why was she fired from the EEOC by Thomas?'

The all-male (and all-white) Senate Judiciary Committee eventually dismissed Hill's accusations and refused the testimony of other corroborating (female) witnesses. To this day, Clarence Thomas remains an Associate Justice of the Supreme Court, arguably its most conservative member.

Michael Kimmel, professor of sociology at New York's Stony Brook University and a specialist in gender studies, believes this was when the 'whisper network' among women began, although in reality it had been murmuring in the winds since the women of ancient Rome had gathered in protest in the Forum.

'When Anita Hill testified,' Kimmel tells me, 'I thought to myself, "This conversation is happening all over the country. Women are telling their husbands, their parents, their children: This happened to me."

'In my opinion, Anita Hill was one of the bravest women in twentieth-century America, because she gave women a language to talk about what had happened to them. But of course, when she spoke, she was vilified. "She was a woman scorned," they said. One reporter said, "She was a little bit nutty and a little bit slutty." This lovely, very sweet, innocent, Baptist girl from Oklahoma.

'So when women spoke publicly, they got vilified, and so what happened is that they went underground and they talked to each other and they told each other these stories. For 25 years they've been telling each other these stories.'

Twenty-seven years later almost to the day, and in similar circumstances, Judge Brett Kavanaugh, Donald Trump's nominee for the US Supreme Court, would be accused of having committed sexual assault as a seventeen-year-old. As with Clarence Thomas, the explosive allegations would throw the Supreme Court nomination process into chaos, while also proving a test case for the #MeToo movement and women's preparedness to break their silence over sexual misconduct.

The country was spellbound and, needless to say, impossibly divided. Here was Dr Christine Blasey Ford, a professor at Palo Alto University and reluctant witness to the Senate Judiciary Committee, up against the very embodiment of male power: a privileged, conservative, white—and white-hot—judge backed to the hilt by the president of the United States and the Republican Party.

Ford's recollection of the assault was indelibly inscribed in her mind. At a high school party in the early 1980s, a drunken Kavanaugh had tried to rape her. He'd covered her mouth with his hand to muffle her screams. He'd groped her, pinned her to the bed; then, later, he'd indulged himself in 'uproarious laughter' with his friend Mark Judge.

Kavanaugh denied it all, and in his furious, tear-filled rejection of the allegations—as well as his extraordinary tirade against Democrats—he became the new rallying point for the right and for all those who saw the #MeToo movement as having gone too far, morphing into a hostile liberal order whose politics of personal destruction overrides due process.

After all the gains by women over the previous decades—and, indeed, the previous twelve months, courtesy of the #MeToo movement—this was a dark moment. Once again, powerful men were choosing to believe a powerful man over a woman who had suffered.

#

(Rape survivor to author): *When I saw Dr Blasey Ford testifying I thought this was me—my emotions, my words, my fear, my shame. And I understood absolutely why she'd held on to it for so long. There is always the same question: Why did you wait so long? I tried, but what do you do if no one wants to help you or listen to you, or believe you? Stand in the streets and scream out: 'Injustice.'*

#

In 1994, three years after the Anita Hill case, Paula Jones, a former Arkansas state employee, accused President Bill Clinton of propositioning and sexually harassing her while he was governor of Arkansas. Jones filed a lawsuit against the president, which ultimately led to his impeachment in December 1998 by the US House of Representatives.

The articles of impeachment were issued on the grounds of obstruction of justice and perjury to a grand jury over Clinton's relationship with 21-year-old White House intern Monica Lewinsky. (The articles of impeachment were defeated two months later in the Senate.)

Other women also came forward with allegations of sexual misconduct by Clinton, including rape, while Lewinsky became a national punchline that revolved around her looks, her intellect and the infamous blue dress that had been stained with presidential semen. Lewinsky revealed in *Vanity Fair* magazine in early 2018 that she'd suffered for years from post-traumatic stress disorder. Only in the wake of the #MeToo movement had she come to realise that the road leading to her affair with Clinton had been 'littered with inappropriate abuse of authority, station and privilege'. (Hillary Clinton's road to her failed presidential bid was also littered with alleged instances of her using her law firm in Little Rock, Arkansas to silence and intimidate some of her husband's conquests.)

There were dozens of other political sexual scandals during the 1990s and into the noughties—men like the married Newt Gingrich, Republican speaker of the House of Representatives, who led the impeachment of Bill Clinton while having an affair with his staffer; John Edwards, former Democratic presidential and vice-presidential candidate, whose career collapsed after he fathered a child with an aide, lied about it, then covered it up; Anthony Weiner, Democratic representative from New York, who was forced to resign from Congress in 2011 after admitting to sending sexually explicit photographs of himself to several women, then repeating his actions after his departure from Congress.

In 2014, decades of alleged sexual abuse by Bill Cosby also turned into a media frenzy after stand-up comic Hannibal Buress performed a 'Bill Cosby routine' at the Trocadero in Philadelphia, accusing America's one-time favourite television 'family man' of raping women. By the time Cosby was found guilty in April 2018 on three counts of aggravated indecent assault, almost 60 women had come forward to accuse him of rape, drug-facilitated sexual assault, sexual battery and child abuse dating back to the 1960s.

In July 2016, Roger Ailes, the once all-powerful head of Rupert Murdoch's Fox News, and a man *Rolling Stone* magazine would describe as one of the people 'most responsible for modern America's vicious and bloodthirsty character', was accused of sexual harassment by former Fox news anchor Gretchen Carlson in a damning lawsuit. Nearly two dozen women reinforced Carlson's accusations with claims of their own—abuses ranging from sexual harassment to psychological torture.

'You know, if you want to play with the big boys, you have to lay with the big boys,' Ailes allegedly told Kellie Boyle, a former Republican National Committee field adviser. The married 29-year-old declined to perform oral sex on Ailes, she told *Fortune* magazine, and the following day was denied an important contract for her communications firm. 'I was really lost for a few years,' she said. 'I had my career taken away from me.'

Ailes was forced to step down as head of Fox News, but continued to maintain his innocence up until his death in May 2017. Among those who leapt to his defence was Bill O'Reilly, the top-rating Fox talk show host, who was himself about to be exposed as an alleged sexual predator.

Then came the infamous *Access Hollywood* tape. On 7 October 2016, two days before the second presidential debate between Donald Trump and Hillary Clinton, the *Washington Post* released a video and accompanying article showing Trump boasting in 2005 of moving on a woman 'like a bitch'.

'I'm automatically attracted to beautiful,' the former reality TV star and future president was heard telling Billy Bush, anchor of *Access Hollywood* and the nephew of former US president George H.W. Bush. 'I just start kissing them. It's like a magnet. Just kiss. I don't even wait. And when you're a star, they let you do it . . . Grab 'em by the pussy. You can do anything.'

In another age, say, at the dawn of the Roman Empire, instead of at the end of the American, Trump's comments might be akin to hearing Tiberius admitting to being fellated by toddlers, or Caligula admitting to sleeping with each of his three sisters, both of which they were later accused of doing.

After watching Trump's performance on the *Access Hollywood* video, Canadian writer and social activist Kelly Oxford decided to tweet a description of her first sexual assault. She then invited other women to share similar experiences. Two days later she added the hashtag #NotOk: 'Women: tweet me your first assaults. they aren't just stats. I'll go first: Old man on city bus grabs my "pussy" and smiles at me, I'm 12.'

The stories came flooding in—women and girls by the hundreds, then the thousands, then the millions recounting the time they were slapped, stalked, groped, forcibly kissed, pressed up against, masturbated on, raped . . . by fathers, uncles, friends, teachers, priests, babysitters, classmates, strangers. In 140 characters, they were disclosing—many for the first time—how they'd been molested, traumatised, degraded, disbelieved and sidelined. In their collective release, they were also censuring the would-be-president, a man who had just defended his 'pussy-grabbing' comments as 'locker room talk'.

In the days and weeks that followed, a total of nineteen women came forward to describe a range of abusive behaviour from Trump: grabbing women's breasts; putting his hand up a woman's skirt on a plane; groping; fondling; forcibly kissing; grabbing genitals; squeezing bottoms; and entering beauty pageant dressing rooms while women and girls were in a state of undress. (As the owner of the Miss Universe franchise, Trump had admission rights to the dressing rooms of fourteen- to nineteen-year-old Miss Teen USA contestants.)

Trump had also been accused previously of rape, or attempted rape, by his first wife Ivana (who later retracted her sworn deposition), then by a former business associate, Jill Harth, who claimed in a 1997 lawsuit that Trump had thrown her against the wall of one of his children's bedrooms at his Mar-a-Lago resort before lifting her dress. A third allegation—later discredited—had come from a woman going variously by the names of 'Katie Johnson' and 'Jane Doe'. She'd filed a lawsuit in New York in June 2016, alleging Trump had raped her at a sex party when she was thirteen years old. She said she was lured to the party by billionaire Jeffrey Epstein, a notorious sex offender who, she further claimed, had forced her into rough roleplay sex with the presidential candidate.

'Immediately following this rape,' she claimed in her lawsuit, 'Defendant Trump threatened me that, were I ever to reveal any of the details of [his] sexual and physical abuse of me, my family and I would be physically harmed if not killed.'

Trump denied all accusations of sexual misconduct, including this latest bombshell, with his legal team branding it 'disgusting' and a 'hoax'.

Katie Johnson dropped the lawsuit on 4 November 2016, four days before the presidential election, although that same day she told London's *Daily Mail* newspaper that her motivation in taking legal action was to prevent Trump becoming president.

'[It would mean] we would have a rapist in the White House,' she said. 'I would feel horrified every single day if I stay in this country.'

On 8 November, Donald Trump defeated Hillary Clinton in the race for the White House and, on 20 January 2017, was inaugurated as the 45th president of the United States. He did so—maddeningly, confusingly—with the help of white women, particularly non-college-educated ones, who chose to reject a highly qualified woman in favour of a man who was overtly contemptuous of women.

If Trump's election was testament to a widespread distaste for Clinton, as well as an expression of white conservatism, self-interest or the resilience of the patriarchy, then so, too, were the demonstrations against the president-elect testament to the exact opposite.

The day after his inauguration, hundreds of thousands of women descended on Washington and other American cities as part of the Women's Marches protests against the new leader of the free world. They were rallying in support of women's rights, reproductive rights and LGBTQI rights, and they were joined by millions of women and men around the world.

The Weinstein scandal erupted nine months later, on 5 October 2017—first in the *New York Times*, where Jodi Kantor and Megan Twohey spelt out the shocking history of sexual harassment and abuse by the Hollywood producer, dating back nearly three decades. If ever there was a shining example of relentless investigative journalism, this was it, and it led to Weinstein being fired three days later by the company he'd created and the resignation of four members of his all-male board.

On 10 October, the *New Yorker's* wunderkind reporter, Ronan Farrow, published the results of a ten-month investigation that added further sensational detail to what was now the most scandalous tale of power and sexual perversion in America (apart from, perhaps, the president himself).

Over decades, Weinstein, the producer of films like *The Crying Game, Sex, Lies, and Videotape, Pulp Fiction, Good Will Hunting, The King's Speech* and *Shakespeare in Love*, and a self-professed public champion of women's rights, had allegedly raped, assaulted, harassed and mistreated scores of women, while using employees to aid and abet a culture of complicity, hiring lawyers to intimidate and silence his accusers and former spies to uncover dirt on women and journalists with allegations against him.

The levee of power, money and industry heft that had long protected Weinstein was finally bursting its banks. Actors like Ashley Judd, Rose McGowan, Gwyneth Paltrow, Angelina Jolie, Mira Sorvino, Lena Headey and Asia Argento were now prepared to give public voice to the whispers that had circulated for years. They would be the first of more than 80 women in the film industry to accuse Weinstein of rape, sexual assault or harassment. Weinstein denied committing any acts of non-consensual sex and, at the time of writing, is seeking to have all charges dismissed.

As Ronan Farrow wrote:

For more than twenty years, Weinstein, who is now sixty-five, has also been trailed by rumors of sexual harassment and assault. His behaviour has been an open secret to many in Hollywood and beyond, but previous attempts by many publications, including the *New Yorker*, to investigate and publish the story over the years fell short of the demands of journalistic evidence. Too few people were willing to speak, much less allow a reporter to use their names, and Weinstein and his associates used non-disclosure agreements, payoffs, and legal threats to suppress their accounts.

Tina Brown was editor of the *New Yorker* between 1992 and 1998, before leaving arguably the best job in American journalism to work for Harvey Weinstein. In 1999, she established *Talk* magazine in a joint venture between the Weinstein brothers' Miramax company and Hearst Magazines, but left their employ in 2002, around the time she first heard the rape allegations against her former boss.

'I gave that lead to Ken Auletta at the *New Yorker*,' she tells me now as we sip coffee at her chosen meeting place, the iconic Regency Hotel on Park Avenue, a few blocks from Central Park. 'Ken started to report the case but couldn't get the girls on the record. He got those facts, he corroborated them, but he couldn't get them to go on the record at that time . . . [Weinstein] was just too bloody powerful.'

Weinstein had brought high profile lawyer David Boies in to scuttle the *New Yorker* story. 'I actually introduced Harvey to David Boies when I was at *Talk*,' Brown says, 'and [his law firm Boies, Schiller and Flexner] basically came at David Remnick [Brown's successor as editor of the *New Yorker*] with every conceivable threat. David just didn't have the girls on the record. And you cannot publish something like that without the girls on the record, which is why it took so long.

'And, of course, this was pre-Trump, and I think the Trump Women's March had really created this mood where women were so angry they were willing to go on the record. A new feeling of rageful feminism had begun and that atmosphere made those women decide, "Fuck it, I'm going to speak."'

Once hailed as 'the best magazine editor alive' and 'the hardest and hottest act to follow in journalism', Tina Brown was 25 years old when she was named editor of the 270-year-old British society journal *Tatler* in 1978. Six years later, she was appointed editor-in-chief of *Vanity Fair* and, over the next eight years, managed to quadruple circulation with a tantalising mix of celebrity interviews, fashion and in-depth foreign affairs stories. Dubbed the 'Queen of Buzz', she then went on to edit the *New Yorker* for six years, before making her ill-fated move into Weinstein's employ. When she left Weinstein's company, she shut herself away to write a biography of Princess Diana as an act of therapy.

'I felt very, very bruised by working for him,' she says, 'because he demoralises you with his terrible bullying and threats—he's just a terrible person. He never sexually harassed me, but he lied all the way through. Everything was just one lie after another, and he just undermines you by bullying. People forget what it's like to be bullied by a very big scary man with a dark ominous voice. He's a frightening character . . . and he treated people disgracefully.

'I used to watch him humiliating people. He used to speak to me humiliatingly in front of people . . . and he was just a pig with starlets. I certainly didn't know he was raping anyone until I left there. Probably only his assistants really knew about the erectile dysfunction injections . . . the disgusting nature of his life . . . because the girls weren't actually talking. But their agents knew a lot. And I actually think that the Hollywood agents were hugely at fault to deliver over young women to Harvey, because they *did* know what was happening.'

Of course they knew what was happening. That and the mafia boss-like behaviour where Weinstein talked business as if he was spreading the language of death. 'Whack him. Kill him. Stuff him. Stick him.' According to Brown it was like listening to the late Italian-American crime boss John Gotti speaking. You're in a meeting, talking about buying the rights to somebody's film, and, according to Brown, for Weinstein it was like 'just make sure you take it to the bitter end and fucking gouge him and just leave him his eyes to cry with'.

I spent my first few years in journalism listening to talk like this, mostly from certain editors and senior reporters on Sydney's *Daily Telegraph* and *The Australian*—Murdoch's men who seemed to measure their manhood through their swagger and ability to instil fear; along with their often-derisive comments about women.

I thought this was how things worked in the media—you were only as good as your ability to get a story *and* withstand the terror of some of your bosses—until I took a job on a magazine staffed almost entirely by women and realised that a workplace could be generous and collaborative.

'You know we're on your side,' one female colleague told me after a particularly gruelling editorial meeting shortly after my arrival on the magazine. I couldn't believe my ears. *On my side? Working together?* You mean there was another way of communicating that was free from foul-mouthed menace?

5

Not okay? Me too

In bed we laugh, in bed we cry;
And born in bed, in bed we die;
The near approach a bed may show
Oh human bliss to human woe

ISAAC DE BENSERADE, À *SON LIT* (TRANS. SAMUEL JOHNSON)

Tarana Burke was a community worker in Selma, Alabama, birthplace of the civil rights-defining Voting Rights Act, when she first coined the term 'Me Too' in 2006. Burke had grown up in the Bronx before moving to Alabama, first to study, then to work as a youth leader and activist among mostly marginalised young women.

A survivor of rape and sexual assault, both as a child and teenager, Burke was constantly struck by the number of young women she met who were revealing their own terrible histories of sexual violence.

'[They didn't know] that these things were criminal acts . . . or incredibly improper acts that had happened to them,' she told a packed theatre at the Sydney Opera House via satellite from Los Angeles in March 2018. '[They were] just sharing, knowing something was wrong, but not understanding how to talk about it, or what to do about it.'

Burke understood only too well this inability to talk about sexual violence. She'd faced the same problem herself a decade earlier, in 1996, when she failed to support a thirteen-year-old girl desperate to share her story.

'I called her "Heaven",' Burke told her Sydney audience, 'because I [didn't] want to talk about her real name. I used to run a youth leadership camp and Heaven was a student in my camp. She was always getting in trouble. I kept her close to me . . . because she was one of our "specials". I recognised something in her spirit—really rambunctious but . . . in a lot of pain.

'And we had a session—we would call them "sister-to-sister" sessions, and all the young girls would come out . . . and it was just a time for them to really talk about anything that was on their mind. But inevitably, almost every year, the girls' conversations would shift to their experience of sexual violence and this particular year, 1996, was no different.

'The next day [Heaven] came to find me . . . and she was just pouring out, pouring out, pouring out [that] she had been molested by her mother's boyfriend. I can still remember feeling like I was holding my breath the whole time, because I loved this child. She had just become so special to me and I just recognised this thing she was saying, but she kept talking until finally, literally, I couldn't take it anymore.

'I recognise now, because I'm older and I have the benefit of reflection and understanding, that I hadn't dealt with my own abuse and the things that had happened to me. And so she just was triggering all kinds of things in me that I didn't have space for.

'So I shut her down in the middle of her story and . . . I could see in her face and her body language, her spirit . . . she was just crushed because she trusted me, and it probably took a lot of courage . . . I *know* it took a lot of courage for her to even come forward and share this.

'And you know, as adults, the thing you want to do the most is not fail children, right? Whether we're parents or counsellors you just don't want to fail them. And in that moment, I was so scared to fail her. I just kept thinking, *I'm not a social worker, I'm not a counsellor, I don't know what to say. What can I say?* But in reality, what was playing over and over in my mind is, *This happened to me too.'*

#

(Rape survivor to author): *I just saw his eyes, but I remember the smell of blood, this sweet iron smell and the feeling when the blood runs down your legs. I was twelve years old. My parents called the police, but the police officer wasn't interested and my father was furious. He took me to the hairdresser to have my hair chopped off. I had very long fair hair and I'd been a very happy person until then. It was like I'd been living on a golden lake and everything was open to me, everything was there. Suddenly I was totally lost. I couldn't drive my boat anymore.*

#

A decade after her conversation with Heaven, Tarana Burke created a non-profit organisation called Just Be Inc., with the aim of helping victims of sexual harassment and assault—predominantly young women of colour—to heal. She gave her movement the name Me Too, and actor Alyssa Milano used it as a hashtag when she posted the following tweet on 15 October 2017—ten days after the first *New York Times* Weinstein exposé:

> Me too.
> Suggested by a friend: 'If all the women who have been sexually harassed or assaulted wrote "Me too." as a status, we might give people a sense of the magnitude of the problem.'

Milano had no idea of the provenance of the phrase 'Me too', but, on finding out, corrected the record on *Good Morning America* by crediting Tarana Burke as the founder of what was to become arguably the most influential social movement since the clamour for civil rights in the 1960s.

The old power of traditional media, exemplified by publications like the *New York Times* and the *New Yorker*, had lit the flame of social media, which—in the words of Jeremy Heimans and Henry Timms in their book *New Power*—'surged across the world like a current'.

'Old power,' they wrote, 'works *like a currency*. It is held by few. Once gained, it is jealously guarded . . . New power operates differently, *like a current*. It is made by many. It is open, participatory, and peer-driven. It uploads and it distributes. Like water or electricity, it's most forceful when it surges. The goal with new power is not to hoard it but to channel it.'

Heimans—who is the co-founder of the Australian technology-powered political movement GetUp!, the global campaigning organisation Avaaz and the LGBTQI rights platform All Out—believes #MeToo succeeded as an epoch-defining moment—as opposed to its predecessor #NotOk—because of the choice of words.

'"Not Okay" is a statement, it's an argument,' he tells me when we meet at his offices on Fifth Avenue, where he now runs Purpose, a New York–based consultative agency for 21st-century social movements.

'Whereas "Me Too" is an action, and it contains within it three [crucial] elements. The first is it's actionable. It isn't just a communication statement, it isn't just a message, it isn't just an argument. It says: "Me Too", here's my testimony."

'So you have a job, which is to share your testimony, you have something you can do. The second element is what we call "connected". So, immediately, the very idea of "Me Too" makes you feel part of something bigger—the word "too"—but also the collective action dynamic that it unlocked was so important.

'Because the reason that people had stayed silent for so long was that you couldn't look to your left or to your right and find someone else who was prepared to share the same story, especially in a particular industry or directed at a particular person.'

The third element that Heimans and Timms identified in their book was its range and reach. It could be extended, adapted, changed, depending on the context, the country, the industry that you were in.

'So people took the idea of "Me Too" and changed it,' Heimans explained. 'In France, it took on a different form. It became "Denounce Your Pig" (#BalanceTonPorc). So in each of these contexts it evolves. And that's partly because the idea is completely ownerless. Even though the history of it was of Tarana Burke originating this idea in a very specific context, it was just not claimable by anybody, which made it much easier to adapt.'

Adapt it did. As Heimans and Timms noted in *New Power*, within 48 hours of Alyssa Milano's tweet, almost one million people had responded with their own.

In just one day, twelve million Facebook comments, posts and reactions were logged . . . No one was the boss of this movement, and no one quite knew where it would go next . . . The most striking thing about #MeToo was the sense of power it gave to its participants: many who had felt for years that they were helpless to stop longtime abusers, or had been afraid of retribution, suddenly found the courage to stand up to them. Every individual story was strengthened by the surge of the much larger current. Each individual act of bravery was, in fact, made by many.

'You've been groped? So have I.'

'You were penetrated as a little girl? So was I.'

'You were assaulted and you've felt dirty, humiliated and responsible ever since? That's how I've felt.'

'You've carried this around with you for decades? Yeah, me too.'

#

(Rape survivor to author): *He threw me on his bed and sat on me, taking both sides of my hair and pulling at my hair. He then tried to take my clothes off. 'Don't touch my legs,' I screamed. 'Take your dirty fingers off me.' I'm a tiny person and he was like a monster. He took me by the hair and threw my head against the wall, several times. Then he spat in my face and licked it away and said to me in a whisper, 'If you kiss me, I'll give you some chocolate.' 'It's over,' I told myself. 'You'll never get out of this alive.'*

#

When American actor Terri Conn read Alyssa Milano's tweet in 2017, she began to relive an experience she'd had with director James Toback in Central Park nineteen years earlier. She started trawling through Twitter for women who had used both the #MeToo and #JamesToback hashtags and, together, they formed a Twitter support group.

They then took their story to Glenn Whipp, an entertainment writer at the *Los Angeles Times*. Within days of Whipp's story being published, 300 women had come forward with their own accounts of Toback's alleged abuse.

Whipp described in graphic detail how Toback had once prowled the streets looking for attractive young women. Introducing himself as the director of films like *Black and White* or *Two Girls and a Guy*, he would entice the women to hotel rooms, movie trailers and public parks on the pretext of an interview or audition.

Whipp wrote:

During these meetings, many of the women said, Toback boasted of sexual conquests with the famous and then asked humiliating personal questions. How often do you masturbate? How much pubic hair do you have? He'd tell them that he couldn't properly function unless he 'jerked off' several times a day. And then he'd dry-hump them or masturbate in front of them, ejaculating into his pants or onto their bodies and then walk away. Meeting over.

Terri Conn recalled at the time being intrigued enough by Toback's credentials to agree to meet the director in New York's Central Park. The meeting was ostensibly to discuss her dream of being in an 'edgy independent film'.

Conn said that Toback took her to a relatively secluded area of the park, where he then suggested to her that the best way of getting to know each other was to look deeply into each other's eyes while experiencing orgasm.

That's when, according to Conn, Toback went down on his knees and began thrusting against her leg, urging her not to look away from him. 'I was shocked and frozen and didn't know what to do,' Conn said. 'I thought if I resisted, it could get worse. He could overpower me.'

According to Conn, Toback quickly ejaculated into his khakis, stood up, then asked her to meet him for dinner later that night to continue the process. She ignored all subsequent phone calls and never saw the director again.

James Toback later denied the accusations in a profanity-strewn interview with *Rolling Stone* magazine:

Toback: . . . The idea that I would offer a part to anyone for any other reason than that he or she was gonna be the best of anyone I could find is so disgusting to me. And anyone who says it is a lying cocksucker or cunt or both. Can I be any clearer than that?

[Rolling Stone]: No, that's pretty clear.

#

After the Harvey Weinstein revelations, Roy Price—the head of Amazon Studios—was outed, then famed fashion photographer Terry Richardson, then author, journalist and broadcaster Mark Halperin, then music publicist Kirt Webster, then actor Kevin Spacey (for alleged sexual misconduct towards boys and young men), then comedian and producer Louis C.K., then television hosts Charlie Rose and Matt Lauer, then dozens of other prominent men in the arts and entertainment industries: actors, playwrights, producers, editorial directors, chief executives, studio heads, editors, publishers . . .

From the American entertainment industry, it crossed over into state legislatures, and on to Capitol Hill, with congressmen from Arizona, Michigan, Minnesota and Alabama (in the form of the appalling would-be Republican senator Roy Moore) all caught up in the widening scandal. Silicon Valley then came under scrutiny.

Up until this point, there were many cynics who believed the #MeToo movement had to a large extent been co-opted by rich, white American women. (They would level this charge even more against the #TimesUp movement which was launched by Hollywood celebrities less than three months later.) But before long the searchlights were trained on restaurants, the automotive industry, hospitals, domestic workers and hotels. In Chicago, female hotel workers were granted the right to install panic buttons on their uniforms; it transpired that bending over to clean a bath or turn down the sheets had always been a hazardous occupation.

In a letter published barely a month after the Weinstein allegations first aired, the national organisation for Latina female farm workers (Alianza Nacional de Campesinas)—representing some 700,000 women labouring in agricultural fields and packing sheds across America—wrote in support of their sisters in the entertainment industry.

They, too, had experienced gender-based violence at the hands of bosses and co-workers. They, too, had suffered in silence, and feared complaining because of the enormous ramifications for their work and livelihoods. 'We do not work under bright stage lights or on the big screen,' they wrote. 'We work in the shadows of society, in isolated fields and packinghouses that are out of sight and out of mind for most people in this country. Your job feeds souls, fills hearts and spreads joy. Our job nourishes the nation with the fruits, vegetables and other crops that we plant, pick and pack.'

From the margins of society these women were voicing common cause with having been preyed upon by men possessed of the power to hire and fire, to blacklist and threaten women's security, economically, physically and emotionally.

'We understand the hurt, confusion, isolation and betrayal that you might feel,' they wrote. 'We also carry shame and fear resulting from this violence. It sits on our backs like oppressive weights. But, deep in our hearts, we know that it is not our fault. The only people at fault are the individuals who choose to abuse their power to harass, threaten and harm us, like they have harmed you.'

Neither was sports immune. Larry Nassar, USA Gymnastics national team doctor, would eventually be sent to prison for up to 175 years for his sickening abuse of more than 150 women and girls.

From the United States, the current then crossed the Atlantic to Britain, where a dozen MPs were accused of unwanted sexual behaviour, and the ruling Conservative Party's defence secretary, Michael Fallon, was forced to resign.

In Australia, Tracey Spicer—a former television journalist and fellow contributor at Fairfax Media—sent a tweet to her nearly 50,000 followers on 17 October 2017 asking about sexual harassment in the media and entertainment industries.

The catalyst for Spicer's tweet had been a visit to her local police station to report a series of highly disturbing Facebook messages from Australian men—professing to be loving husbands, fathers and grandfathers—threatening sexual violence. At the police station, an officer casually remarked on the #MeToo movement shaking America, and how rare it was for Australian women to approach police about their own harassment and abuse. That was all the encouragement Spicer needed to send a tweet that would soon have her dubbed 'the avenging angel of Australian feminism':

'Currently, I am investigating two long-term offenders in our media industry. Please, contact me privately to tell your stories.'

Spicer was overwhelmed by allegations from more than 500 women, and the names of 65 men. (At the time of writing, thousands of women had contacted Spicer with direct experiences of rape, harassment and assault.)

The first man to be exposed during this period was Don Burke, the celebrity gardener who, in his heyday, hosted the most popular program on Australian television, *Burke's Backyard*. In a joint investigation by Fairfax Media and the ABC, Burke was exposed as a 'psychotic bully, misogynist and sexual predator' who, for years, had indecently assaulted, harassed and terrorised women, particularly female employees. The allegations ranged from lunging at breasts, lifting up skirts and boasting about the size of his penis to suggesting various sexual positions to female employees and insisting a female employee join him in watching a video of a woman having sex with a donkey.

In another instance Burke reportedly explained to a young female reporter in the late 1980s why he'd bought a horse for a young relative: 'Because I love watching her rub her cunt on its back.'

'I was absolutely and utterly repulsed by the man,' the reporter recalled. 'I felt compromised, I felt violated, I just felt disgusted. I took the tape recording to the head of publicity [of the Nine Network] at the time and said I want action. And the next day I received a bunch of flowers and that was the end of it.'

As with Weinstein's company, Nine management had known of Don Burke's behaviour for years but failed to act. 'They didn't really give a damn,' one former senior network employee said. 'He was just too popular a celebrity.'

Six weeks later, in another joint Fairfax/ABC investigation, award-winning Australian actor Craig McLachlan was accused by three women from the 2014 musical *The Rocky Horror Show* of having indecently assaulted, harassed and intimidated them, both on and off the stage, while inhabiting the role of alien transvestite Dr Frank-N-Furter.

McLachlan vehemently denied the allegations, and launched defamation proceedings against the two media outlets, as well as one of his accusers, former co-star Christie Whelan Browne. McLachlan said his career had been 'annihilated' and his life ruined. (These defamation proceedings were delayed in January 2019, after Victorian police charged McLachlan with one count of common law assault, seven counts of indecent assault and one of attempted indecent assault. The defamation proceedings were postponed to be heard after McLachlan had faced criminal charges in the Melbourne Magistrates Court.)

As in other countries, there was an immediate backlash to the airing of these allegations. Here was lack of due process—trial by Twitter, a celebrity-obsessed media circus, a conflating of shocking abuses with minor indiscretions, a tarring of all men with the same brush, a descent into 'victimhood', a new puritanism, more finger-wagging from feminists . . .

Germaine Greer—never a woman to sidestep a controversy or igniting one herself (remember her 'big arse' comment directed at former prime minister Julia Gillard, and her description of Weinstein's accusers as 'career rapees')—waded into the murky waters by defending Craig McLachlan's legal presumption of innocence.

'He hasn't been proved guilty of anything,' she said. 'Now it's becoming if you're in a position of power or influence, you can't make a pass at somebody, because it will be considered to be inappropriate use of influence, force and so on. How do you express desire without putting pressure on people?'

Just weeks earlier, Oscar award-winning actor Geoffrey Rush had also issued defamation proceedings against the Rupert Murdoch–owned *Daily Telegraph*, which had reported inappropriate behaviour during a 2015 Sydney Theatre Company production of *King Lear.*

In an affidavit submitted to the Australian Federal Court in April 2018, Rush's lawyer said the four-time nominated and one-time Academy Award winner had suffered 'tremendous emotional and social hardship' because of the accusations. They had turned him into a virtual recluse, causing him to wake each morning with 'a terrible sense of dread'. He vehemently denied any inappropriate behaviour.

Four months later, Eryn Jean Norvill—the actress at the centre of the allegations who had played the role of Lear's daughter Cordelia—agreed to testify on behalf of the *Telegraph*, following a judge's initial decision to throw out the newspaper's 'plainly deficient' defence. In their amended document, lawyers for the *Telegraph* stated that during a 2015 preview performance of *King Lear*, the acclaimed Australian actor had allegedly 'moved his hand so that it traced down [Norvill's] torso and across the side of her right breast'. In an earlier Federal Court hearing, lawyers alleged that Rush had repeatedly touched his STC co-star in a manner that made her uncomfortable. Not only had he ignored her requests to stop, he'd also allegedly followed Norvill to the female toilets at an after-party on the final night of the production, waiting outside her cubicle until Norvill had told him to 'fuck off'.

The three-week trial in Sydney's Federal Court proved a sensation, with illustrious names like two-time Oscar nominee Judy Davis and stage legend Robyn Nevin taking the witness stand. Nevin told the court she believed the allegations against her old friend Geoffrey Rush were baseless. She had played the Fool in the same *Lear* production and had seen nothing untoward. Nevin also denied ever saying to Norvill (as Norvill claimed she had): 'Oh, I thought Geoffrey had stopped doing that. Poor Jane.' (This last a reference to Rush's wife, Jane Menelaus.)

Norvill accused Nevin, an enormously powerful figure within the Australian arts community, of enabling (along with other senior actors) Rush's alleged inappropriate behaviour towards her during the *Lear* rehearsals. In a telling exchange, Rush's barrister, Bruce McClintock SC, said to Norvill: 'It's ludicrous to suggest . . . Ms Nevin . . . would ever have tolerated an act of sexual harassment of a younger actor.'

'No it isn't,' Norvill replied. 'We are from different generations; maybe we have different ideas about what is culturally appropriate in a workplace.'

Like Dr Christine Blasey Ford's appearance before the US Senate Judiciary Committee, Eryn Jean Norvill was mortified to have found herself in the public eye. She'd made her complaint privately to the Sydney Theatre Company, and then declined to formalise that complaint. Not only had she not wanted Rush to know of her complaint, she'd also refused point blank to speak to the *Telegraph*. The Murdoch-owned newspaper had published anyway.

Compared to the forensic probing and scruples shown by the *New York Times'* and the *New Yorker's* investigations into Harvey Weinstein, the *Telegraph's* 'investigation' looked like a drive-by shooting. Eryn Jean Norvill's life was upended as the media hounded her day and night. She felt isolated and terrified. And this was before the relentless cross-examination that would see her accused by Rush's lawyers of telling 'a whole pack of disgusting lies' in an attempt to 'blacken and smear' their client's name.

It was an infuriating spectacle to witness, particularly given that by agreeing to testify Norvill was potentially helping to save the *Telegraph* from an enormous defamation payout.

On 11 April 2019, Federal Court judge Michael Wigney found the *Telegraph* had defamed Rush with a 'recklessly irresponsible piece of sensationalist journalism'. He ordered Rush be paid more than $850,000, with the prospect of millions more in aggravated special damages. The judge rejected the testimony of Norvill, declaring he was 'not ultimately persuaded that Ms Norvill was an entirely credible witness.' It was a profound rebuke, and a devastating blow to the #MeToo movement in Australia.

Norvill stood by everything she'd said at trial. 'I told the truth,' she declared in a statement to the assembled media after the verdict. 'I know what happened. I was there . . . I would have been content to receive a simple apology and a promise to do better, without any of this.'

She then added: 'We are living through complicated and rapidly changing times. We need to make genuine cultural change in our professions and industries. We can do it, but only if we acknowledge and confront, with honesty, the problems and the complexities of the power imbalances in our workplaces. It has to be possible for a young woman working in theatre who feels unsafe in her workplace to get that situation fixed.'

The entire script could have been borrowed from ancient times, a point not lost on Julia Baird, writing with deadly aim in the *Sydney Morning Herald* shortly after the trial ended, and five months before the verdict was delivered.

'Think of Medusa,' she wrote. 'She was a beautiful maiden, once. But we forget her story, the origins of her myth. We remember she could turn men to stone with her rage, that she was monstrous and ugly and to be feared. We forget that as a young woman she was raped in the temple of Athena, by the god of the sea, Poseidon. And for this, she was cursed. Punished for being a victim.'

Baird was not just writing about Eryn Jean Norvill's public ordeal. She was also referring to ABC state political reporter Ashleigh Raper who had just released an explosive statement outlining allegations of sexual harassment against the New South Wales state Opposition leader Luke Foley. Raper, like Norvill, had been publicly exposed against her will, in this case by the New South Wales Minister for Corrective Services David Elliott, speaking under parliamentary privilege.

In October 2018, Elliott had accused Luke Foley of drunkenly harassing an unnamed ABC journalist at a Christmas function in 2016. He was deliberately setting loose the hares. Raper had never sanctioned his comments, because she wanted the matter to remain private. She only decided to release a public statement because media and political interest had built to fever pitch, and because Luke Foley had allegedly reneged on his pledge to her to resign as Opposition leader.

'This is a position I never wanted to be in and a statement I never intended to make,' she said, before outlining her version of what happened at the end-of-year Christmas event in 2016: 'The party moved from Parliament House to a Martin Place bar after a number of hours. Later in the evening, Luke Foley approached a group of people, including me, to say goodnight. He stood next to me. He put his hand through a gap in the back of my dress and inside my underpants. He rested his hand on my buttocks. I completely froze.' Foley then left the bar.

ABC journalist Sean Nicholls witnessed the incident, but Raper swore him to secrecy. Like Eryn Jean Norvill, she chose not to make a formal complaint for reasons she now wanted to explain.

'It is clear to me that a woman who is the subject of such behaviour is often the person who suffers once a complaint is made. I cherished my position as a state political reporter and feared that would be lost. I also feared the negative impact the publicity could have on me personally and on my young family. This impact is now being felt profoundly.'

Luke Foley resigned as Opposition leader while angrily denying the allegations and threatening to sue for defamation. He later withdrew that threat, although the damage was done. Within a 24-hour period, we'd witnessed a young actress and a young state political reporter accused of lying over matters neither had wished to speak about publicly.

Julia Baird didn't bother to hide her crackling fury, noting the double penalty imposed on women whose alleged assaults entered the public domain against their will. First the exposure, then the denunciation, where they were then cast as 'playthings, provocateurs' and 'hysterical fabulists.' Here, all on the one day, she observed, was television footage of a strutting post mid-term American president who had once boasted of grabbing women's genitals with impunity, an Australian politician (Foley) looking like a man hell-bent on destroying a woman's reputation to save his career, and an Australian actor's (Rush) barristers seeking to demolish a woman's version of events in court.

This was no 'partisan politics,' she wrote. This was the patriarchy in full flight, although thankfully, some of Foley's (male) Labor colleagues condemned the former Opposition leader's hypocrisy, giving some gossamer thread of hope to the prospect that more men will begin denouncing the outing of women in this fashion.

6

The hunting ground

I don't ask you to love me always like this, but I ask you to remember. Somewhere inside me there'll always be the person I am tonight.

F. SCOTT FITZGERALD, TENDER IS THE NIGHT

I arrived in the French Riviera town of Cannes on 14 May 2018, three days too late to witness Cate Blanchett lead an extraordinary, first-time protest at the international film festival—82 actresses, female producers, directors, writers, cinematographers and editors marching arm in arm to demand equal pay and an end to sexual harassment. The number 82 was no accident. It was the number of female-directed films that had been selected for the festival's esteemed Palme d'Or competition during its entire 71-year history, compared with 1645 films directed by men.

'Women are not a minority in the world, yet the current state of our industry says otherwise,' Blanchett declared in her capacity as president of the Cannes Film Festival jury.

'We expect our institutions to actively provide parity and transparency in their executive bodies and provide safe environments in which to work. We expect our governments to make sure that the laws of equal pay for equal work are upheld. We demand that our workplaces are diverse and equitable so that they can best reflect the world in which we actually live. A world that allows all of us in front and behind the camera, all of us, to thrive shoulder to shoulder with our male colleagues.'

On 20 May, Italian actress Asia Argento delivered an inflammatory address to 3000 dignitaries at the film festival's closing ceremony.

'In 1997, I was raped by Harvey Weinstein here at Cannes,' she told her spellbound audience during her presentation of the Best Actress Award. 'I was 21 years old. This festival was his hunting ground. I want to make a prediction: Harvey Weinstein will never be welcomed here ever again. He will live in disgrace, shunned by a film community that once embraced him and covered up for his crimes.'

She then zeroed in on other alleged predators in the room. 'Even tonight,' she said, 'sitting among you, there are those who still have to be held accountable for their conduct against women, for behaviour that does not belong in this industry, does not belong in any industry. You know who you are. But most importantly, we know who you are. And we're not going to allow you to get away with it any longer.'

Argento was speaking barely three weeks before a fresh hell would visit her when her boyfriend, celebrity chef Anthony Bourdain, took his own life in a hotel room in north-eastern France, and thirteen weeks before Argento herself would be targeted as a sexual abuser by a young male actor.

Let's deal with Weinstein first.

Argento's claims of being raped by Harvey Weinstein were first revealed in that era-defining piece of journalism by Ronan Farrow in the *New Yorker* in October 2017— a 10,000-word essay which, together with a *New York Times* investigation that same week, finally blew the lid off decades of monstrous behaviour by the Hollywood film producer. Farrow and the *Times* investigation team would later win the Pulitzer Prize for Public Service.

The scene of Weinstein's alleged crime against Argento was the illustrious Hotel du Cap-Eden-Roc in Antibes, a once-obscure nineteenth-century villa that had been transformed into an iconic winter destination for the rich and famous during the 1920s. Ernest Hemingway and F. Scott Fitzgerald had visited there for long sojourns, Fitzgerald eventually immortalising the place as Hotel des Étrangers in his last completed novel, *Tender is the Night*. Marc Chagall sketched from his beachside cabana during the 1960s. Winston Churchill, Charles De Gaulle and John F. Kennedy's family all occupied rooms on different occasions, while Elizabeth Taylor and Richard Burton conducted a tryst there before choosing it as their honeymoon destination.

According to Argento, Weinstein lured her there in 1997 with an invitation to a party he was throwing. She was led upstairs to Weinstein's room by one of his producers, but found no party, just Weinstein's hulking presence. (The producer has denied any role in bringing Argento to the hotel.)

Initially, Weinstein was solicitous, lauding her work. He then left the room and returned wearing his signature bathrobe, holding a bottle of lotion. 'He asks me to give him a massage. I was, like, "Look, man, I am no fucking fool", but looking back, I am a fucking fool. And I am still trying to come to grips with what happened.'

Argento said she reluctantly agreed to massage Weinstein, but that the Hollywood kingpin then pulled her skirt up, prised her legs apart, and performed oral sex on her, as she repeatedly begged him to stop. She was terrified, so she began feigning pleasure. Perhaps, she reasoned, this would end the assault.

'I was not willing,' she told Farrow. 'I said, "No, no, no." . . . It's twisted. A big fat man wanting to eat you. It's a scary fairy tale.

'The thing with being a victim,' she continued, 'is I felt responsible. Because, if I were a strong woman, I would have kicked him in the balls and run away. But I didn't. And so I felt responsible.' Argento described the incident as a 'horrible trauma'.

Farrow: 'Argento recalled sitting on the bed after the incident, her clothes "in shambles," her make-up smeared. She said that she told Weinstein, "I am not a whore," and that he began laughing. He said he would put the phrase on a T-shirt. Afterward, Argento said, "He kept contacting me." For a few months, Weinstein seemed obsessed, offering her expensive gifts.'

This is where the story grows more complex. Argento admitted she eventually succumbed to Weinstein's advances, drawing close enough to accompany him on dinner dates and be introduced to his mother. She had consensual sexual relations with Weinstein on numerous occasions over the next five years, although she labelled the encounters one-sided and 'onanistic'. Their first encounter after the alleged assault in Cannes occurred several months later, just prior to the release of the Miramax-distributed, British–American film *B. Monkey*, in which Argento played a starring role.

'I felt I had to,' she said, 'because I had the movie coming out and I didn't want to anger him.' She was also convinced Weinstein would destroy her career if she didn't submit to his advances.

In speaking to Farrow, Asia Argento was fully cognisant of how this contact with Weinstein would be used to attack her credibility. That was part of the problem. The initial assault had laid its tripwire. Every time she saw him she felt overpowered. 'Just his body, his presence, his face, bring me back to the little girl that I was when I was 21. When I see him, it makes me feel little and stupid and weak. After the rape, he won.'

There was more to come.

In August 2018, the *New York Times* revealed that in the months following Argento's public revelations about Weinstein, the Italian actress and director had paid US$380,000 to a 22-year-old American actor and musician as hush money for her alleged sexual assault of him. The young man was Jimmy Bennett, best known for his role as a six-year-old actor in Eddie Murphy's 2003 film *Daddy Day Care* and as a young James T. Kirk in the 2009 film *Star Trek*.

In documents sent to the *Times* via encrypted email, Bennett accused Argento of sexually attacking him in a California hotel room in 2013, two months after his seventeenth birthday, when Argento was 37. (Bennett was ten months shy of California's legal age of consent.) The two had first met in 2004, when seven-year-old Bennett was cast in the Argento-directed and co-written film *The Heart is Deceitful Above All Things*. Argento was playing the role of Sarah, a drug-addled mother, opposite Bennett's abused-son character Jeremiah, who is raped and co-opted by his mother into becoming a cross-dresser.

According to documents viewed by the *Times*, Argento and Bennett maintained intermittent contact over the ensuing years. Bennett likened their relationship to a 'mother–son' connection, which is how Argento referred to their relationship when she tagged Bennett in an Instagram post on 9 May 2013, the day of their reunion at the Ritz-Carlton hotel in Marina del Rey.

'Waiting for my long lost son my love @jimmymbennett in trepidation #marinadelrey smoking cigarettes like there was no next week,' Argento wrote in a selfie caption.

'I'm almost there!:) 5 min,' Bennett responded underneath the photograph.

In her hotel room, Bennett contends, Argento poured him a drink then showed him a flurry of notes she'd been writing to him on hotel stationery. The *Times* reported:

> She then kissed him, pushed him back on the bed, removed his pants and performed oral sex. She climbed on top of him and the two had intercourse, the document says. She then asked him to take a number of photos.
>
> Later that day she posted a close-up of their faces on Instagram with the caption, 'Happiest day of my life reunion with @jimmymbennett xox,' and added that 'jimmy is going to be in my next movie and that is a fact, dig that jack.'

That post and others (along with photos) were included with Bennett's notice of intent to sue Argento in November 2017, one month after Argento had publicly accused Harvey Weinstein.

According to Bennett, Argento's allegations against Weinstein had re-triggered his own trauma. Now he wanted $US3.5 million in damages for the emotional distress, assault and battery he had suffered, presumably to compensate him for the calamitous drop in his earnings—an average of $US540,000 per year down to $US60,000—that had been caused by the trauma.

The *Times* noted that Bennett had felt 'extremely confused, mortified and disgusted' on his way home to Orange County on the afternoon of his reunion with Argento. A month later, however, he'd tweeted Argento a message saying, 'Miss you momma!!!!!', along with a photograph of an engraved bracelet Argento had given him to commemorate the movie they'd starred in nine years earlier.

Five months after sending his tweet, Bennett filed a lawsuit in the Orange County Superior Court, claiming his parents had banned him from the family home and cheated him out of at least US$1.5 million in earnings held in a family trust. He was broke and two months behind on his rent.

Given Argento's prominent role in the #MeToo movement, the *Times*' revelations were a bombshell. After five days of silence, Argento issued a statement denying any sexual encounter with the young actor.

'I am deeply shocked and hurt by having read news that is absolutely false,' she said. 'I have never had any sexual relationship with Bennett,' adding that his claim amounted to 'a longstanding persecution'. She also revealed that it was her late partner Anthony Bourdain, and not her, who had paid Bennett, and that this was intended as a gesture of financial help to a troubled young man.

The *New York Times* stood by its reporting, noting that, among the documents sent to the newspaper, was a 'selfie' dated 9 May 2013 showing Argento and Bennett lying in bed together. Under the terms of Bennett and Argento's agreement, the photograph and its copyright had been given to Argento.

The next day the American celebrity gossip website *TMZ* posted text messages exchanged between Argento and a friend which, if authentic, clearly showed Argento admitting to sex with Bennett. 'I had sex with him it felt weird. I didn't know he was a minor until the shakedown letter,' she wrote. Then, 'The public knows nothing, only what the NYT wrote. Which is one sided. The shakedown letter. The horny kid jumped me.'

In another text Argento showed her friend a photograph of the note Bennett had reportedly written to her on Ritz-Carlton stationery following their reunion: 'Asia, I love you with all my heart. So glad we met again and I'm so glad your [sic] in my life. Jimmy.' Bennett then kept sending Argento unsolicited nudes of himself.

In another text to her friend, Argento said, 'It wasn't raped [*sic*] but I was frozen. He was on top of me. After, he told me I had been his sexual fantasy since [*sic*] was 12.'

Not surprisingly, Harvey Weinstein—through his lawyer Benjamin Brafman—seized on the Argento accusations, accusing the actress of 'a stunning level of hypocrisy' that demonstrated how threadbare her allegations against Weinstein were.

'What is perhaps most egregious,' Brafman said, 'is the timing, which suggests that at the very same time Argento was working on her own secret settlement for the alleged sexual abuse of a minor, she was positioning herself at the forefront of those condemning Mr. Weinstein, despite the fact that her sexual relationship with Mr. Weinstein was between two consenting adults which lasted for more than four years.'

At one level, the Argento allegations were a gift to those wanting to undermine the credibility of the #MeToo movement; at another, they were a sobering reminder that issues of sexual misconduct, power and privilege were not always the provenance of one gender.

7

La grande cause

*Women are not altogether in the wrong when they refuse
the rules of life prescribed to the World, for men only
have established them and without their consent.*

MICHEL DE MONTAIGNE, *ESSAYS*

Marlène Schiappa, the French Minister for Gender Equality, greets
me in her office in central Paris, the French national flag fluttering
outside her window, a photograph of her country's youthful,
not-yet-embattled president inspecting us from above her desk.

In 2017, after winning an astonishing victory in the French
presidential elections, Emmanuel Macron announced that gender
equality was the *grande cause* of his five-year term, and that he
was appointing Schiappa, a former blogger and daughter of a
Corsican father and Italian mother, to tackle the country's gender
pay gap and to punish street harassment with on-the-spot fines.

In her previous incarnation, Schiappa had edited a book called
Letters to My Uterus, a collection of sixteen essays by women
addressing their menstruation, sex life, pregnancies, menopause,

experience of endometriosis and their shaming by the medical system. She had also appeared on stage in Paris in March 2018, performing one of the monologues in Eve Ensler's *Vagina Monologues* ('My vagina is angry,' she told her audience of 800) and since her appointment as minister had campaigned against *les violences obstétricales*—the harrowing procedures women often underwent during childbirth, including unnecessary episiotomies.

But it was sexism in general, and sexual violence and harassment in particular, that Schiappa wanted to focus on, along with the gender stereotypes her president had first become aware of as an investment banker, prior to his entering politics. (Macron had reportedly attended numerous board meetings where few women were present. When they were—and chose to speak—the men would often look away or down at their phones.)

This was part of the background for Macron's powerful speech on the International Day for the Elimination of Violence Against Women (25 November) in 2017, when he described French society as 'sick with sexism', before calling for a minute's silence for the 123 women—one every three days—killed during the previous twelve months.

Four days prior to my meeting with Schiappa, the National Assembly— France's lower house of parliament—had passed a bill curbing sexual harassment and defining the term more specifically as anything that 'infringes the freedom of movement of women in public spaces and undermines self-esteem and the right to security'.

Marlène Schiappa has felt this insecurity all her life, from the time she was a young girl growing up in the working-class Parisian neighbourhood of Belleville.

'When Virginia Woolf wrote *A Room of One's Own*, she said the home was the most dangerous place for a woman,' Schiappa tells me now in halting English, her press secretary interpreting beside her. 'For me, that's not the case. I think the street is the most dangerous place.'

Schiappa recounts how when she and her sister ventured out as teenagers—to school, the supermarket, to meet friends—young men would follow them, catcalling, harassing, sometimes even groping. Invariably, the two girls would take alternative routes to stay out of harm's way.

'Our father used to tell us that our neighbourhood was peaceful because when he went out no one bothered him. And we said, "We can't do that because we're girls. It's peaceful for you because you're a man . . . but if we go out, we'll be followed."'

Schiappa had recently overheard her eleven-year-old daughter and a friend swapping strategies for dealing with predatory behaviour. 'My daughter said, "Watch out if there's a group of guys coming, you need to look straight in front of you." And her friend said, "That's not my technique. I pretend to be on the phone or listening to music."'

On-the-spot fines in France will now range from 90 to 750 euros for persistent catcalling and aggressively lecherous street behaviour, or anything else that causes women discomfort in public. This includes 'asking a woman for her phone number ten times in a row, or following her down several streets'.

Criticised by far-right lawmakers as a 'witch hunt against men', Schiappa counters that the bill is an example of the exact opposite.

'We want to preserve seduction, chivalry and *l'amour à la francaise* by saying what is key is consent. Between consenting adults everything is allowed—we can seduce, talk—but if someone says "no", it's "no" and it's final.'

This notion of legal consent has even extended to children in France where, shortly after my visit to Paris, the National Assembly pulled back from setting fifteen as the minimum age at which a minor can accede to a sexual relationship with an adult. Under current legislation, sex with a child under fifteen is regarded as an offence. The onus of proof, however, rests on prosecutors to prove that there was force in order for it to classify as rape.

#

There is probably no city in the world that tingles with sex quite like Paris.

Throughout its tawdry, tragic, artistic, revolutionary and lovelorn history, it has been a lure for miscreants of all kinds—anarchists, bohemians, absinthe-soaked writers and painters, libertines, dandies, whores, after-dark adventurers and, indeed, men like the infamous Marquis de Sade who, in the late eighteenth century, stuffed himself with food and masturbated while writing his massive opus on sexual perversion, *The 120 Days of Sodom*, over 37 days while held prisoner inside the Bastille.

Sade's name was to become a byword for sexual cruelty—or 'sexual sadism disorder'—but he was more complex than that, simultaneously repellent and fascinating. A French nobleman, soldier, revolutionary politician and philosopher, his writings were an exploration of fantasies, depravities, fetishes and vices (particularly sodomy)—all the things that, as Simone de Beauvoir would later write in support of him, investigated 'the darker side of humanity'.

Sade's aim, as Andrew Hussey explained in *Paris: The Secret History*, was also to challenge religion-based morality and the multitude of ways in which moralising crusades restricted people's sexual freedom and pleasure.

Parisians have always 'taken a chauvinistic pride in their horror of prudery', Hussey noted, citing as a prime example the distress many felt for the manner in which town planning ruined people's (or was that just men's?) pleasures during the nineteenth century, culminating in Baron Haussmann's mid-century redesign of the city.

The first and clearest example of this emerged when street names began to be sanitised in the overcrowded, brothel-filled neighbourhood of Les Halles in 1809—rue Tire-Boudin (Sausage or Cock-Puller Street), for example, became rue Marie-Stuart; rue de la Pute-y-Muse ('Idling Tart' Street) turned into rue Petit-Muse.

'The rues du Petit et du Gros-Cul ("Big and Little Cunt" streets), Gratte-Cul ("Scratchy Cunt"—this street contained some of the favourite brothels of Casanova) and du Poil-au-Con ("Hairy Cunt") also disappeared at the same time [but] . . . the establishments that had inspired the street names continued to offer their customers the democratic tradition of freedom of choice.'

It was that so-called 'freedom of choice' which—nearly 170 years later—prompted a group of 100 French women, including writers, performers, academics, businesswomen and film star Catherine Deneuve, to condemn aspects of the #MeToo movement (and its French counterpart #BalanceTonPorc—Denounce Your Pig) in an open letter to Le Monde newspaper.

Published just three months after the #MeToo movement had exploded, the letter defended men's 'freedom to bother' as an indispensable part of sexual freedom.

'Rape is a crime,' they wrote. 'But insistent or clumsy flirting is not a crime, nor is gallantry a chauvinist aggression. As a result of the Weinstein affair, there has been a legitimate realisation of the sexual violence women experience, particularly in the workplace, where some men abuse their power. It was necessary. But now this liberation of speech has been turned on its head.'

The women argued that the #MeToo movement had incited a campaign of public accusations that had placed relatively harmless men in the same category as sex offenders without giving them an opportunity to defend themselves.

'This expedited justice already has its victims, men prevented from practising their profession as punishment, forced to resign ... while the only thing they did wrong was touching a knee, trying to steal a kiss, or speaking about "intimate" things at a work dinner, or sending messages with sexual connotations to a woman whose feelings were not mutual,' they wrote.

They also argued that, instead of empowering women, the #MeToo movement and its French equivalent had begun to serve the interests of 'the enemies of sexual freedom, of religious extremists, of the worst reactionaries', and those people who believed women were 'separate beings, children with the appearance of adults, demanding to be protected'.

'A woman can, in the same day, lead a professional team and enjoy being the sexual object of a man, without being a "promiscuous woman", nor a vile accomplice of patriarchy,' they said.

In conclusion, the writers returned to the concept of self-victimisation and called on women to accept the downsides that come with freedom. 'Accidents that can affect a woman's body do not necessarily affect her dignity and must not, as hard as they can be, necessarily make her a perpetual victim. Because we are not reducible to our bodies. Our inner freedom is inviolable. And this freedom that we cherish is not without risks and responsibilities.'

The response was predictably fast and furious. Leïla Slimani, a French-Moroccan writer and journalist who won the country's premier literary prize, the Prix Goncourt, in 2016, condemned the letter's authors with a short, withering critique.

'I am not asking to be protected, but to exercise my rights to security and respect,' she wrote in the newspaper *Libération*.

'I am not a victim, but millions of women are. That is fact and not a moral judgement.'

Asia Argento (who, as discussed in the previous chapter was allegedly raped by Harvey Weinstein in 1997) denounced Deneuve and her co-authors in a tweet: 'Catherine Deneuve and other French women tell the world how their interiorized misogyny has lobotomized them to the point of no return.'

I ask Marlène Schiappa about the Deneuve letter and the minister offers a curious response. Previously, she has been on record as saying the letter contained a potpourri of ideas, some of which were 'not uninteresting', some of which were 'profoundly shocking.'

She now takes up the 'not uninteresting' ideas first, by referring to Virginie Despentes, the French maid-turned-prostitute-turned freelance rock journalist and pornographic film critic, who caused a sensation in France in 1993 with her debut novel, *Baise-moi* (*Fuck me*), which was turned into a 'rape and revenge' film of the same name seven years later. 'Thelma and Louise on crack,' one critic described it. Both novel and film told the story of two young women who embark on a crime spree after being gang-raped in a park by three men. One woman struggles and screams, the other remains detached, arguing later that because she 'can't prevent anyone penetrating her pussy', she doesn't leave anything precious inside it.

Despentes was, in part, writing of her own experience at the age of seventeen, when she was raped while hitchhiking home from Paris to the north-eastern city of Nancy. After her ordeal, she continued hitchhiking, travelling to music events, sleeping in train stations and declaring this period as one of the most rewarding in her life. Despentes was not resiling from the horror of rape, nor the way rape was used against women as a 'weapon of war'. She was arguing for women to value their 'ability to get over it, instead of lying down obligingly in the anthology of trauma'.

This is the point that seizes the imagination of France's Minister for Gender Equality now. 'I think there is a debate to be had here which is interesting. When a woman has been aggressed, or raped, or harassed, she has to present herself to other men like damaged goods. But there is no *one* way for a woman to react or present herself. We have to listen to every victim, every woman . . . because there is no one way to react.'

Conversely, the most shocking aspect of the open letter, Schiappa says, was the writers' downplaying of 'relatively minor forms of sexual harassment', such as men masturbating, or rubbing themselves, against women on buses and subways.

She confirms now what she told France Culture radio recently: 'We have immense difficulty convincing young women that when a man rubs his genitals against a woman in the metro without her consent, it is an act of sexual assault that can lead to three years in prison and a 75,000-euro fine.'

In 2016 a national study by the National Federation of Transport Users (FNAUT), revealed that 83 per cent of French women had reported being taunted or intimidated about their appearance on public transport. The famed Paris metro system was among the worst.

'Almost all women say they have been exposed to gender-based violence in the subways,' Schiappa tells me finally. 'It's really dangerous and it has consequences in all women's lives. Because you can't go to a school, you can't go to gym, you can't go outside to have a social life, you can't go on the streets . . .'

#

I am on a train from Paris to Zurich the day after meeting Marlène Schiappa. A French woman asks if she can take the seat beside me. I say yes not only because the seat is empty, but because she happens to be extremely beautiful.

Her name is Murielle and she says she is heading home for the weekend to Dijon. She works in cybersecurity and has a book on Tibetan Buddhism in the seat pocket in front of her. This proves an opening for our conversation because I'd recently written a story about the spectacular fall from grace of Tibetan Buddhist teacher Sogyal Rinpoche after accusations by former students of sexual abuse.

We discuss Rinpoche, then move on to her cybersecurity work, and how the French interior ministry is now using the latest cyber tools to combat online sexual harassment. I mention the book I am writing and how, only yesterday, I'd spoken with Marlène Schiappa about men regularly masturbating on the French public transport system.

'Does this really happen? I ask Murielle. (I know—it's amazing how quickly you can tackle the big subjects with a perfect stranger.)

'My sister was on the metro in Paris recently,' she replies. 'She was going to Gare du Lyon, and she was with a friend, talking to him while holding onto the pole in the middle of the train. The train was packed and everybody was pressed up against each other, so it was normal to feel something against her back.

'But when she got out of the train, onto the platform, her hand went to her bottom. She could feel something on her back, a movement of some kind. And that's when she felt a wetness, and she took back her hand and there was semen all over it.' Murielle's disgust was palpable.

She then offers some insights about women's power deriving from nature, and the importance of the doula in assisting women before, during and after childbirth. She also mentions—and don't you just love this about train trips—a traditional community in Papua New Guinea where, as an initiation rite, the father penetrates his small son with a red pepper. That way, she says, the son knows what it feels like to be a woman.

I am keen to continue my conversation with Murielle, but the train is already pulling in to Dijon. '*Alors, voici mon arrêt*,' she says. '*Enchanté*. Nice to meet you.'

I reply it had been nice to meet her too, although what I really want to say is: 'Might you want to have a drink sometime when I return to Paris?'

I'm aware this might make some readers—women particularly—cringe. (And, indeed, some early readers of the manuscript have expressed their doubts.) But I think this is worth exploring further: both my compulsion to ask her out *and* why women would cringe at this.

I'm a single man on a TGV train and a beautiful French woman has asked to sit next to me. Would I have agreed if she hadn't been beautiful? Yes, I would have. And would I have struck up a conversation with her? Again, yes. I'm a friendly guy—to both women and men.

But what about her perspective? Maybe she was asking to sit next to me because there were no other seats in the compartment, or because the seats were facing north, in the direction we were heading, or some other reason I'll never know. Whatever the case, her sitting next to me had nothing to do with me, and everything to do with her right to sit where she wanted, undisturbed. Fair enough.

Then, after we'd just had a conversation about her sister being pressed against on a train, I was thinking about asking her out. Surely that makes me little better than the revolting man on the Paris metro, just a less crude version. Woman enters man's line of sight, is polite and conversational, and man, typically, reduces woman to her only value—her attractiveness, and the unspoken possibility of a sexual encounter with her.

I get it, but here's another truth. This was no run-of-the-mill conversation. We were both engaged—mutually and curiously from where I sat—in a nonstop 90-minute discussion about Buddhism, cybersecurity and sex. Who would want to deny that kind of conversation, or its potential sequel? (Plenty of people, you say, which is why I'm exploring it.)

If I had asked Murielle out—which I didn't—and she'd said no, and I'd then proceeded to harass or reproach her for rejecting me, that would be one thing. But if, as was the case, we were two consenting adults on a train going to Dijon, enjoying an intellectual joust, possibly even a playful flirt, that would be another thing. Wouldn't it?

And isn't this the story of the ages? Isn't this how every couple, family, generation, lineage forms—through the mating game and the dance of seduction? Isn't that why we watch romantic comedies and listen to love songs? Isn't this fundamental to our very humanness, to the evolutionary and biological impulses that enable us to form relationships and perpetuate the species? How else would we get together? Besides which—and maybe you think I'm protesting too much—women are sexual creatures too. According to most—if not all—women I know, they want to be considered attractive and desired.

The question then, surely, is how men are showing their interest. Are they showing it with respect and courtesy, by reading and listening to the cues, by taking no for an answer? Or are they showing it with aggression or a sense of entitlement?

It's not the try-on that's wrong, I'd argue; it's the way the try-on happens. Women are justifiably terrified of being assaulted, or worse. Men are fearful of having their reputations and livelihoods destroyed over miscues and overplayed hands.

So, maybe my instinct to ask Murielle out for a drink makes you wince, but I hope men never lose the best ways of trying it on. Because, if we do, women will never be asked out, babies will never be born and, never mind climate change, the human race will cease to exist.

Actually, scrap that last ridiculous statement. That's me being a typically defensive male thrashing around in the death throes of a fading world. Women could do the asking out, as they increasingly do, and as they should.

8

Here, there and everywhere

When you're accustomed to privilege, equality feels like oppression.

BRIAN SIMS (THE FIRST OPENLY GAY PERSON ELECTED TO THE
PENNSYLVANIA HOUSE OF REPRESENTATIVES)

It's taken us tens of thousands of years to get to the #MeToo and Time's Up movements, not to mention all the struggles women have engaged in over the past century and a half to achieve equal rights before the law.

But, just as most slave owners were never able to comprehend the humanity of their slaves, let alone the hell of slavery, it's probably equally true that most men—including me—have never been able to fathom the privileges of our gender, or measure the extent of social discrimination that's been directed towards women throughout history.

Patriarchy? What patriarchy?

Let's imagine, though, that the founding document of human rights from the French Revolution in 1789 was called the Declaration of the Rights of the Woman and of the Citizen, instead of the Declaration of the Rights of Man and of the Citizen. Men might have responded with the same indignation Mary Wollstonecraft did when she wrote her famous riposte to this cornerstone document of the Enlightenment, *A Vindication of the Rights of Woman.*

Or imagine that the second paragraph of the American Declaration of Human Rights had stated that 'all women are created equal', with no mention of men.

Imagine that throughout the nineteenth century a married man had no rights to his own earnings or inheritance, that his body and his children belonged to his wife; that before he married he was subject to the authority and discipline of his mother. (Actually, that might have improved things.)

Imagine that a white man was only granted the right to vote in the United States in 1920 (and, if he was black, 1965), and not until 1928 in the United Kingdom (only then if he was 30 years old with 'proper qualifications'), or 1944 if he was a Frenchman, or—wait for it—1971 if he was a Swiss man. (Australia can at least take a bow on this front, having become the second country in the world after New Zealand to grant suffrage to women, in 1902.)

Imagine if higher education were considered an almost non-existent privilege instead of a right, and that for most of history a man was ineligible for leadership positions or political responsibility; that a man was discriminated against—and very often dismissed from his job—on the basis that he was married or about to become a father. Or that he was overlooked for a job he was perfectly qualified for in favour of *a woman*. Or paid less for doing the same job. Or seen as the perfect—or imperfect—adornment to his wife.

Imagine that when a man went to work he had to endure unwelcome touching, comments on his body, or worse. Imagine if he was overweight and forthright and was mocked whenever he spoke up, or if, say, he happened to be a redhead and was pestered on the train by hordes of young women who wanted to know whether he had red pubic hair or not. (Just an example plucked from the deep blue.)

Imagine if he was duped and badgered into sex; or that when he was a victim of violence, particularly rape, it would be suggested to him—sneeringly, contemptuously—that he'd asked for it because of the way he'd dressed (perhaps his pants were too tight or too loose), or the way he'd smiled, or that he was lying about the incident, only to then be required to relive the burden of his abuse under cross-examination in a court of law.

Imagine if his name happened to be Rob Batty, instead of Rosie, and that he'd been made Australian of the Year because he'd campaigned tirelessly to raise awareness of domestic violence after his wife had bashed and stabbed to death his child, only to then be abused by prominent women in the media.

Imagine if he had seen 34 of his fellow Australian men—maybe his son, brother or father, or just ones of his mates—murdered in the first 27 weeks of 2018, many by partners or former partners, or that one in three men had experienced physical violence since the age of fifteen, one in five sexual violence.

Imagine—and, yes, I know this is an intolerable concept—that whenever he decided to say something in a group, a woman would interrupt, dismiss, contradict or ignore him, or actually explain something to him that he already knew. That would be *womansplaining*, right?

Yes, it would, and at this point it's worth retelling a story Rebecca Solnit wrote in 2008 for the online publication *TomDispatch*. Called 'Men Explain Things to Me', it is now credited with having ushered in the term 'mansplaining'.

In 2008, Solnit and her friend 'Sallie' attended a party at a luxury cabin in the hills above Aspen, Colorado. They were the youngest women at the gathering and, as they were preparing to leave, the host invited them to stay a little longer. He'd heard Solnit was a writer.

'So,' he said, 'I hear you've written a couple of books?'

'Several, actually,' she replied.

The host asked Solnit what her books were about. Solnit had written seven or eight by this stage, so she mentioned her most recent one, *Rivers of Shadows: Eadweard Muybridge and the Technological Wild West*, published in 2003. It was about the industrialisation of life and the annihilation of time and space.

The host interrupted Solnit to ask whether she'd heard about the 'very important' book on Muybridge that had just been released. He didn't wait for an answer before launching into an exposition of the book's contents, his eyes fixed on the horizon, his face a study of grave authority. (Perhaps he was recalling the lines of British diplomat Lord Chesterfield, who wrote in a letter to his son in 1748: 'Women are to be talked to as below men, and above children.')

Solnit's friend Sallie tried to interject. She wanted their host to know that the book he was describing was written by her friend, the very same Rebecca Solnit seated in front of him! The host didn't hear her or, if he did, ignored the comment and continued with his analysis.

'That's *her* book,' Sallie tried again, several times, until finally her words registered. The host turned ashen. How to reconcile the fact that the book he'd read about in the *New York Times Book*

Review a few months earlier was actually written by the very person—the *young woman*—sitting in front of him? The world was shifting off its axis.

Only when Solnit and her friend were well out of earshot did they burst out laughing, even though they knew it was no laughing matter. Solnit herself acknowledged this four years later when she drew an arc from that 'minor social misery' of 'mansplain[ing]' to the 'violent silencing and even violent death' that women suffer around the world.

'This is a struggle that takes place in war-torn nations,' she wrote in the new introduction to her essay, 'but also in the bedroom, the dining room, the classroom, the workplace, and the streets.'

It is the same point then prime minister Malcolm Turnbull made when honouring Eurydice Dixon after her murder in Melbourne in June 2018. 'Not all disrespect of women is violence against women,' he said, 'but that is where all violence against women begins.'

#

So, let's talk about the workplace, because, almost from its inception, the #MeToo movement was never going to be just about generations of female rage over sexual violence; that was merely the tip of the spear. The movement was, as Jeremy Heimans and Henry Timms explained in *New Power*, a movement powered by the currents of technology that would constantly adapt itself to different industries, cultures, countries, communities and contexts.

It was about deep-rooted inequalities not just in the entertainment industry, but across all industries. It was about women being respected and heard, and about them taking their rightful seat at the top table. It was about equal pay, power dynamics and discrimination, both structural and casual. It was about the commodification and commercialisation of women and the way they were so often forced to curry favour—professionally and personally—to advance their careers or merely to attain economic security.

It was about sex in the digital age, and how advertising, marketing, music, porn and video games reduced and cheapened women as a matter of course. It was about how a culture used female sexuality to sell products, then slut-shamed women for being sexually active. It was about everyday fear and safety, and being believed, rather than dismissed or ignored. It was about how men measured the value and worth of half the human race, and what it was that made women feel patronised, uncomfortable or, worse still, violated, either physically, verbally or both.

As I've been pondering this, Australian Greens senator Sarah Hanson-Young recounted how her colleague, libertarian Senator David Leyonhjelm, responded to her when she decided to vote against a motion for legalising pepper sprays, mace and tasers as a way of preventing sexual assault and murder.

'You'll have to stop shagging men now, Sarah,' Leyonhjelm yelled across the chamber as the vote was defeated. Afterwards, when Hanson-Young sought an apology, Leyonhjelm told her to 'fuck off', before doubling down on his position. Hanson-Young decided to launch legal action.

'For years,' she explained later in a comment piece published by *The Guardian*, 'I have winced and tried not to flinch at innuendos about my dress, my face (being told by older men that I don't smile at them enough) and my apparent sex life. What started as mutterings while I would be on my feet speaking, or during a debate, slowly over the years has become slurs that are now shouted across the chamber floor.'

Hanson-Young then made reference to the misogyny experienced by Julia Gillard as prime minister, which included being labelled 'deliberately barren' by one of her conservative opponents, and having the then Opposition leader, Tony Abbott, speak to an anti-carbon tax rally in 2011 in front of placards screaming BITCH and DITCH THE WITCH.

Gillard responded eighteen months later with one of the most commanding political speeches ever delivered by an Australian prime minister, in which she lacerated Abbott for his sexism and double standards. The 'misogyny speech' went viral around the world.

'I will not be lectured about sexism and misogyny by this man,' Gillard declared. 'I will not. And the Government will not be lectured about sexism and misogyny by this man. Not now, not ever. The leader of the Opposition says that people who hold sexist views and who are misogynists are not appropriate for high office. Well I hope the leader of the Opposition has got a piece of paper and he is writing out his resignation. Because if he wants to know what misogyny looks like in modern Australia, he doesn't need a motion in the House of Representatives, he needs a mirror.'

Now, six years later, an older white male politician (Leyonhjelm) was debasing a female politician (Hanson-Young) who'd been overwhelmingly supported by her colleagues in rejecting a motion he wanted passed. Sarah Hanson-Young was having none of it. She was cresting the zeitgeist.

The #MeToo movement has given women across the world the encouragement to speak out. And like so many others that have come before me, yesterday I decided that I've had enough. I've had enough of pretending the slurs and taunts aren't there, enough of pretending that they don't throw me off my game while I'm speaking. I once had a male Senator—who had been drinking—come sit next to me while I was on my feet during a late night Senate debate. He sang nursery rhymes in my ear while I was trying to speak.

Later, on the ABC's *7.30* program, Hanson-Young said she would be pursuing legal redress, in part out of solidarity with women less able to defend themselves than she was. 'I'm doing this because the women on the factory floor or the flight attendant who has things like this hurled at her, comments made, many of those women can't stand up.'

#

Flight EK 414 Dubai to Sydney: I am watching *The Newspaperman*, a documentary about the legendary *Washington Post* editor Ben Bradlee, whose enormous influence on American journalism spanned decades. The documentary reveals that in 1962, at a party on board John F. Kennedy's presidential yacht, *Sequoia*, to mark the president's 46th birthday, the president of the United States chased his friend Ben Bradlee's wife Antoinette ('Tony') to the bathroom and, outside the toilet, sexually assaulted her.

As the credits roll the following conversation takes place across the aisle from me:

Flight attendant: 'Can I take your tray, sir?'

Passenger (Australian male): 'I'd prefer you took the tray from my bedroom when we get back to Sydney.'

Flight attendant: 'I beg your pardon, sir?'

Passenger: 'You heard me.'

Flight attendant: 'I think that is highly inappropriate, sir.'

Five minutes later another conversation, this time between me and a second flight attendant who has just been alerted by her colleague to this previous conversation:

Me: 'Does this sort of thing happen often on flights?'

Flight attendant: 'It happens more with male colleagues than passengers.'

Me: 'Has it happened to you?'

Flight attendant: 'Yes.'

Me: 'Would you mind telling me about it?'

Flight attendant: 'Well, I had an experience once with the purser, who seemed like such a lovely, gentle guy. We were all back at the hotel after our flight and one of the attendants had a headache, so she asked me whether I had any paracetamol. I said yes. The purser overheard our conversation, and 30 minutes later he came to my door to ask for paracetamol as well, so I brought them to the door. He then asked me for some water. I went back into the room to get the water and, as I did, he pushed his way in and started to try to kiss me and undress me. I told him to stop, but he kept holding me by the neck, trying to force himself on me. I finally got him to leave, but my regret is I never reported him because I was only 22 and had just started flying and I was scared of losing my job.'

\#

Ever since the upheavals of the #MeToo movement disrupted the established order, the media has been instrumental in breaking stories about the extent of sexual harassment and bullying in places of employment. At the same time, the media has been among the worst culprits—gatekeepers with their own dark secrets to protect.

As we've seen in America, many of those accused have been giants of their industry, part of a growing list of 'Shitty Media Men' that was created anonymously in October 2017 and is now the subject of a federal lawsuit. (In January 2018 Moira Donegan, a former assistant editor at the *New Republic*, revealed that she had been the one to start the list.)

The men include, of course, Harvey Weinstein, Roger Ailes and Bill O'Reilly, but also Matt Lauer, co-anchor of *Today* on NBC, accused of sexually assaulting and exposing himself to a female staffer and sexually harassing several other women; Charlie Rose, co-host of CBS's *This Morning*, accused of exposing himself, grabbing breasts, bottoms and genitals, as well as making lewd phone calls; Leslie Moonves, former chief executive of CBS Corporation, accused by twelve women of sexual harassment, including retaliation for sexual favours not granted; Mark Halperin, senior political analyst for MSNBC, accused of pressing his genitals against several women (make that his erect penis); and Sean Hannity, Fox News confidante to Donald Trump, accused of blacklisting a guest because she declined an assignation in his hotel room.

Here in the Australian media, trammelled as we are by some of the strictest defamation laws in the western world, only Don Burke has been held to account for his unrestrained hands and smut-soiled language, even though there's a small army of female journalists who've been subjected to threats and abuse for years for daring to wade into contentious issues, or, from some quarters, for daring to exist at all.

In September 2018, the ABC's Virginia Trioli delivered a stirring speech to the Women in Media conference on the Gold Coast, where she outlined the multitude of ways in which male colleagues and others had tried to diminish her during her 28 years as a journalist. Comments on her breasts, her 'fuckability', a series of crude drawings sent to her—all these normalised infringements and degradations that had caused so many other talented women to flee the profession.

Earlier in the year, veteran reporter Candace Sutton wrote about the 'vile and obscene campaign of bullying' directed against her in 1990 by Tim Ferguson, a member of the Doug Anthony

All Stars comedy trio—letters signed by Ferguson with 'love and breast cancer', 'love and leukemia' and 'cunnilingus'. Ferguson later issued a formal and unreserved apology.

There are few prominent women in the media without some kind of horror story to tell. Van Badham, columnist, critic, playwright, novelist and vice-president of the Media Entertainment and Arts Alliance in Victoria, has been subjected to sexual violence, workplace sexual harassment, internet abuse, media abuse and intellectual property theft. She's been beaten by a male partner, hospitalised by another man's sexual violence, alienated by the justice system and, on the day of her father's funeral, assailed by a flurry of disgraceful tweets and pornographic images.

Columnist and author Helen Razer went public in September 2018 about being stalked and threatened with rape and murder when she was a young ABC radio announcer. Neither the death threats against her, nor the constant shadowing of her by this man, nor his turning up to her workplace, nor the jar of urine sent to her by courier, nor the requests for protection by her union, nor, indeed, Razer's own panic attacks and acute depression, caused her boss to act. Rather, he suggested she 'just fuck the guy because that would scare him off'.

Clementine Ford, the author of *Fight Like a Girl* and *Boys will be Boys*, has endured years of obscene attacks. She's been called 'an evil scumbag slut', 'a whore', 'a dumb cunt', a bitch who should kill herself or, alternatively, be gang-raped by men infected with AIDS. She's been accused of ruining men's lives and having 'penis envy'. She is 'fucking delusional,' 'evil' and 'unfuckable' (this last according to right-wing provocateur Milo Yiannopoulos who, during an appearance in Adelaide in 2017, displayed a photograph of Ford as a fifteen-year-old with that caption underneath).

Think of most workplaces and there's a problem. It's the grocery shop owner in a Tasmanian town that I can't name—there's only one grocery store in the town—who has been consistently groping his female staff for the past 30 years. It's the air traffic controller in Queensland who, over a period of five months, made crude comments and sucking noises to his female colleague—every day, every shift—while rubbing his genitals and sticking out his tongue. The woman eventually suffered an emotional breakdown.

It's farmers and cattle station owners who have pressured young backpackers into providing sexual favours in return for signing off on their one-year working holiday visas. It's the insurance company boss who subjected his female employee to repeated sexual harassment, intimidation and bullying—putting his hand up her dress, telling her he wanted sex 'because you need to have a baby', then turning up regularly at her house uninvited.

It's here, there and everywhere, coded into the system and architecture of where we work and how we live—in the White House, the US Supreme Court, Congress, the British House of Commons, the French National Assembly, Australian parliaments—both federal and state, the Swedish Academy, the United Nations, the Vatican, Hollywood, media and entertainment, big business, small business, the legal sector, the rural sector, the military, the music industry—from hip hop to opera, the arts world, academia, medicine, science, sport, publishing, libraries, university campuses, hospices . . . Have I missed anything? Oh yes, let's not forget the scandals at charities like Oxfam, Save the Children, Médecins Sans Frontières, Care International, the Norwegian Refugee Council . . . *What's the weight and measure here in an impoverished third world country? A kilo of flour for a blow job?*

And it's thanks to the #MeToo movement that people who might otherwise have remained silent have finally stepped through the looking glass to describe the not-so-alternative universe they have always inhabited.

Australian Sex Discrimination Commissioner Kate Jenkins said as much when in June 2018 she announced the world's first national inquiry into sexual harassment in the workplace.

'This spotlight on sexual harassment has turned the tide and created a clear and unprecedented appetite for change . . . Over the course of the next year, we will speak with individuals and organisations from all over Australia about their experiences. We will consider the economic impact of sexual harassment, the drivers of these behaviours and the adequacy of the existing legal framework.'

In Australia, a shocking 45 per cent of the population of eighteen- to 29-year-olds report having been sexually harassed over the past five years. But, of course, it's not only sexual harassment. It's discrimination, conscious or unconscious, barefaced or subtle, conducted in plain sight or undercover, that continues to affect half the population. You're pregnant so you lose your job. You've had a child, but you can't get back into the workforce. You're denied a raise in salary, even though your male counterparts are earning more and performing less. You're doing double the work, but he's getting the praise. You're on the receiving end of sexual slurs or putdowns and discriminatory remarks—all the smaller aggressions that undermine your sense of safety and belonging.

You're Julie Bishop, Julia Banks, Kelly O'Dwyer, Lucy Gichuhi, Sussan Ley, Ann Sudmalis—a growing number in a limited list of women in the Australian Liberal Party (Julia Banks has, of course, since quit the party and Julie Bishop and Kelly O'Dwyer have decided to quit politics altogether)—and you've endured years of bullying machismo and blatant sexism from your male colleagues.

You're Lisa Wilkinson, bright star in the firmament of Australian television, and you leave the Nine Network's *Today* program after ten years because of the pay disparity between yourself and your co-host, Karl Stefanovic. (According to the Workplace Gender Equality Agency, Australian women earn 15.3 per cent less than men for doing the same or comparable work.)

You're Carrie Grace, the BBC's China editor, and you've been breaking major stories for 30 years when you discover after a salary list is made public that your remuneration is 50 per cent less than some of your male colleagues.

You're Claire Foy and you've lit up the small screen as Queen Elizabeth II in the top-rating Netflix television series *The Crown*, only to learn that your co-star, Matt Smith, playing Prince Philip, has earnt 200,000 pounds more than you. (The BBC eventually apologised to Foy and compensated her.)

You are overlooked time and again for senior leadership or board positions because you 'don't have the right credentials', there's 'too much oestrogen' in the company already, 'we already have one woman on the board', or your name isn't Dave or Steve because, seriously, in 2017 there were more Daves (eight) and Steves (seven) running the top 100 companies on the London stock exchange than there were women CEOs (six); and, according to the *New York Times*, there are more men named John running large companies in the United States than the total number of women.

Tomas Chamorro-Premuzic, professor of business psychology at University College London and Columbia University, addressed these themes and more for the *Harvard Business Review* in 2013; namely, the inability to discern between confidence and competence, and the conspicuous blind spots that lead so many people to conclude that men are better leaders than women when often the reverse is true.

> When it comes to leadership, the only advantage that men have over women (e.g. from Argentina to Norway, the USA to Japan) is that manifestations of hubris—often masked as charisma or charm—are commonly mistaken for leadership potential, and that these occur much more frequently in men than in women.
>
> The truth of the matter is that pretty much anywhere in the world, men tend to *think* that they are much smarter than women. Yet arrogance and overconfidence are inversely related to leadership talent—the ability to build and maintain high-performing teams, and to inspire followers to set aside their selfish agendas in order to work for the common interest of the group.

Chamorro-Premuzic is an international authority on psychological profiling and identifying leadership talent, and years of research have confirmed to him that the best leaders are usually the self-effacing ones. Whether this springs from nurture or nature, the fact remains that this trait is far more common among women than men. Conversely, men are far more arrogant, manipulative and risk-prone than women.

No surprises there, perhaps, but 'the paradoxical implication,' he wrote, was

> that the same psychological characteristics that enable male managers to rise to the top of the corporate or political ladder are actually responsible for their downfall. In other words, what it takes to *get* the job is not just different from, but also the reverse of, what it takes to *do the job well*. As a result, too many incompetent people are promoted to management jobs, and promoted over more competent people.

The mythical image of a 'leader' embodies many of the characteristics commonly found in personality disorders, such as narcissism (Steve Jobs or Vladimir Putin), psychopathy (fill in the name of your favorite despot here), histrionic (Richard Branson or Steve Ballmer) or Machiavellian (nearly any federal-level politician) personalities.

Unfortunately, this was not because these larger-than-life figures were unrepresentative of the 'average manager'; rather, the average manager failed precisely because he possessed many of these same characteristics.

Most leaders—whether in politics or business—fail. That has always been the case: the majority of nations, companies, societies and organizations are poorly managed, as indicated by their longevity, revenues, and approval ratings, or by the effects they have on their citizens, employees, subordinates or members. Good leadership has always been the exception, not the norm.

So why encourage women to adopt these dysfunctional leadership traits when it is flexibility, creativity, modesty, vision—the very qualities of a transformative leader—that is required? Chamorro-Premuzic explained:

There is no denying that women's path to leadership positions is paved with many barriers, including a very thick glass ceiling. But a much bigger problem is the lack of career obstacles for incompetent men, and the fact that we tend to equate leadership with the very psychological features that make the average man a more inept leader than the average woman. The result is a pathological system that rewards men for their incompetence while punishing women for their competence, to everybody's detriment.

That's not to say some women don't make bad bosses. Obviously they do. But it does suggest that cultures perpetuate themselves and, if it's mainly men running the show, particularly white Anglo men, then it's their values which will be propagated.

Australia's former Race Discrimination Commissioner, Tim Soutphommasane, made a similar observation in July 2018 with the publication of a University of Sydney Business School report into cultural diversity among Australia's top 100 ASX companies.

Australian boardrooms were 'pale, male and stale', with many male board members claiming they preferred to associate with those who looked and sounded like them. (One female director reported she was more likely to be asked for a recipe than for her opinion.) Australian boards, among the most hidebound in the western world, were stacked with Anglo men displaying all the traditional traits of male leadership, while women, particularly of non-Anglo backgrounds, faced the 'double jeopardy' of neither making it to executive level nor being elevated to the board.

Avivah Wittenberg-Cox has seen variations on this problem in more than 80 countries as a consultant to corporations on leadership and gender issues. 'Every country is on the spectrum,' she tells me, 'but where people think particular countries sit is usually wrong. Eastern Europe, for example, is much more gender-balanced than western Europe, Asia is usually more gender-balanced than the Anglo-Saxon world. The Anglo-Saxon world keeps thinking it's more advanced when it's actually much further behind a lot of other cultures.

'Among the corporate clients I work with, their internal gender map is very indicative of these cultural differences. Like in Russia (oligarchs aside), their international companies are run by women, and the guys are all drunk and having trouble. In China, the political hard power is still male-dominated, but the economic power is much more gender-balanced.'

Canadian-born and London-based, Wittenberg-Cox has been one of the world's leading authorities on leadership, gender and business for nearly 25 years. In 1996, she founded the European Professional Women's Association in Paris (now the global Professional Women's Network) and, four years later, conducted the first gender board review across Europe, together with the prestigious executive search firm Egon Zehnder.

In 2005, she founded 20-first, a global consultancy designed to help companies achieve gender balance. One of her starting points—then and now—was to present to executive teams a graduation speech delivered by the late American writer David Foster Wallace to the students of Ohio's Kenyon College in 2005. It began with the parable of two fish:

'There are these two young fish swimming along and they happen to meet an older fish swimming the other way, who nods at them and says, "Morning, boys. How's the water?" And the two young fish swim on for a bit, and then eventually one of them looks over at the other and goes, "What the hell is water?"'

The point of the fish story, Wallace told the graduating students, was that the most obvious realities were often the hardest to detect, let alone talk about. The same applied to cultures—political, national or organisational. Those who possessed the power were blind to those who didn't. And many had never learnt how to listen, nor seen the reason to do so. They listened in ways that reconfirmed what they already knew or thought they knew. They listened by exchanging facts and corroborating—or refuting—the data being presented. They nose-dived on the first rule of empathy, which was to try to see the world through someone else's eyes.

Wittenberg-Cox cites an example of a corporate leadership team of 50 people who gathered in Italy recently for a two-day talk on gender balance. They had flown in from all over the world to brainstorm ideas. On the first morning, the chief executive officer—an Australian—walked into the room and said: 'If anybody here still needs the moral case for gender balance explained, they shouldn't be working for this company. The business case has already been proven—it will gain us 34 per cent return on equity.'

So far so good. Sort of. But then he said: 'I don't want any fuzzy talk. I'm expecting actionable deliverables from this session,' before proceeding to speak in rugby metaphors to a room comprising more than 50 per cent women. Then he walked out as brusquely as he'd walked in.

'This guy didn't understand the first thing about listening, and what it takes to engage women,' Wittenberg-Cox tells me during an interview in London. 'He was using his existing masculine leadership default style in order to rev up the audience . . . and he didn't even know that he didn't know, because nobody was going to tell him.'

It's a problem Wittenberg-Cox sees a lot of, particularly in Anglo-Saxon countries, where senior executive teams are still waiting for 'proof' that gender equality is advantageous for a company. They're also still wanting to address the issue as a conversation for women rather than for society as a whole.

'All these senior teams say, "Prove to me that gender balance is going to be good for our business," and my response is: "You want to wait for proof when 60 per cent of the talent and 80 per cent of your market is female? You want proof that gender balance in leadership is going to help you?"'

(In a landmark 2015 report, the McKinsey Global Institute provided some of that evidence by looking at 'gender equality indicators' in 95 countries. In pure economic terms, McKinsey found that US$28 trillion would be added to annual global GDP by 2025 if women's participation in the economy was equal to men's—roughly the equivalent of the combined American and Chinese economies today.)

'I work a lot in Australia,' Wittenberg-Cox says, 'where we do thousands of interviews with senior executives on this stuff, and the issue is completely framed as a women's issue. It's about women's networks, women's coaching, women's mentoring, women's empowering.

'We need to be more gender bilingual. We need to talk about customers, talk about talent, talk about managers, talk about opportunity, not keep talking about women. It drives me crazy how "progressive" leaders always start by saying, "We're going to be nice to women and allow them to be flexible with their children."'

In Wittenberg-Cox's view, a 'gender bilingual leader' creates a workplace that balances personal and professional requirements, and understands the imperative for employees to be able to do two things at once—care for their families *and* deliver on results in ways that don't break them.

'And good leaders do that in a way that is positive, inspiring and constructive,' she says. 'They don't keep saying it's about *women*—which is where we are now—because if you say, "I really support women," that alienates men. It's just about promoting the best talent which, today, just happens to be female.'

Wittenberg-Cox believes that when women first started rising to senior management or board positions in the early 1970s, they played by the rules of the patriarchy and, in fact, were selected on the basis they were more 'masculine-brained'. That was the system's design: men chose women whom they believed were 'strong and powerful' then, very often, turned against those same women because they possessed these preferred 'masculine' qualities.

As more women moved into positions of power, however, the rules of the game began to shift. The system would adapt to women instead of the other way around. 'The Nordic countries are interesting for this reason,' Wittenberg-Cox observes, 'because they're more gender-balanced politically. That's where parental leave legislation started up, as well as board quota legislation which, in Norway, was introduced by a man, but in a much more gender-balanced environment. And when that happens politically you become less focused on foreign policy, economics and the military, and more focused on social systems, education and health care.

'And in companies that are more gender-balanced, you can see this immediately. They tend to be more feeling workplaces that end up being less competitive, more flexible, more output than input driven, much less ready to put up with self-marketing bullshitters who talk about themselves.

'But this only comes by design. This is not a natural evolution at all. It's an enlightened, proactive decision to adapt and shift to more gender-balanced systems. It takes a lot of work and leadership and intention, and it's a huge issue that bumps up against entrenched power systems.'

In trying to contextualise the #MeToo moment, Wittenberg-Cox takes the view that rather than this being a hinge point, it is more a continuum of the gains made by women over the past century—the vote, the pill, quotas . . . 'It's just a rising power of women, steadily, slowly. Not as fast as some people would like, but in terms of human history, it's unbelievable what 100 years has wrought in terms of power between the sexes.

'And the pressure is growing. Social pressure, investment pressure, even shareholder pressure, investment fund pressure. Slowly but surely, every year it gets a little more. So, if the twentieth century was about the rise of women, then the 21st century is about the adaptation of men to that rise.'

If intelligence is the 'ability to adapt to change', as Stephen Hawking once said, that might mean men stepping back, stepping aside, getting out of the way in order to make more room for women. Otherwise, despite all the advances over a century, the pace of change will continue to feel glacial, although who can forget that glaciers are melting faster than anyone thought possible.

9

Augustine confessions

What cannot be said will be wept.

SAPPHO

Like a lot of boys coming of age in the Swinging Sixties and Seventies, I grew up obsessed with girls and sex.

I never ate dirt, snails, daisies or my rubber galoshes to impress the girl of my dreams, as Romain Gary confessed to in his memoir, *Promise at Dawn*. But maybe that's because no girl ever dared me; perhaps I would've if she had.

But the pursuit and longing was endless, and as my friends and I moved into our early teenage years, we had codes for how far we'd managed to get with a girl at a party before reporting in. There was 'upstairs outside', and 'upstairs inside', and 'downstairs outside', and, 'downstairs inside'. If you got 'downstairs inside' you were a legend, although when I was first asked by a friend if I'd reached that heavenly place, I had no idea what he was talking about.

'Did you go upstairs outside with her?' he asked after a party. I was thirteen at the time.

'Absolutely,' I replied, even though the house was single storey and there were no balconies.

'What about downstairs inside?' he pressed.

'Look,' I said, as nonchalantly as I could, 'we've been down there most of the night.' Which we had been, talking and drinking Fanta, probably with a dash of Galliano stolen from the parents' drinks cabinet.

I loved talking to girls. And this was from the time I was a little boy, long before I'd played spin the bottle, or learnt the art of self-pleasuring, or read Philip Roth's taboo-busting *Portnoy's Complaint*, in which his lust-ridden character Alexander Portnoy recounted his teenage years of feverish masturbation, including his sickening—and riotous—defilement of a piece of liver en route to a bar mitzvah lesson.

I thought about the opposite sex endlessly, and as I grew up, it became an almost all-consuming desire: resting my head against the soft fullness of a breast (pendulous or pert, it didn't matter), was an exquisite lullaby; being enfolded by a woman, entering a woman, was a thrilling voyage of discovery, as well as a homecoming to the warmest, safest place I'd ever been. In some ill-defined way, it was like possessing and transcending the world all at once, and it was enough to make you want to cry for the sheer joy of being human.

Did I think mostly about my own rapture? Almost certainly as a teenager and young man. Did I ever pressure a partner to go beyond where she wanted to go? Yes—most probably I would have said, on a few too many occasions, 'Are you *sure* you don't want to?' Did I objectify females by viewing sex as a victory, or mark of my manhood, my *coolness*? Yes, I did, but—and, this is no excuse—what other markers were there for becoming a young man in Australia besides sport and sex?

Did I ever physically abuse a woman? Never. Harass a woman? To the best of my recollection—and, believe me, I've raked endlessly over my past to test this—no. Did I ever trample a girl or woman's heart? Absolutely. Did my heart get trampled as well? You better believe it.

Did I have an affair while I was married? Yes I did. Did I ever confuse work and love? Oh dear, yes to that as well. After my marriage ended I employed a brilliant young singer, writer, teacher and friend to be my PA. (I know, what was I thinking?) She was more than twenty years younger than me, a radiant spirit, whip smart, funny, kind and beautiful, the perfect salve for a broken heart, and, yes, I fell for her—although, thank goodness, I never made a move. The sheer terror of being rejected was enough to prevent that.

What I did do, though, was when I realised (a) that I didn't have enough work for her, and (b) that given my unrequited feelings, the idea of working and travelling with her was simply too much to bear, I let her down (financially) and let her go, and even though I think I can say we salvaged the remnants of our friendship, I am not proud of the episode.

What am I doing here, though, with these Augustine confessions? I guess because we live in an age of radical transparency, I'm trying to get in first. In their book *New Power*, Jeremy Heimans and Henry Timms describe this approach as an example of 'occupying' oneself, a term adopted from the world of protest in the form of the Occupy movement.

Their favourite example is independent 2018 Arizona gubernatorial candidate Noah Dyer, who used his campaign website to hang his own 'dirty' laundry out to dry. (Dyer's campaign was ultimately unsuccessful.) In a section called 'Scandal and Controversy', Dyer says of himself:

Noah has had both deep and casual sexual experiences with all kinds of women . . . He's had group sex and sex with married women. He has sent and received intimate texts and pictures, and occasionally recorded video during sex.

Noah has always been forthright with his partners. All of his relationships have been legal and consensual . . . Noah is unapologetic about his sexual choices and wishes others the same safety and confidence as they express themselves.

Thank you, Noah, for erecting the scaffold and handing me the noose.

My first sexual experience was definitely not legal, although perhaps it was consensual. I'm still not sure. Can a fourteen-year-old boy consent to being seduced by the 37-year-old mother of his ex-girlfriend? Probably not; certainly not by today's standards.

For years I big-noted myself to my male friends about how I'd lost my virginity to an older woman when I was still wearing shorty pyjamas. (They had trains on them.) I even joked about this in a memoir, published a few years ago, to describe my excitement when she beckoned me into her bedroom one night. It was after she'd invited me to accompany her and her daughter to a screening of *The Graduate*, in which Anne Bancroft, playing Mrs Robinson, seduces greenhorn college graduate Benjamin Braddock, played by Dustin Hoffman.

Watching the film proved a prelude to the real thing, but the way I described this life-altering episode in my memoir was designed only for comical effect. I was sleeping on the couch when the mother summonsed me. It was late at night and the train carriages on my pyjamas had already begun to hoot and holler.

Once in bed with her—at her insistence—she'd put her hands down my pants, and my trolley had 'leapt from the rail yard, and gone searching for a tunnel through the shorts, and into the waiting clutches of my veteran conductor. No kissing, no fondling, no lovemaking, just a passionless late-night shunting from Bewilderment Station to Mercy Street'.

I was rather proud of that train metaphor at the time, but in recent years I've come to the same conclusion that many of my female friends reached once they heard or read the story. By law, I was obviously too young to consent to what had happened. By law, she had breached her position of authority and trust. On both counts, she was almost certainly guilty of aggravated sexual assault.

Did I feel that at the time? No. Did I keep going back for more? Yes. For nine months. Did that make me a willing participant? Yes, but probably only to the extent that a fourteen-year-old boy has any idea what he's doing. Did it affect my life and inform my view of women? I don't think so, although the hard disk of memory is always selecting and erasing.

Keep digging, David, you've got to unpack this thing. It must have made you cynical about women. It must have damaged your sense of trust.

No, sorry, I can't locate that feeling.

Actually, who am I kidding? Of course this must have taught me the wrong way of thinking about sex and, yes, it might even have changed my neural pathways, although this is pure supposition. But how would I know, given there's been no *before* and *after* study. At the time, it felt like a badge of honour. Now it reads like what it was: abuse.

And yet I don't feel damaged. I don't feel like a man who was abused once as a teenage boy, although I must admit that when

I read Haruki Murakami's *Men Without Women* recently I did wonder whether that line about being forever fourteen and 'waiting for a gentle wind to stroke my innocent penis' applied to me and, perhaps, to all men.

But was I taught anything about respect and consent from this woman during the nine months she led me astray? No. Was I taught anything about the way women were designed to receive pleasure, about the difference between the clitoris, the vagina and the G spot? You've got to be kidding. I don't think I discovered the complexity of the female anatomy until I was in my late forties, and only then because I decided to attend a 'female orgasm' workshop in Byron Bay run by an Australian tantric master, Andrew Barnes.

A short, chubby man with five diplomas in bodywork and 'sacred sexuality', Barnes had studied at the feet of American sex educator Betty Dodson, the so-called 'great-grandmother of masturbation' and the woman widely recognised as having popularised the delightfully named Hitachi Magic Wand.

Barnes's workshops were sell-outs all over Australia as well as the United States and Britain. Women were saying he'd changed their lives. Some were leaving his sessions ecstatic with—and liberated by—what they'd discovered; others were sad that it had taken them this long to become properly acquainted with their bodies.

Barnes had decided to conduct a men-only workshop in Byron Bay, and my wife had encouraged me to attend, if only from a sense of journalistic curiosity. I was reluctant, partly because I thought I already had the territory charted. (*Ha, who's the chump here.*) Did I know, for example, there was a female prostate gland housed in the urethral sponge and that a woman could ejaculate out of that sponge like a man? *No, I didn't.* Did I know that if you stimulated the G spot, you were also stimulating the female prostate, and that this was an area of the anterior vaginal wall, possibly the anterior root of the clitoris, which, when aroused, could lead to an ejaculation of up to a cupful of alkaline fluid? *Can you run that by me again?*

Barnes used slides and geometric diagrams to show us the clitoris. First the clitoral hood (or prepuce) covering the head or clitoral glans; then, back from the head, along the clitoral shaft, to the clitoral legs, known as clitoral crura. All this concealed behind the labia minora and a winding course of nerves, blood vessels, sponges, bulbs and flapping skin.

Did I know anything of this? We know the answer to that now—and, to the dismay of Andrew Barnes, who considered it a tragedy, neither did most women and girls. Not only did they not know what they were supposed to look and feel like, they also had the weight of thousands of years of history telling them they *shouldn't* know.

'Pussy is our true north, our meter reader, our highest power,' Regena Thomashauer wrote in her bestseller *Pussy: A Reclamation*, twelve years after this Byron Bay workshop. 'We don't trust her because we don't know her. Straight women have spent way more time handling cock than we've spent handling pussy.'

According to Barnes's figures—and I still find this hard to believe—70 per cent of women in America died without ever experiencing a vaginal orgasm, with 25 per cent never enjoying clitoral orgasm. (According to author Naomi Wolf, the figure is closer to 29 per cent of women never experiencing orgasm during intercourse.)

How could this be? Was it because the candle of shame had been burning for centuries around female sexuality and because, as Barnes put it, 'We are not teaching young girls about their bodies, so how will they know about their bodies as women? Why am

I still getting 50-year-old women coming to my workshop who have never had an orgasm in their life?'

The Victorian era epitomised the hyper-anxieties surrounding the vagina when the historic role of midwives—and their approach to sexuality and birth—was progressively banished by the rise of a new profession: male gynaecologists.

'The midwives' approach to sexuality and birth,' Naomi Wolf wrote in *Vagina: A New Biography*, 'had been to advise, and to support natural processes; the male doctors' model of dealing with the vagina and uterus was, rather, one of "heroic medicine," or impatient, sometimes violent, intervention.'

British gynaecologist William Acton asserted in his 1875 dissertation, *Functions and Disorders of the Reproductive Organs*, that 'masturbation may be best described as an habitual incontinence eminently productive of disease'. However, this should not be a problem, he maintained, because 'the majority of women (happily for them) are not very much troubled with sexual feeling of any kind'.

Acton's treatise went through eight editions in twenty years to become one of the most widely referred to books on female sexuality in the English-speaking world.

During this period, clitoridectomies were also introduced as a way of dealing with the 'moral leprosy' of female masturbation, and as a cure for any signs of nymphomania. The chief exponent of this practice from the mid-1850s was Dr Isaac Baker Brown, a prominent British gynaecologist and one-time president of the Medical Society of London.

Brown believed that female masturbation triggered eight stages of progressive disease: hysteria, spinal irritation, hysterical epilepsy, cataleptic fits, epileptic fits, idiocy, mania and, finally, death. In his opinion, only the removal of the clitoris could prevent the hellish slide towards an inevitable and ghastly end.

'Dr Brown became famous and sought after for his "cure",' Wolf continued, 'which took argumentative, fiery girls, and, after he had excised their clitorises, returned them to their families in a state of docility, meekness and obedience.'

Baker was later expelled from the London Obstetrical Society in disgrace, and his practice condemned in British medical circles. But clitoridectomies would take hold in the United States, and continue up until the middle of the twentieth century. It is, of course, still widely employed across broad swathes of Africa and, to a lesser extent, the Middle East.

'Before the war on drugs, the war on terror, or the war on cancer,' write Christopher Ryan and Cacilda Jethá in *Sex at Dawn*, 'there was the war on female sexual desire. It's a war that has been raging far longer than any other, and its victims number well into the billions by now. Like the others, it's a war that can never be won, as the declared enemy is a force of nature. We may as well declare war on the cycles of the moon.'

#

Some further confessions.

Nine years ago my wife and I separated after 23 years of what had been a predominantly happy marriage.

I walked out the door and into a fifteen-month self-imposed exile in the Australian bush, not because I didn't love her, nor because I was indifferent to the silent rain of tears streaming down my younger daughter's face that dreadful day of departure. Quite the contrary. I was haunted for years by the pain I'd caused, and that reflected image of parental betrayal in my daughter's eyes.

I left because I'd given up. I left because there was nothing I felt I could do to dislodge the view my wife had formed of me over many years: A husband who had restricted her opportunities, thwarted her professional ambitions, sought his own rewards and successes at the expense of hers. A man blind to the howls of protest from women, despite all his declarations—indeed his writings—to the contrary.

I couldn't recognise the man she saw me as, because I saw myself as someone quite different. That man was a good provider and an even better father. He was progressive, respectful, sincere and kind. He supported women's equality, and he would never dim his wife's lights—or allow them to be dimmed—in order for his own to shine brighter. Yet apparently that's what I did, without ever meaning to—although just as nothing is ever entirely clear in nature, neither is it ever entirely clear in a marriage.

What does seem clear, however, is that the very thing she feared most was the very thing she became during our 23-year marriage. She would serve as chief cook and bottle washer. She would prepare most of the family meals, take care of the laundry, tend the garden, do our finances, while also working as an arts curator and urban designer, together with raising our two daughters.

I lost count of how many times she asked me to take over the accounts, prepare a meal once a week, join her in the flowerbed, clean the pool . . . only to be met with the same excuse: I had a story to write and the deadline was urgent.

As both judge and party to these episodes you might take this with a grain of salt, but I did vacuum the house. I did clean up after dinner most nights. I did read to my daughters and help them with their homework. I did cook the occasional meal. I also spent too much time travelling for work, living in my head, lost in my self-absorption, thus breaking whatever fair division of labour I'd pledged myself to.

It's taken me a long time to face this, but the deeper, harder truth of our marriage is that it was never equal, despite my protests to the contrary. The reciprocity and sharing were never there because I never really stopped to fully examine—let alone relinquish—my own entitlements. I had the wind at my back; why alter course?

'I believe that what we become depends on what our fathers teach us at odd moments when they aren't trying to teach us,' wrote Umberto Eco, the Italian novelist and literary critic.

What my father taught me when he wasn't trying to teach me was that my job was more important than my wife's, my role as breadwinner more important than hers and, in so far as any adjustments would need to be made for those early years of child-rearing, they were hers to make, not mine—even if she was earning more than me or her career was on a sharper upswing than mine.

My father rose to the top of his industry as a magazine publisher and rarely, if ever, cooked a meal. I never saw him carry his dishes to the kitchen or, heaven forbid, wash up afterwards. I never saw him change a light bulb, hang a painting, water the garden, remove leaves from the gutter, fix a lawnmower, lay a tile, build a shelf or restore a piece of furniture. In that sense, he was about the most un-Australian man I ever knew. He had more important things to do, like run the publishing company he had founded in 1959, a company that was to publish Australian *Vogue* under licence from the American-owned Condé Nast Publications. It was a big job, and for a German Jewish boy who had fled his homeland on the eve of World War II, arriving in Australia via New Zealand at the age of 22, it was a hell of a job brief. And, so, when he wasn't working or socialising—which he was most of the time—his greatest pleasure was to be found in the silence and concentration of books, or the form and poise of a Beethoven symphony.

My mother, a musician by training, a bookseller by trade, fully accepted that the tasks of child care and household belonged to her, even though during the course of my growing up it was usually housekeepers and nannies who fulfilled these roles, not her. Her job was to administer these functions, while yielding to the demands of my father.

As you can see, though, I didn't come from a demographic that often produces the most wounded of men, the kind that Australian novelist Tim Winton described as often being put together from 'spare parts'. I was never beaten or abandoned by my father. I was never subjected to the horrors of war. I was never anyone's cheap labour, or human detritus thrown on the economic scrap heap. I was never made to feel useless in the eyes of my children or my community. I was never forced to doubt where I belonged, or to sense that I was nothing more than a sorry footnote in someone else's story.

I had advantages. Straight, white, educated, middle-class, male advantages, and just to be able to acknowledge that right here seems to be an advantage all unto itself. It doesn't cost me much, certainly not the last vestiges of my self-esteem, to say so.

But the problem with having always had a leg-up is that it can often blind you to another's disadvantage. You only ever see the life that has produced, nourished and paid for your own privilege, nothing of the catalogue of oppression that is visited upon others.

The Kennedy brothers, Jack and Bobby, were like that when they confronted the reality of the civil rights movement in America in the early 1960s. They thought of themselves as well-meaning, broad-minded reformists; they had no clue what it was to live as black Americans, because nothing in their reality corroborated the truth of segregation.

'You don't know what's happening on the other side of the wall,' said James Baldwin, the American author and social critic, 'because you don't want to know.'

You don't want to know, or you don't even know that you don't know.

This seems important to mention now in the context of what the #MeToo movement might be able to teach us men who are trying to pay attention. What does the world look like to a woman, and do we men want to know about it?

In the article that inspired this book, I wrote that 'it takes a moment like this in history for men to truly wake up'. I thought I'd been awake during my marriage. I thought I'd understood women's collective complaint. I'd read the works of numerous feminist authors, profiled numerous women, worked for brilliant female editors and, through all of this, believed I'd come to see how my own entrenched biases, assumptions and sense of entitlement had been shaped by the mere fact of being a privileged white male.

There was some truth to this, but the bigger truth, *the truer truth*, was that I was kidding myself if I thought I was awake during those years.

I'd never imagined sufficiently what it was like to walk down a darkened street at night as a woman. I'd never really imagined what it would be like to be pressed against on a crowded train; to be ignored or talked over repeatedly; to know that my value at work was often predicated on my sexual attractiveness to my boss or my fellow colleagues. I'd never visualised what it would be like to have someone indecently expose themselves to me; to have to devise strategies each day, often unconsciously, just to feel safe. Nor had I envisaged what it would be like to be shamed, sneered at, or reduced to the parts of me that could be breached.

There was all that, but there was also this: I'd never given enough thought to equality of regard and equality of opportunity; about how power gets expressed in every aspect of life—in kitchens, living rooms and boardrooms, on casting couches and film sets, on university campuses and in doctors' surgeries, on farms and in restaurants and factories, in law firms and television studios, across industries, blue collar and white. I'd never thought enough about the hazards and disappointments of living in the world as a woman.

'The more complete a privilege,' wrote William Gibson, the Canadian-American pioneer of cyberpunk fiction, 'the more thoroughly we take it for granted, often to the point of being profoundly unaware of having it.'

I'm only really starting to understand this now as I plunge deeper into these black waters—remembering, reflecting, recoiling (at myself) and rethinking all that I was taught or assumed as holy writ. Because, once you start seeing the systems and structures that have been in place for centuries, it's impossible not to see them everywhere. And I don't think I'd ever truly seen them before.

'There's only room in this marriage for one of us to work full-time,' my wife said to me one evening after arriving home late from work to find our daughter in hysterics in the arms of a new au pair, the house in disorder, and me still in my home office with nothing prepared for dinner.

As she'd uttered these words, she'd hurled a wineglass across the living room—a bull's-eye shot from the couch, which, on reflection, had announced the end of the cosy arrangements I had clung to since we'd first uttered our marriage vows.

For years I'd refused to see how my ambitions could possibly be overwhelming the woman I loved; nor could I see how her resentments were a symptom of the assumed prerogatives men had been carrying for centuries. I understood this in theory, but certainly not in cold, hard practice. My needs counted more. My projects counted more. My interests counted more.

'There's a huge amount of unexamined privilege that men go about in the world with,' said Tim Winton on the Seven Network's *Interview*, hosted by Andrew Denton, in June 2018.

[They think] that they've got where they've got just because they're good, and a lot of the time they've got where they've got mostly because they're a bloke. They have an enormous tailwind, and if you're not actually conscious of that, then you don't understand that for so many people, particularly girls and young women, they have a headwind. It's changing, but it's still there, and a bloke who can't see that is a bloke who's just adding to the problem, he's adding to the headwind.

In other words, if respect and true equality were at the heart of what women had been clamouring to achieve—in the workplace and at home—then it was sheer artifice on my part to pretend I'd ever fully understood this clamour, let alone done something to address it.

The tragic symmetry of this is that my life would have been better if my wife's life had been better; that if I'd understood the value in relinquishing some of my unacknowledged freedoms, both our lives would have improved.

10

The man box

A man in manacles doesn't fully understand the threat he poses to others. Even as he's raging against his bonds. Especially as he's raging against his bonds.

TIM WINTON, *THE GUARDIAN*, 2018

Eve Ensler, author of *The Vagina Monologues*, had every reason to fear and despise men, and to be reluctant to hear what ails them; from a young age, she was beaten, bruised, choked and nearly murdered by her father. Yet her efforts to survey the ruined landscape of female suffering—visiting rape camps, establishing safe houses for women across the world, creating a global movement to stop violence against women (first V Day, then One Billion Rising)—ultimately took her into the heart of male darkness.

In her 2006 book *Insecure at Last*, she described meeting a soldier in Kosovo in the late 1990s who seemed both physically and mentally paralysed. His name was Agrim and for some reason, she wrote,

He looked at me, threw his arms around my neck, and started weeping. No, it was more like wailing. I have never heard a sound like that. He would not let go.

Then his weeping wailing began to build and release. It could not be controlled or stopped. It resounded through the neighbourhood. People from the village began to gather around.

I held on to Agrim, but, honestly, I wanted him to stop. All these years I had told myself I wanted men to be vulnerable, to have their feelings, to cry. All of a sudden it felt like a lie. I did not want this man to be so destroyed, so out of control. I wanted him to have answers and be tough and know the way and make everything work out.

Ensler understood how part of her was terrified of men being lost, how she needed them to be tough and assured. She also understood how many years she'd been carrying men's 'invisible pain' in order not to see their weakness or shame. Holding Agrim in her arms, 'this weeping liquid man'—as she described him—was her undoing, pulling her 'out to sea in the wild waves of his crying'.

It was as if I were holding the secret story of men in my lap. Centuries of male sorrow and loss, centuries of unexpressed worry and doubt, centuries of pain. I suddenly understood violence and war. I understood retaliation and revenge. I understood how deep the agony is and how its suppression has made men into other things.

I understood that these tears falling down Agrim's face would have become bullets in any other case, hardened drops of grief and rage directed toward a needed enemy. I saw how in fighting to live up to the tyranny of masculinity, men become driven to do anything to prove they are neither tender, nor weak, nor insecure. They are forced to cage and kill the feminine within their own beings and consequently the world.

I first read this passage more than a decade ago, and the words have remained with me. That's partly because they were delivered by a strong feminist, but also because they spoke to what it is in men that causes them to inflict such monumental hurt on women, other men, children and themselves. *They are forced to cage and kill the feminine within their own beings and consequently the world.*

Carl Jung, the Swiss psychoanalyst renowned for his theory of the collective unconscious, called this feminine within a man the *anima*—the 'unconscious woman' that contains all the feminine personality qualities inside a man that can either be expressed, if allowed, or repressed and removed. These are the qualities of tenderness, compassion, vulnerability, friendship, relatedness, creativity, imagination and intuition.

Conversely, he called the masculine within a woman the *animus*—the 'unconscious man' that holds the archetypal masculine traits of courage, assertiveness, analytical thought, decisiveness and a drive for achievement. (The Chinese describe this polarity as yin and yang, the complementary female and male principles operating in nature.)

In Jung's worldview, all of us carry these archetypal qualities inside us—feminine and masculine—but from childhood we create gender identities and roles, consciously or unconsciously, to conform with the often-crippling sexual stereotypes society imposes.

Girls wear pink, and isn't that a pretty dress? Boys wear blue and play with Lego and trucks, and aren't you strong? Women are nurturers. Men are providers. Women are sensitive. Men are tough. We all know the drill; and we all know that identity politics today is, in part, a furious backlash to these oversimplified and limiting concepts.

For men, these stereotypes are particularly destructive, as Tony Porter, an internationally recognised American author and educator, pointed out in his inspirational 2010 TED talk in Washington DC.

I grew up in New York City, between Harlem and the Bronx. Growing up as a boy, we were taught that men had to be tough, had to be strong, had to be courageous, dominating, no pain, no emotions, with the exception of anger, and definitely no fear.

[We were taught] that men are in charge, which means women are not; that men lead, and you [women] should just follow and just do what we say. That men are superior and women are inferior; that men are strong, that women are weak. That women are of less value, property of men, and objects, particularly sexual objects.

Porter later came to describe this collective socialisation as the 'man box', a term first coined by Paul Kivel in his 1992 book, *Men's Work: How to Stop the Violence That Tears Our Lives Apart*. This 'man box' contained all the ingredients for how men came to define their masculinity. Some of those ingredients, Porter said, were 'absolutely wonderful', others were so 'twisted' that it required deconstructing and redefining the very concept of manhood.

Porter used his own parenting to illustrate the point. When his daughter Jay was little, she could come crying to him anytime she liked and Porter would comfort her. 'Daddy's got you,' he'd say.

With his son Kendall, the opposite was true. Whenever he heard him cry, a clock would start ticking in his head. His son had about 30 seconds to stop before he'd start saying to him, 'Why are you crying? Hold your head up. Look at me. Explain to me what's wrong. I can't understand you.' And then through sheer frustration, together with a sense of responsibility for building his son into a 'man', Porter would say, 'Just go to your room. Go on, go to your room. Sit down, get yourself together and come back and talk to me when you can talk to me like . . . *a man.*' His son was five years old.

Porter was mortified. 'My God, what's wrong with me?' he'd ask himself. 'What am I doing? Why would I do this?' And the answer took him back to his own father.

He then related a story from his teenage years. His brother Henry had just died and the burial was being held in Long Island. Porter's family was about to be driven home from the cemetery to the Bronx—a two-hour drive that first required a toilet stop. 'The limousine empties out,' Porter recalled.

My mother, my sister, my auntie, they all get out, but my father and I stayed in the limousine, and no sooner had the women got out, than he burst out crying. He didn't want to cry in front of me, but he knew he wasn't going to make it back to the city, and it was better [to have me there] than to allow himself to express these feelings and emotions in front of the women.

And this is a man who, ten minutes ago, had just put his teenage son in the ground, something I just can't even imagine. The thing that sticks with me the most is that he was apologizing for crying in front of me, and at the same time, he was also giving me props, lifting me up, for not crying.

This fear of expressing emotion, of being seen as weak or feminine, Porter said, kept boys and men paralysed—just as Eve Ensler noted with her Balkan soldier, Agrim. They are held hostage inside the 'man box', from which there is often no escape.

'I can remember speaking to a twelve-year-old boy, a football player,' Porter finished, and I asked him, 'How would you feel if, in front of all the players, your coach told you you were playing like a girl?'

I expected him to say something like, 'I'd be sad, I'd be mad, I'd be angry,' or something like that. No, the boy said to me, 'It would destroy me.' And I said to myself, 'God, if it would destroy him to be called a girl, what are we then teaching him about girls?'

#

In 2018 two of Ireland's most prominent rugby players, Paddy Jackson and Stuart Olding, stood trial in a Belfast court for the rape and sexual assault of a nineteen-year-old woman. For nine weeks the case horrified and polarised the nation.

Two other men, Blane McIlroy and Rory Harrison, were also charged: the former with exposure, the latter with perverting the course of justice and withholding information. All four men denied the charges and were eventually acquitted, causing uproar over the perceived toxic male culture in elite sport and issues around consent.

The Ulster case resulted from a party in 2016. The young woman went to Paddy Jackson's house in the early hours of 28 June and, according to her testimony, was raped by both Jackson and Olding. A third man, McIlroy, also tried to get involved.

Much of what happened that night was revealed in court through text and WhatsApp messages. One damning text message sent that night from the complainant to a friend read:

There was one guy I really didn't like and I was like right I'm going to go now. Went to get my shoes but my clutch was upstairs . . . and Paddy Jackson came up behind me. He'd already tried it on earlier and I firmly told him where to go. The next thing I'm bent over the bed. I have bruising on my inner thighs. I feel like I've got bruising. They were so rough I've got my period a week early.

The complainant spent eight days on the witness stand being interrogated by each of the defendant's lawyers, with her underwear being carefully handed to—and inspected by—each juror.

The following week, Jackson's lawyer, Brendan Kelly, accused the woman of having taken a morning-after pill soon after the party, so that she could present herself as 'a classic rape victim'. The lawyer also reminded her that 'drunken consent' was 'still consent'.

In WhatsApp group chats the day after the alleged rape, Olding, Jackson and McIlroy referred to themselves as 'legends' and 'top shaggers' who were doing a 'bit of spit roasting' the previous night on a woman who 'was very loose'. It was like a 'merry go round at the carnival'.

Rory Harrison, the man accused of perverting the course of justice and withholding information, was described by the complainant 'as a really nice guy' because he accompanied her home in a taxi to make sure she was okay. He followed this at midday with a text message to see if she was 'feeling better'.

An hour later, in a series of exchanges between Harrison and McIlroy, Harrison told his friend, 'mate the scenes from last night were hilarious,' to which McIlroy replied, 'It was a good night, I loved it.' Harrison then said he 'walked upstairs and there were more flutes than the 12th of July'.

Blane McIlroy then posted to a different WhatsApp group a photo of three other girls at the same party the previous night sitting on his knee. The caption reads: 'Love Belfast sluts.'

Shortly before Paddy Jackson and Stuart Olding were arrested, Blane McIlroy sent another WhatsApp message to a friend:

'Pumped a girl with Jacko on Monday. Roasted her. Then another on Tuesday night.'

That same day, and shortly before McIlroy was called in for questioning by the police, he and Harrison had the following text exchange:

McIlroy: 'Do you know who this girl even is, this is ridiculous, surely it's all just gonna get dropped?'

Harrison tells McIlroy the complainant's name.

McIlroy: 'What age, what school?'

Harrison eventually replies: 'Hopefully it'll be thrown out. Just a silly girl who's . . . done something then regretted it. She's causing so much trouble for the lads . . .'

So much trouble for the lads? That's the choice as many men see it—defend the woman under pain of ridicule from other men, or laugh it off with the boys by showing contempt for the woman, thereby demonstrating 'manhood'.

Many boys are taught early that to avoid the bullies they have to side with them. They join the gang in order to look tough. They trash talk the girls, because heaven forbid they might like one themselves and be labelled weak. They go along with her mistreatment, because there might be a terrible price to pay if they don't. Never mind what they really feel; putting one's heart on the line carries too many risks.

This denial of the feminine is deeply imbued in men and it's learnt first in the schoolyard, then burnished bright with posture, swagger, flexed biceps and a curled lip in sporting clubs, universities, the military and corporate boardrooms. The message is often unspoken, but it's loud and clear: Join us, or suffer the consequences of derision.

'I remember being ridiculed when I tried to break free of this mould,' one of my younger daughter's friends, Drew Rooke, tells me. 'Confessing your love to a girlfriend at school when you were fourteen or fifteen made you a total wanker if that got around the schoolyard. God help you for your standing in the schoolyard.

'That was such a lame and pathetic thing to do. "How gay are you?" The idea of loving someone was seen as pathetic, and that ridicule I think comes from a longing to want to love someone. All the guys who paid me out for that wanted love as much as I wanted love.'

#

Perhaps as men we take our cues from our fathers. From the way they expressed—or failed to express—their emotions, weaknesses, vulnerabilities. Or the way they showed us—or failed to show us—their devotion.

In that sense, I think I was lucky. My father called me 'darling' my whole life, and he always greeted and farewelled me with a kiss or a declaration of love. In our quieter moments, up until the time he died four years ago, we were always able to discuss the usual male topics of work, sport and politics, but also relationships, matters of the heart, the things that often felt unsayable. There was even a time, as an adult, when I allowed myself to cry in his arms.

That has often made me feel different from most of my male friends, because even today there are few I know who can speak with any abiding affection about the men who helped bring them into the world.

One old school friend left Australia 30 years ago, largely because of the hurt his father inflicted on him from the time he was a little boy. When he was sixteen, his father called the police to escort him from his home because he'd found him experimenting with cannabis. His father didn't speak to him again for almost a decade. Five years after my friend had been banished and come to live with my family, he saw his father walking towards him down George Street in Sydney. 'Hello, Dad,' he said tentatively. His father stared at him briefly, then kept walking.

Another friend was repeatedly bashed and thrown against walls as a boy when his father returned home from the pub. His mother often copped a hiding too.

Yet another man I know, a carpenter with dashing good looks, warm and funny to strangers, once tied his six-year-old son to a pole and left him out in the midday sun. That was his way of teaching his little boy a lesson after the boy had said he was bored being on the building site with his dad. 'I'll show you what bored is,' his father replied.

I know men (and women too, of course) whose fathers died early, or walked out on the family when they were young, never to return. I know men whose fathers were rarely, if ever, at home, so consumed were they with their work or whatever went on after work. I know men who, rather than face up to their own corporate follies or misdeeds, publicly humiliated the sons who were working for them. I know a man who still laments the fact that his father never once told him he loved him. His father is dead, but he's still waiting.

I remember another close friend telling me how, when he turned ten years old, he was informed by his father that they could no longer kiss each other goodnight. 'You're a man now,' his father said. 'We'll shake hands.' My friend felt both chuffed and crestfallen by this sudden declaration. Chuffed because he'd been anointed a 'man'; crestfallen because he knew something priceless had just been ripped from him.

It was 22 years before these two men would embrace again, and only because the son spontaneously pulled his father towards him one night and hugged him. 'Dad, I've been wanting to do this for years.' The pair wept in each other's arms.

Australian psychotherapist Steve Biddulph—author of the seminal book *Raising Boys*—has thought about these issues for almost 40 years, and he describes this sorrow for lost contact and love as 'father hunger', a term first coined by Jungian writers.

'This "father hunger",' he tells me when we meet at his home in Tasmania on an afternoon of soft falling rain, 'is the sorrow for lost contact and love; the simple need to be affirmed and valued by older members of one's own gender—not just our fathers, but uncles, teachers, grandfathers, gay or straight, and of different ethnicities and natures. Each boy needs to create a masculinity that is his own, and to do that he must experience a wide range of masculinities from different kinds of men. This is especially the case when his own father is a terrible, or not very relevant, example of manhood.

'Role-modelling is the way the human brain learns almost all complex behaviours, attitudes and skills, and so boys need to know good men close up. All of us are a bundle of the good people, male and female, we have known. But we have let that enrichment disappear on the male side, and many boys today have never seen what a good man looks like close up.'

Biddulph believes this is a key insight into the defective nature of male psychology, an impairment that began during the Industrial Revolution. For the first time in history, men abandoned their agricultural communities and went in search of jobs in the cities, thereby splitting their family roles between home and work. Men were no longer working alongside women and children; they were miles away in factories and mines.

'In a break with eternal tradition,' Biddulph wrote in his best-selling book *Manhood*, 'boys began being raised solely by women.

The lack of male input into growing boys created a huge break in the family fabric, yet we adjusted to it and soon assumed it was normal. The possibility that boys might need fathering for many hours a day, not just minutes, and that uncles and grandfathers had a critical role in male mental health, was forgotten.'

For 30 years, Biddulph has travelled Australia and the world talking to men about fathering, encouraging them to become more engaged, inviting them to talk about their own boyhoods.

'When I meet with groups of young dads,' Biddulph tells me, 'I conduct a survey and the results are always the same. About 30 per cent of men report that they don't even speak to their fathers. Their relationship is non-existent. Another 30 per cent have a somewhat prickly or difficult relationship. They do sometimes spend time with their father, but it's a painful and awkward time. Around another 30 per cent fare somewhat better—they visit their father or phone him regularly, show up for family get-togethers, go through the motions of being a good son, and yet discuss nothing deeper than lawnmowers. Fewer than 10 per cent of men are friends with their father and see the relationship as deep and sustaining. Only about one man in ten says, "My father is fantastic. He's an emotional backstop in my world."'

By contrast, many women absorb an entirely different type of role-modelling, from which they naturally develop a capacity for intimacy and connection. Biddulph says, 'They have spent hours a day, over years of their lives as girls, in deep conversation and exposure to good people of their own gender, which boys just don't get. As a counsellor you find this all the time—the man just doesn't seem to have found a voice, beyond clichés or platitudes. And that's why men feel so liberated and alive when they start talking to other men, and find shared depth and experience.

'Women tell me, "Finally I know what he is thinking and feeling!" And of course, a man who can express himself, and think about his inner self, is far less likely to hurt others on impulse, take his own life on impulse, or act stupidly in any number of ways.'

Each culture produces its own kind of man. An Irishman is not an Indian, a man from Kansas is entirely different to one from Kenya. Men wheel prams all over Denmark, something we've only just begun to see in this generation's Britain where, Biddulph says, a 'typical British father was like a log of wood, except that from time to time, he blazed out in violent rage, or an alcoholic blur, or lashed out with a verbal coldness that made millions of sons feel that they never measured up'.

We know all manner of men—good men, dangerous men, corporate men, artistic men, alpha and beta men, terrifying and tender men, physical and bookish men, gregarious men, silent men, old-world men, New Age men, rescuers, narcissists, hopeless romantics, cynics . . . For Biddulph, however, one of the common denominators, certainly throughout the western world, is the correlation between the time a father spends with his children and a child's sense of self-worth.

'A father's absence from his daughter's life has been found in research to increase her chances of risky sexual behaviour, experiencing teen pregnancy, doing poorly in school. For sons, it prevents them from seeing the fullness of what it means to be a man. There is no access to the interior world of male feeling.

'There's been a vast improvement in this over the past twenty years because of how much time fathers are now devoting to their children. But generations of men have carried the legacy of this gaping hole.'

In the early days of giving talks around the world, Biddulph noticed certain men leaving the theatre. He assumed they were bored or indifferent, or felt they had better things to do. Then, at one gathering in the British Midlands, he was told by ushers that they'd seen men leaving in tears, although who can say why. Perhaps because of the grief of their own broken relationships with their fathers. Perhaps because, as the nineteenth-century American poet Henry Longfellow wrote, 'Often times we call a man cold, when he is only sad.'

11

Hammer blows

You do not stop hungering for your father's love even after you are grown up.

PAUL AUSTER, *THE INVENTION OF SOLITUDE*

For all my father's tenderness, I still remember his often long, impenetrable silences, particularly as old age began to overwhelm him. These silences were born, I'm sure, from his troubled German youth, where he was shunned at school for being Jewish, and then force-marched through the streets of Nazi Germany and pelted with rotten fruit by jeering crowds. He never forgot the indignity of Kristallnacht, the 'night of broken glass', when Jewish homes, businesses and synagogues were destroyed across the country.

My father's silences also probably mirrored his own father's, although, in my grandfather's case, this had more do with the injuries he sustained in the trenches during World War I and then bore throughout his life with stoic acceptance.

Perhaps we all know a version of this male silence. Certainly, in the Australian context, it's easy to see how our ideas of masculinity were shaped by our felon origins for one, but also the Great War which saw hundreds of thousands of husbands, fathers, sons and brothers return home as husks of the men they'd once been—that is, if they returned home at all. Everywhere, households were enveloped by the muteness of male anguish.

'We've militarised men and commodified women for thousands of years,' Steve Biddulph tells me, as we continue our talk at his home in Tasmania. 'War became one of the definers of masculinity and we're still raising boys as soldiers of empire—which is why they don't cry. If we need you to go and die in the trenches of France, or in Iraq, we don't want you to complain about it. Similarly, if you're a policeman pulling bodies out of cars, or you're a surgeon tending horrific injuries, you don't want a man to burst into tears. It can be a positive thing to suppress your emotions. The problem is when it becomes a lifelong characteristic.'

Biddulph describes a place in Rotorua, New Zealand, where Maori men were traditionally known to do their weeping after battle. There's a hot spring there that runs into a stream, before tumbling over a waterfall.

'The Maori said this was their ritual place. They used to wash the blood off themselves there, and then do their weeping so that they could release the warrior mode. After that, they could go back to being safe, trusting men again with open hearts.

'We've never done that, not since World War I. And it was a century of hammer blows. We've never grieved or raged against the monumental waste, and we're now in the fourth or fifth generation since that war.'

In Australia, there is also the enduring power and myth of the bush, which defined ideas of manliness for generations—squatters, soldier settlers and farmers who, alone in nature, controlled and governed themselves as they attempted to control and govern the land. It was a hard-boiled self-sufficiency, and it came at great cost, not just to the land and its original inhabitants, but to the way in which men were able—or unable—to communicate. The elemental silence of the bush seemed to find its ghostly reflection in the reserve of the men who sought to tame it.

'The bush has always been as much for hiding pathologies as repairing them,' Don Watson wrote in his exquisite rendition of the Australian landscape and character, *The Bush*. 'The no-speak rule of old persists. In the city, opinion corrodes the outer layer of existence; in the country it eats the inner.'

All the stock definitions of masculinity that prevent boys from dealing with the 'storms and subtleties' inside their hearts. Only yesterday, as I wrote this, one of my oldest and dearest male friends told me that he didn't think he'd cried since he was nine years old. That's more than half a century ago. 'I'm hard-wired not to cry,' he said. 'I was nine when my father died, and I was determined not to cry in front of my friends, or even myself. But I think by that time I'd already decided I would never cry. That's because only girls cried, so it's almost like I *can't* cry now. It's baked in. It would be like weeing in your pants, which is just like tears coming out the other end.'

This is the suppression of pain that Eve Ensler referred to—'the caging of the feminine'—which, if unexpressed, can harden and direct its fury outwards. Quite possibly, this is the first act of violence that the patriarchy commits: a wholesale assault on the qualities of softness and vulnerability, of emotional attachment and spirit that reside inside a man. That's the desecration of the feminine right there.

In the previous chapter Tony Porter referred to this cage as the 'man box'; Steve Biddulph calls it the 'mask', and in a recent article in the *Sydney Morning Herald* he described what this concealment does to boys and men.

As a young man, I felt an enormous blank inside me every waking second, and the men I have worked with in hundreds of seminars and groups all describe this in the same way. We had simply no idea how to do male. But we had to do it nonetheless.

So to deal with this, every day, we clamped on a mask, and hoped it would last until night. That no-one would notice. Teenage boys are the ones who first find and choose these masks, and it's no accident that they become the bulk of the shooters, the terrorists, and so on. Nine times more likely to go to prison. A hundred times more likely to rape.

And, according to the Australian Bureau of Statistics, three times more likely to commit suicide. In 2016, 2866 people died by suicide; 75.1 per cent of them were male.

Mid-teen boys look at the available range of standard masks, try out a couple, and then clamp the one that seems most successful onto their face and live with it the rest of their lives. In the UK there are four or five standard masks. The tough guy. The cool dude. The hard-working go-getter. The funny guy . . . The depressed alcoholic clown is a very identifiable kind of British male, loveable and not usually dangerous, but suicide prone and intensely lonely beneath the veneer.

The masks do a terrible thing to these young men—they isolate even as they protect. They have mates but no true friends. Their parents feel them slipping away. When they become adults, the women and children in their lives get no sense of connection, and soon their families start to fall apart. The man may explode, or just drift into addiction to work, alcohol or drugs. Either way it's a dismal life.

#

Anyone who has worked down the coalmine of youth suicide, homelessness, mental health, juvenile justice or the education system—be it here in Australia or in other western countries—knows there is a crisis in masculinity, and they've known it for years. Boys' school retention rates lag well behind girls'; literacy levels are lower; drug overdoses, road trauma, workplace fatalities, unemployment and youth suicide are higher.

Men are living, on average, six years less than women, and in four out of five marriage breakdowns, they're the ones being left. Among boys and young men there is more obesity, homelessness, schizophrenia and attention deficit disorder than ever before. Young men are entering university in fewer numbers. In schools the majority of children with behavioural problems are boys; so, too, those with learning difficulties. Boys and young men take more risks than girls. They play harder, drive faster, die earlier. Their problems are apparent from an earlier age, with primary and preschools reporting depression, anxiety and violent conduct. And on the question of violence, they are more likely to be murdered, robbed or physically assaulted than women.

These are all factors that fire the righteous anger of the men's rights movement, and you only need to scan some of their websites to grasp how deeply some of these men resent being seen to be the ones holding the power.

The way they see it, the Family Law Act favours women, child support agencies favour separated mothers, and the claims and statistics proffered for the levels of physical assault by men on women are exaggerated. They accuse western feminists of not caring about women in the developing world.

They consider influential television programs like the ABC's *Q&A* as a bully pulpit for feminists who routinely ignore domestic violence against men. They see patriarchy as a myth—*patrimalarkey*, one calls it—and point to the reigns of Queen Elizabeth I, Mary Tudor and Mary Queen of Scots. (Didn't Queen Elizabeth I rape and pillage Ireland? Didn't Mary Tudor burn 300 Protestants at the stake?)

They see misandry at every turn, with negative stereotypes foisted repeatedly on men—our Y chromosome is defective, our capacity for pain lower, our ability to think laterally questionable, our aptitude for multitasking inferior, our emotional intelligence more stunted.

They point to how many cheating wives there are (most studies show the numbers are higher for men), how many false rape accusations are made (in fact, false rape accusations constitute less than 10 per cent of reported rape cases, possibly as low as 2 per cent), the unacknowledged number of women hitting men (in many cases they're hitting back), the lack of men's shelters (almost certainly true), and the number of men who are forced into penetrative sex by women using threats and blackmail (I'll pass on this one). And they look to men like Canadian psychologist and author Jordan Peterson, and American author Warren Farrell, as their intellectual figureheads.

'The weakness of men is the façade of strength,' Farrell wrote in *The Myth of Male Power: Why Men are the Disposable Sex*, first published in 1993 and now a standard text of the men's movement.

The strength of women is the façade of weakness.

When a man tries to keep up with the payments by working overtime and is told he is insensitive, or tries to handle the stress by drinking and is told he is a drunkard, he doesn't feel powerful, but powerless.

When he fears a cry for help will be met with 'stop whining,' or that a plea to be heard will be met with 'yes, buts,' he skips past *attempting* suicide as a cry for help, and just *commits* suicide. Thus men have remained the silent sex and increasingly become the suicide sex.

A self-declared champion of feminism during the 1960s and 70s, Farrell shifted his focus to men's issues when he realised that, as an educator, he'd been listening mainly to women. When he *had* been listening to men, he'd often criticised them for their 'chauvinism', 'sexism' and 'defensiveness'. He'd failed to appreciate their sense of 'powerlessness'.

The Myth of Male Power is Farrell's appreciation of that power-lessness; his 'ten glass cellars' (the invisible barriers that keep men in hazardous jobs) as opposed to the 'glass ceilings' (the invisible barriers that keep women out of certain jobs). This, he wrote, was testament to men's 'disposability'.

Since its first print run a quarter of a century ago, *The Myth of Male Power* has proved one of the most durable—and biting—remedial cures for the perceived domination of feminist voices in the gender debate. And, as with all arguments that are furiously contested, some of Farrell's assertions have merit.

There's no doubt that the various definitions of masculinity have sold boys and men a bill of goods; that suicide—'death by loneliness'—takes young men's lives far more than young women's; that anywhere we care to look, we find confused, broken, angry boys and men ready to inflict damage on themselves and others. (And, according to a recent *Washington Post* report, more likely, because of a 'fragile masculinity'—read erectile dysfunction and hair loss—to vote for a posturing male like Donald Trump.)

They feel attacked, hard done by, discarded, stranded in a dislocated world not of their making. They see deregulation, downsizing, outsourcing, corporate engineering and corporate malfeasance at every turn. They see old ideas of loyalty, productivity and service rendered obsolete by a perilous job market. They see themselves and their sons swept out to sea in a shifting tide, lost to drugs, gangs, brooding silences, pornography and video games. They see their utility lost, and they look at women rising through the economy—new graduates, customers, stakeholders, executives, professors, female-dominated health and services industries—and blame feminists and feminism for their predicament.

They feel *Stiffed*, as Susan Faludi wrote in her book of the same name twenty years ago. 'Women see men as guarding the fort, so they don't see how the culture of the fort shapes men. Men don't see how they are influenced by the culture either; in fact they prefer not to. They would rather see themselves as battered by feminism than shaped by the larger culture.'

It's the same point Michael Kimmel makes when we meet at his home in New York on a gorgeous late spring afternoon in 2018. 'It wasn't feminist women who outsourced your jobs,' he says, talking to these men directly, particularly the online male storm troopers of hate. 'It wasn't immigrants who gave you those predatory loans. Yes, you got screwed. But you're delivering your mail to the wrong address.'

#

Michael Kimmel is an international authority on men and masculinities, and, as distinguished professor of sociology and gender studies at New York's Stony Brook University, is known for his female-friendly comments. That's why he's regarded as one of the world's pre-eminent male feminists, and why I decided to seek an interview with him, blissfully unaware—as I suspect he might also have been—of the accusations of sexual harassment that would be levelled at him just over two months later. (And, yes, we will come to that in later chapters.)

Michael Kimmel grew up in a middle-class Jewish household in Brooklyn and both his parents worked—his father as a chiropractor, his mother as a psychoanalyst. It never occurred to him, therefore, that a woman could not be as ambitious as a man, nor that her career path should ever be blocked.

Another shaping influence was his time living in the San Francisco Bay area during the mid-1970s. He was in graduate school and his then partner worked at a shelter for battered women.

'We had one car and it had a stick shift,' Kimmel recalls. 'She didn't know how to drive a stick shift, so when we would get a phone call from the shelter, I drove the women. I drove women to the hospital, I drove women to the shelter, I got kids out of the house. And I had lived a fairly middle-class suburban life. I had no idea that men beat up women. It never really touched me, but it does something to you viscerally, when you're listening to somebody on their way to the hospital, say to you, through a broken jaw, "Well, sometimes I deserve it, but this time I didn't."

'So I said to my partner after [one] particular event, "You know what? I'm going to come work with you at the shelter. This is really important. I really want to do something. This is really getting to me." And my partner said, "You can't work there; you only even know where it is because I don't drive a stick shift."

'She said, "Why don't you go talk to the men who beat the women up?" I looked at her like she must be mad. I said, "I don't want to go talk to them. They beat women up. I don't like them. I want to talk to the women." And she said, "You have a natural constituency of half the human race. Go talk to them.'"

So that's what Michael Kimmel did. He went and trained in a 'batterers' intervention project in order to counsel men convicted of violence against women. The men had been given a choice between incarceration and therapy.

'Their motivation to show up to therapy groups was very high,' he says. 'Their motivation to do anything about it was very low, because all they had to do was show up [and] check their names.

'That was the moment I realised that I had to start doing work in this area. That I did have a constituency, I did have a contribution to make. I did have a way that I could, as a man, engage with the issues that women were raising in the mid-1970s.'

Kimmel has been engaging with these issues ever since and, in his relentless efforts to promote gender equality, he has delivered the International Women's Day annual lecture at the European Parliament, the European Commission and the Council of Europe, while also developing programs for boys and men throughout Scandinavia.

He has written eleven books, including *Manhood in America*, *Guyland: The Perilous World Where Boys Become Men*, *The Guy's Guide to Feminism* and his latest, *Angry White Men: American Masculinity at the End of an Era*. Researching *Angry White Men*, he crisscrossed the country talking to college students, white supremacists, neo-Nazis, Tea Party activists and men who'd lost contact with their children, all the while taking the pulse of white men. In the resulting book, he lays out in stark terms what has become so palpable in America and, to a lesser degree, Australia: the raw fury of men who feel robbed and deceived, who are casting around for someone, or something, to blame. He wrote:

They're angry at immigrants, who, they believe are displacing them in the workforce. They're angry at fat-cat capitalists, who, as they see it, downsize and outsource them out of their jobs, demolish communities, and then jet off in their private planes, only to golden-parachute onto some tax-haven island. They're angry at feckless bureaucrats who are deaf to their cries for help. They're angry at women, who, they argue, are beautiful, sexy and sexually available—yet turn them down with contemptuous sneers.

And the result is an explosion of white male American anger unlike anything seen before in the country's turbulent history. Upper class, middle-upper class, lower-middle class, working class, skilled, unskilled, farmer, shopkeeper, small businessman.

They feel they've borne the weight of the world on their backs, and they can't hold it up any longer. And now, suddenly, some of these regular guys are re-inventing the American Revolution with Tea Party, Minutemen and Patriot organisations, while others are further out there, organising militias and joining survivalist cults, waging war on 'feminazis,' rampaging through their workplaces, promoting protectionist and anti-immigrant policies.

They're listening to angry white men like Rush Limbaugh . . . and other radio hosts who lash out at everyone else as the source of their woes. They're trying to roll back the gains made by women and minorities in corporate and professional life and resisting their entry into the ranks of soldier, firefighter, and police officer.

And these men's sons, according to Kimmel, are either busy destroying the galaxy in their video games, or actually opening fire on their classmates. Some of them are exploding at work, slaughtering co-workers, supervisors and plant managers before, usually, taking their own lives.

Few observers notice the *gender* of these vitriolic legions. Few, if any, couple the increase in American anger with the growing gulf between women and men. The gender gap—politically, socially, and economically—is as large as it has ever been. It's not 'Americans' who are angry: it's American *men*. And it's not all American men—it's *white* American men.

Yet the truth is that white men are the beneficiaries of the single greatest affirmative action program in world history. It's called 'world history.'

Not surprisingly, Kimmel doesn't win too many popularity contests among men's rights groups with views like this. As with women who dare to articulate the grievances of their sex, he is often viciously attacked. His Twitter feed is living, vibrating proof of it.

'Here's one,' he says, scrolling through his phone. '"You know nothing about masculinity or being a man." Here's another, "How dare you call yourself an expert in male roles when all I see is a liberal apologist who delights in attacking traditional male roles."' He grins at that one.

Any more, I ask? 'Yes, "Stop being such a self-loving, male-bashing misanthrope and show some pride in being a man. Your pandering to female approval is as disgraceful as it is obvious."

'Here's another one, "You're an embarrassment to the Jewish people." I'm okay with that. But where's that other one I recently got? Here it is: "You fucking genocidal Jew, why don't you talk about angry black men? They're the ones that commit epidemic violent crime, [you] fucking genocidal piece of shit."

'Hold on, here's another: "You are a dirty criminal kike Jew. If you ever come to Germany again and try to agitate white women against white men and children, I [sic] cut your throat in front of all spectators."'

Michael Kimmel says he understands the distress of legions of men because—to quote Henry David Thoreau—'the mass of men lead lives of quiet desperation'. He just disagrees with their conclusions.

'The traditional definition of masculinity doesn't make men feel very good,' he says. 'It leaves them without many friends, stoic, unemotional, robotic. They rarely like their family, they don't know anybody, and they don't feel vulnerable or intimate with anybody.'

And in Australia it produces thousands of men—trollers, stalkers, harassers, slappers, killers, men who promise (or are too proud) to change, whose disrespect and mental cruelty knows no bounds.

In the case of public figures like Mark Latham, Senator David Lleyonhjelm and broadcaster Alan Jones, these are men who seem so devoid of self-reflection, and so filled with self-righteousness, that they continue raging at the dying of the light.

12

Brick by hurtful brick

The greatest enemy to man is man who, by the devil's imagination, is a wolf, a devil to himself and others.

RICHARD BURTON, *ANATOMY OF MELANCHOLY*

In its boiled-down version, the impulse for the men's liberation movement of the 1970s was a recognition that, if women needed liberation from their traditional sex roles, so too did men. Men felt exiled from their homes. They felt lost in soulless jobs. They felt their 'success' was dependent on their earning capacity and ability to endure.

Betty Friedan, widely acclaimed as one of the pioneers of the second wave of feminism with her 1963 book *The Feminine Mystique*, expressed sympathy for these grievances in her epilogue to mark the tenth anniversary of her book's publication.

How could we ever really know or love each other as long as we kept playing those roles that kept us from knowing or being

WOMEN, MEN, AND THE WHOLE DAMN THING

ourselves? Weren't men, as well as women, still locked in lonely isolation, alienation, no matter how many sexual acrobatics they put their bodies through? Weren't men dying too young, suppressing their fears and tears and their own tenderness? It seemed to me that men weren't really the enemy—they were fellow victims, suffering from an outmoded masculine mystique that made them feel unnecessarily inadequate when there were no bears to kill.

American poet Robert Bly tapped into this collective longing with his 1990 international bestseller, *Iron John: A Book about Men*. Focusing on the destructive effects of remote—or non-existent—fathers, Bly's book took his readers on a part-Jungian, part-Grimms fairy tale march through the mists and myths of time, back to a pre-industrial age when 'male energy' had not been so diluted. Bly had produced a mud map for how boys might grow into healthy manhood by connecting with the hairy 'wild man' inside.

Along with the works of American mythologist Joseph Campbell, *Iron John* became one of the most influential texts of the so-called 'mythopoetic men's movement', resulting in men's groups springing up around the world with their emphasis on Native American rituals like drumming, chanting and sweat lodges.

We had them in Australia, too, and I was one of those who joined, although I never chanted, only crawled into one sweat lodge, and I can't remember ever beating a conga. But some of my closest friends are the men I came to know in this group twenty years ago—each of them successful in his own way but, like me, drawn to the possibility that, in a place of mutual trust, we might be able to let our guards down. We might be able to talk in ways often difficult for men to navigate—conversations around our career disappointments, our health, our marriages, our children, our parents, our fathers . . . yes, always our fathers. Conversations that might breech the double walls of the heart.

'What Bly tapped into,' offers American professor of sociology and gender studies Michael Kimmel during our May 2018 interview in New York, 'is that men need the company of other men. They need to be emotional. There were things I hated about his work, but what I loved was that it was explicitly counter-homophobic. That homophobia is what keeps men from recognising that they need the companionship of other men. They need to be close to men, they need contact, emotional vulnerability, real close friendships, meaning.

'And I thought he got that. He got the fact that men need other men in their lives. We can't ask women—this is now the feminist part of me coming through—to answer all our emotional needs. We need men in our lives and Bly sensed the same thing that Warren Farrell and the men's liberation did, which was that men are not happy.'

Where men's right activists peeled off from the men's liberation movement was that they not only sought the solidarity of other men, they invariably took to blaming women for all that had gone wrong. Feminism was an assault on their identity, rather than a call for fairness and equality.

'My question is,' Kimmel explains, '"Why are men unhappy?" The men's rights guys say, "Because women have all the power." And I say because women *don't have enough power*. Because we're still gender unequal. So when men have more equality in the home, when they do more housework and child care, they live longer, they're happier, their children are happier, their wives are happier. So I'm saying let's be more equal; not less. It's not women who are making us unhappy. I think that their diagnosis is entirely wrong.'

A perfect example of this misdiagnosis, he says, is the way men's rights activists deal with violence. 'What we know from social science is that violence is the only behaviour attitude and trait in which there's a significant gender difference. And the men's right guys would not disagree with that. Why? Because they would [point] to testosterone. Men are biologically programmed to be more aggressive, more violent than women. Of course we are, that's the testosterone factor, and they might even celebrate that.

'So why, when we put two people in a house, do we suddenly pretend that that's not true? Here's what's true: if you ask a man and a woman who are married to one another, "Have you ever used violence in your relationship?", it is true that an equal number of women and men will say yes.

'Now if you ask them who initiated it, if you ask them how severe it was, if you ask them how many times it happened, if you ask them whether it was offensive or defensive—for example, "Did you use violence to control or hurt somebody else, or did you use violence to keep the person from hitting your children?" —then it begins to look like what women have been saying all along, which is that men are overwhelmingly the perpetrators of violence.'

The question, then, for men's rights activists, according to Kimmel, is how can you have it both ways? How can you assert that men are more often the victims of (male) violence in the public domain than women but then refute it when it comes to violence carried out in the home? How can you also fail to see that, in the case of divorced couples, nearly 100 per cent of the violence is male to female. So, too, virtually all the stalking, the ex-spousal murders, the ex-spousal rapes . . . it's almost always men.

Also, when the studies find there are equal numbers of men and women committing violence, that doesn't include couples who are no longer together, nor does it include sexual violence. In other words, it doesn't include rape.

Says Kimmel: 'It's only, "Have you ever used any of these tactics: hitting, punching, slapping, hitting with a newspaper, hitting with a book, hitting with a frying pan, punching, kicking . . .", a whole long list of these things, and an equal number of women and men say yes.'

Kimmel has met many men who've been hit by their wives or partners. He says his heart goes out to them. 'Nobody should be beaten up by somebody who professes to love them. I get that. But why is compassion a zero-sum game?

'If there are men who have been victims, I'm all for hearing their stories, I'm all for ministering to them and supporting them. I don't want to dismiss them and I don't want to pretend they don't exist. I think we should have an endless capacity for compassion. We don't need to ration it.

'I share the diagnosis that men are in trouble. There's a lot of distress we need to attend to. But it's not a competition. It's not like we have a finite amount of attention here. We need to have adequate funding for counsellors in schools so that boys don't pick up assault weapons. (Of course you don't have assault weapons [in Australia] to pick up, but we do.) Men's rights activists are right, in a way, to be resentful. We should pay more attention to these things . . . they're right to pay attention to the consequences of gender inequality for men, but where they go wrong is they don't pay attention at all to the privileges men get through inequality.'

And that's another misdiagnosis—or, more accurately, a gigantic presumption born from centuries of male dominance: the world belongs to white men, and, if it doesn't, it should. This is British artist and author Grayson Perry's thesis in *The Descent of Man*, where 'Default Man'—the white, middle-class, heterosexual, usually middle-aged man—normally holds the keys to power. He doesn't see his own biases. He doesn't see the way his habits, beliefs and traditions have been formed. He can't quite see the equal value of other cultures. He doesn't notice how, and by whom, laws have been legislated, buildings designed, corporate lobbies furnished, films made, history books written, because they've all been constructed according to an 'ideology of masculinity' that's plaited into the fabric of society.

'When talking to men about masculinity,' Perry wrote, 'I often feel I am trying to talk to fish about water.' (There's that fish metaphor again, as encountered in chapter eight in a graduation speech from American writer David Foster Wallace.) 'Men live in a man's world; they are unable to conceive of an alternative.' (Grayson Perry, it should be noted, is a transvestite.)

'White male power has [seen] itself as the neutral identity against which all others are measured,' Perry continued ' . . . [and] having been unaware of the myriad ways they are privileged, they feel feminism is an attack on their core identity rather than a call for equality. Men's rights groups seem to be rallying points for what psychotherapists would call persecutors from a victim standpoint.'

Michael Kimmel gives this another name. 'Aggrieved entitlement.' Several years ago, he took part in a television talk show alongside four men, each of whom believed he'd missed out on a job or promotion for which he was qualified. They felt wronged, mistreated—thus the title of the show: *A Black Woman Stole My Job*.

'My response to them,' Kimmel says now in the gathering dusk of his Brooklyn apartment, was: "I have a question about one word in the title. I want to know about the word *my*. Where did you get the idea it was *your* job? Why isn't the title of the show "A Black Woman Got *the* Job"? Because without confronting men's

166

sense of entitlement, we'll never understand why so many men resist gender equality.

'Where these men are right is they pay attention to the consequences of gender inequality for men. But where they go wrong is they don't pay attention at all to the privileges men get through inequality . . . In gender relations, the disconnect is that men are in power and don't feel powerful and there's three ways you can [look at] that. "Men don't feel powerful because women have all the power, so let's get it back." That's the men's rights group. The "mythopoetics" said, "We don't feel powerful, so let's go off to the woods. Here's the power chanting, the power drumming, the power rituals, the power breakfasts." And the pro-feminist men said, "The fact that you don't feel powerful despite the fact that men have the power is how patriarchy works." Because patriarchy is not just men's power over women, it's also some men's power over other men. It's a system that's designed to make most men and women feel powerless. And that has been my position all along—men's power and men's powerlessness are linked.'

#

On 1 August 2018, nine weeks after I interviewed Michael Kimmel, the *Chronicle for Higher Education*, a Washington DC–based news service for American academia, reported that the professor had been accused of sexual harassment. An unnamed former student claimed that, six weeks into her graduate studies program, Kimmel suggested they sleep together. The anonymous accuser also claimed Kimmel had told her that her attractiveness meant she would have to work harder for equal recognition. The allegations were made a week before Kimmel was due to be honoured with a major award by the American Sociological Association (ASA) for his extensive research on the role of women in society.

In written comments to the ASA, which he shared with the online publication *Inside Education*, Kimmel asked that his award be delayed for six months so that the allegations could be properly vetted.

'I have been informed that there are rumours circulating about my professional conduct that suggest I have behaved unethically,' he wrote. 'While nothing has been formally alleged to the best of my knowledge, I take such concerns seriously, and want to validate the voices of those who are making such claims. I want to hear those charges, hear those voices, and make amends to those who believe I have injured them.'

Kimmel added that he hoped the American Sociological Association would not act on 'rumours', and that 'those making these accusations will file a complaint with the [organisation's] Committee on Professional Ethics so that these accusations can be formally addressed'.

Two days later, Debra Guckenheimer, a research associate in gender studies at Stanford University, issued a blistering online rebuttal to Kimmel, claiming his response disempowered and silenced his accusers, and failed to acknowledge the risks for graduate students and junior faculty in coming forward. This was particularly so given that the ASA had 'zero' track record of ever holding a sociologist publicly accountable.

Guckenheimer then sought to hoist Kimmel with his own petard by quoting his own comments on the subject: 'Sexual harassment persists,' Kimmel wrote in the *Harvard Business Review* in January 2018,

because of three factors: the sense of entitlement that some men feel toward the women they work with; the presumption that women won't report it or fight back; and the presumed support—even tacit support in the form of not calling out bad behavior—of other men . . .

So, where do we go from here? After decades of accepting sexual harassment as the status quo, we have to take some of the weight off women's shoulders. It's simply not their responsibility alone to talk about and enforce workplace equality. We must call out the sexist behaviors of other men because it's wrong and because it undermines women's confidence and effectiveness in the workplace.

Guckenheimer then called on Kimmel to 'acknowledge and believe the survivor' even if her account didn't fit with his own 'sense of self'.

#

This much should be obvious by now: it's hard to know how to be a man. You grow up with the mask, and all the insecurities concealed behind the mask. You find yourself inside a 'man box', where the fear of being seen as weak cripples you psychically, robbing you of many of your natural human emotions. You live with the peer pressure to objectify and denigrate girls to prove your manhood under threat of ridicule or violence from men (and let's not forget possible ridicule and disdain from women). You spend hours each day watching porn, playing video games, having your brain rewired in the opposite direction of connection and intimacy. You follow the rituals of power and the bristling hostility and pecking order that men impose on each other. You become a cast-off in a hyper-capitalist, hyper-masculinist world in which you are measured only by your economic utility. You feel devalued, excluded, unprotected, confused and lonely as hell.

And then there's shame as well, because there's no telling what a man might do when he's plunged into shame, real or perceived. Carry out an act of hideous revenge by throwing his little daughter off the West Gate Bridge, as Arthur Freeman did in Melbourne in 2009, on his daughter Darcey's first day at school. (He even turned his hazard lights on before he hauled her from the front seat.) Kill his wife and three children (and later himself) as Geoff Hunt did in 2014 on his farm in Lockhart, New South Wales. Murder his entire family on a property near Margaret River, south of Perth, as Peter Miles did in 2018.

Launch a Jewish Holocaust, a Rwandan genocide, a Serbian ethnic cleansing?

That might not be shame, pure and simple—let's toss into the boiling pot a wild, primitive rage and bigotry as well—but there are probably few women on this earth who aren't aware of the core fragility that lies at the heart of the masculine ego and how easy it is for a man to feel loss of face. They often know it better than the men themselves.

#

(Flight attendant to author): *I know a man who is very dangerous when he's insecure. I was in a very bad relationship with him and I could tell from the beginning—it was just an alarm—because he kept mentioning the things I owned. I built my own home and when I talked to him about it I could see he was ashamed. He became angry really fast. I felt very scared once when he went to the kitchen to get a knife, but mostly he was an emotional abuser. He wanted to crush me to make himself feel better. He became so abusive that I left him but he's been stalking me ever since. He leaves notes on my car saying, 'I'm watching you. I'm still here.'*

\#

Women are terrified of a man's shame—as they should be. The consequences are often horrific. And so women often try to accommodate that shame, tiptoe around it, or back away from it, lest the world blows up.

In their book *The Spirit Level: Why Equality is Better for Everyone*, authors Richard Wilkinson and Kate Pickett quote James Gilligan, a psychiatrist at Harvard Medical School, who has studied violence for more than 30 years. A former director of mental health services for the Massachusetts prison system, Gilligan has made it his business to study the most violent offenders in prisons and prison mental hospitals. His conclusion: most acts of violence are attempts to ward off or eliminate shame, and replace it with its opposite—pride.

The authors wrote:

> Time after time, when talking to men who had committed violent offences, [Gilligan] discovered that the triggers to violence had involved threats—or perceived threats—to pride.
>
> Sometimes the incidents that led to violence seemed incredibly trivial, but they all evoked shame. A young neighbour walking disrespectfully across your immaculate lawn ... the popular kids in the school harassing you and calling you a faggot ... being fired from your job ... your woman leaving you for another man ... someone looking at you 'funny.'

None of this excuses the unchecked male aggression we see so routinely, but it might help to explain it. You start out in life sensitive, vulnerable, full of wonder, open to the world and all its possibilities; then, after a certain age, these qualities are shamed, beaten, bullied out of you by the culture and, often, by the men who run our nations, corporations, legal firms, advertising agencies, film industries, media outlets.

As Australian writer Tim Winton told Andrew Denton on his program, *Interview* in June 2018:

[It's just so sad] to see these boys who are reservoirs of tenderness drying up and becoming this narrow, cracked, dry creek that runs on for the rest of their lives for so many. They start out with all the colours in the pencil box and then somehow, from fourteen onwards . . . you just see more and more pencils have been taken off them. And in the end, they get to middle age and they've got black, purple and dark blue. 'There's your colours—go live a life with that.'

With so few colours in the spectrum with which to draw, it's no wonder that what so often passes for masculinity is the persistent brutality of the male libido, something the #MeToo movement has finally shone a global spotlight on.

American Buddhist teacher John Bell laid it out eloquently in a lengthy online post for *yes!* magazine in 2017 when he asked:

What happened to boys to make this [sexually aggressive] behaviour so pervasive?

What happened to men that they support a [US]$96 billion porn industry that produces, by some estimates, 13,000 films a year (compared to Hollywood's 600 films), has 420 million websites, and sees 68 million search engine requests for porn every day?

. . . No one is born a rapist, a sexual abuser or a porn addict; even the creepiest, sleaziest and most dangerous of these men began as sweet little boys. What happened?

What happened, according to Dr Arne Rubinstein, chief executive of Rites of Passage Institute and author of the bestselling book *The Making of Men*, was that boys never actually grew up. Their bodies did, but their minds didn't. They got stuck in a 'boy psychology'—the very antithesis of what makes for 'healthy man's psychology', indeed a healthy society.

'After puberty,' he tells me, shortly after landing in Sydney from his home in northern New South Wales, 'boys can become angry and lost because they're still operating from boy psychology. And to understand this boy psychology, you only need to picture the typical behaviour of a seven-year-old in the playground. He wants to be acknowledged all the time. He sees himself as the centre of the universe. He takes no responsibility for his actions. He finds it difficult to deal with his emotions. And he wants his mother. He wants her to do everything for him, tell him how wonderful he is, cook for him, pick up his clothes.

'Whereas in the healthy man's psychology, a man sees himself as part of the universe, not the centre of it; he takes full responsibility for his actions, he deals with his emotions and he looks for a healthy relationship with the feminine.

'And my belief—and a lot of my work—is based on the fact that we don't create a way for boys to move into this healthy man psychology, so we end up with a lot of men who still think they're the centre of the universe, they still want power, they're still incredibly competitive, they still can't handle their emotions, and they're still looking for a mother.

'If you ask a lot of women if they know any men who are still in this boy psychology stuff, the majority will say, "Yeah, I married him." And that's not appropriate when you're a man. When you're a man in a real relationship, it's a two-way thing. It's about supporting another person. It's about how we can actually work together and really love each other genuinely.

'We live in a world still ruled by boys who want acknowledgement and power, and who think it's okay to treat women in an abusive way—that women are actually there for their gratification and to serve them. The role-modelling and mentoring for boys and teenagers is very poor, and the messaging is terrible.

'So that's what our organisation does—it gets men to help the next generation think about what it means to have a healthy relationship with both the masculine and the feminine.'

We've all grown up with the clichés that boys don't cry. They don't show fear. They keep a stiff upper lip. They suck it up, lest they be labelled a 'girl' or a 'pussy'—all these stock phrases that shame the idea of being soft, compassionate or kind-hearted.

And what replaces this, as John Bell also observed, is a 'strutting of male power'—perhaps the perfect image for the caricature of machismo currently on display in the White House. Perhaps, also, the perfect image of what men do not just to women, but to gays, queers, transgender people, bisexuals and, of course, other straight men—anyone considered different or a threat.

'For many men,' Bell wrote,

> the beckoning archway of human need for closeness and love gets bricked up, brick by hurtful brick, until the only pathway for those real needs narrows to a small keyhole called sex. Add testosterone, unrelenting sexual advertising and media images, and boyhood training to be aggressive to get what you want, and we can start to understand how sex for men becomes so fraught, compulsive, or desperate.

Add to this also the fact that men are taught to take charge, to hold the reins of power, to feel superior to women, to expect women to serve them in exchange for protection and security, and to refrain from showing feelings other than anger or toughness, and it should come as no surprise that we've got a problem of epic proportions.

13

In the shadows of Saddam

The wound is the place where the light enters you.

RUMI

Zainab Salbi's first #MeToo moment was with Saddam Hussein, although she only came to realise this many years later.

She was sixteen years old, living in Baghdad with her family, when her mother, Alia, began to notice the way Saddam would look at her daughter. He would breathe her in, just as an animal might its prey.

Salbi's father Basil, an Iraqi commercial airlines captain, had been reluctantly drafted as Saddam's personal pilot in the early 1980s. From that point on, there was nothing he nor his family could do to avoid spending time with the Iraqi dictator. You simply didn't say no to Saddam Hussein.

Saddam was not only a mass murderer, he was also a serial rapist. He institutionalised rape at the top echelons of the state security apparatus, abusing women as a means of sending political messages to friend and foe alike. He raped city women and village women. He raped his colleagues' and friends' wives and daughters. He had his secret police abduct women from the streets for his own pleasure. He sent select men off to war so that he could rape their wives while they were at the front. (A modern-day echo, perhaps, of King David sending Uriah the Hittite to the front line so he could take possession of his wife, Bathsheba.) Saddam allowed his elder son Uday, notorious as 'the rapist of Baghdad', to establish 'rape palaces' in the capital where he violated and tortured women before passing them on to his bodyguards and friends.

Salbi's mother, Alia, knew some of this, but could reveal nothing to her daughter, at least not until Saddam was dead. The walls had ears. Instead, she sent Zainab to America, into an arranged marriage with a much older dissident Iraqi businessman.

Salbi initially railed against her mother's demands, only relenting out of respect and love for her. Her mother was not to know that by saving her daughter from Saddam she would be sending her into the arms of another rapist.

Salbi was twenty years old when she married the 33-year-old Iraqi businessman. Her initiation into sex came on the night of her wedding.

'I went to him in my nightgown feeling shy,' she wrote (with Laurie Becklund) in her compelling memoir, *Between Two Worlds: Escape from Tyranny, Growing up in the Shadow of Saddam*:

> I had never had sex before, but I also knew how a kiss can melt the heart. He asked me to lie on the bed and spread my legs apart. I did. Then he suddenly was on top of me, an uncomfortable stranger pressing into me. He didn't say anything. There was no kiss, no caress at all, no tenderness

or effort to help me relax. There were just humiliating shoves and then he stopped.

Three months into their marriage, shortly after her 21st birthday, they had a heated quarrel, the latest in a series of arguments in which her husband repeatedly referred to her as a 'whore'. Salbi refused to have sex with him. 'He screamed at me and threw me down on the bed,' she recounted.

Then he flipped me over onto my stomach and forced my head into the pillow. He held my head down and started penetrating me from behind, hurting me as he had never hurt me before.

'Fuck you,' he cursed again and again. I cried into the pillowcase until my voice disappeared. I couldn't breathe, and I was afraid I was going to die of suffocation. I vividly remember how powerless I felt. Finally, I consciously stopped resisting and took my soul away, leaving my body an empty shell for him to abuse so he only had the illusion of power over me. In some painful faraway place, I counted each second until he finished. Then he got up, put on his clothes, and walked away as if I were a piece of dirt he was leaving behind.

I hobbled out of bed and turned on the shower. I stayed in the white plastic enclosure for an hour, sobbing and trembling in pain. 'Ightisab,' I thought in Arabic. 'Rape.'

Within days Salbi had fled her marriage. It was Christmas night, 1991, nearly five months after the first Gulf War had been launched following Saddam's invasion of Kuwait. Less than eighteen months later, Salbi read a Time magazine story about 'rape camps' in Bosnia-Herzegovina and Croatia. As in so many other conflicts, women had become just another 'field of battle'. Salbi responded to this crisis by founding the humanitarian and development organisation Women for Women International, its principal aim being to help women survivors of war and rape. She was 23 years old. She started in the Balkans with 30 women and, by today's reckoning, has assisted more than half a million women through the delivery of US$120 million in aid to countries like Nigeria, Rwanda, the Democratic Republic of Congo, Afghanistan and Iraq.

'I heard women speaking in different languages about the same stories of sexual violence,' she wrote. 'So often when brutal armies invaded, it didn't matter whether they called themselves rebels or soldiers, they claimed women along with disputed territories. It wasn't a matter of politics, but patriarchy. Yes, it had been happening since the beginning of time.'

While urging other women to voice the outrages visited on them, the one thing Salbi was unable to do herself was speak about her own violation. 'It took me until I was 35 years old,' she tells me when we meet in New York in May 2018, 'to realise that all these years I'd actually been working out my own psyche. I couldn't speak up, so I repeated the pattern of going to countries that were similar to where I'd grown up—in wars.'

'I urged women as an outsider to speak out and break their silence. I wanted to empower them and give them money and resources, so they could have safety . . . only to realise that I'd been really working out my own issues. That's why I had to write my memoir. I thought I had no story.

'So to link it to #MeToo, I swear I had no story of my own. I grew up in privilege. I had private planes and private cars and helicopters. I had jewellery and diamonds and brand names. I had no story. These poor women did, but I didn't.'

But then a Congolese woman relayed to Salbi how she and her daughters had been raped by militia, then stripped of all their worldly possessions. It was a cry from the doomed edges of a benighted land and Salbi asked the woman for permission to tell her story.

'Tell it,' the woman answered. 'If I could tell the whole world what happened to me I would. But I can't, so you go ahead and tell the world.'

That was the moment Salbi realised there was a thread connecting her own story to the collective story. She realised at last that, despite all appearances to the contrary, she was carrying an abiding shame—the shame of having known Saddam Hussein; the shame of having been forced into an arranged marriage; and, of course, the shame of having been raped by her first husband.

'How could I be a feminist who has gone through that?' she asks rhetorically. 'And that's the reason I'm so excited about Hollywood, that women are speaking about what happened to them—and it's not Hollywood so much as the elite and the privileged of America and the world. Because their hiding was similar to my hiding. "I'm okay, I have all of these things. I don't have a story, it's these poor women who have a story."

'And when you acknowledge, "No, I have a story too, and, yes, it came with material privilege" . . . that is true sisterhood for me . . . when we all own our stories and share [them].'

#

In February 2018, the American Public Broadcasting Service began airing a five-part series on the #MeToo movement and the countless issues we've been forced to examine since lightning struck America, sending its thunderbolts rolling and crackling across the world.

The PBS series looked at the impact of popular culture on women in the workplace and the social costs of pay inequity and gender discrimination. It examined masculinity in crisis and the hidden cultural biases of patriarchy. It explored the influence of gaming and pornography, and it sought to ask the questions: 'How did we get here. Where to now?'

The series was wide-ranging and incisive, and Zainab Salbi was the perfect choice of moderator to bring together voices from across America.

Since founding Women for Women International and writing her memoir, Salbi had written several other books and in 2015 launched *The Nida'a Show*, a television program dedicated to tackling women's issues in the Arab world. (It opened with an interview with Oprah Winfrey, her first exposure to an Arab audience of millions.) That same year Salbi was also made editor-at-large for Tina Brown's Women in the World, an annual summit for women leaders, activists and change agents.

Over the years, Salbi had been showered with accolades: a 2010 nomination for *Harper's Bazaar*'s 21st-century heroine; *Arabian Business* magazine's choice for one of the world's 100 most powerful Arab women; inclusion in *Foreign Policy* magazine's 100 Leading Global Thinkers; *Fortune* magazine's selection as one of the Most Influential Women on Twitter; *People* magazine's choice as one of 25 women changing the world . . .

It was instructive, therefore, to meet her in person—around the corner, as it turned out, from where, only a few days earlier, Harvey Weinstein had appeared in court charged with rape.

I began by asking her whether she saw any connection between her own experiences in Iraq and the cries of women now being heard around the world.

'For sure,' she replies unblinkingly. 'The common thread is the pattern of men in power and how blind they are to the magnificence of their power and how they abuse it. Sometimes they're aware of it. I think Harvey was aware of it. But sometimes they're unaware. They take for granted the entitlements they have and the fear they impose.

'My first encounter with this was with Saddam Hussein. You could write an analysis of it [because] it's exactly the same behaviour, the same patterns [as other men] —except Saddam Hussein was a dictator, whereas these other guys, Harvey Weinstein, Charlie Rose . . . I don't want to name names, but so many names . . . they were the moral leaders, the intellectual leaders. They did not commit the crimes and atrocities Saddam did . . . but you can't criticise a dictator for these patterns when you actually have them inside yourself . . .'

As Salbi sees it, these dynamics of power, authority and oppression happen everywhere. Sometimes the abuse that stems from it is clear and unmistakeable; other times men—as with some of the accused in the #MeToo movement—proffer the excuse that they thought the woman liked them. They are blind to their own power and how normalised the exercise of that power is.

During her research for the PBS series, Salbi investigated the music, advertising and gaming industries' deliberate investment in the over-sexualisation of women. She was aware of this culture of objectification, but was still shocked by its range and scope.

'I discovered the gaming industry—forget about porn; I don't know how many boys [watch porn], but games, they're all playing. And how a female figure is presented and how a male figure is presented is fascinating. The female is always hypersexualised. Her nipples are always erect. Her lips are always puffed, she is orgasmic: "Come to me, baby, right now." So this is teenage boys' encounter with females, even in stupid games.

'It creates a disconnect when they encounter women . . . that she might be sensitive, that she might want this or that. So we need to look at what we are producing in content material in our society, and what that content is communicating about women. We have to look at all industries—at the money behind the objectification of women. We have to look at the commercialisation of women's sexuality. We have to look at all of it to really change our culture.'

In other words, we can project all we like on to the Harvey Weinsteins, Donald Trumps or Saddam Husseins of the world—their predations are clearly defined and easy to condemn—or we could look further at the more everyday conduct that women are now calling out.

#

Aziz Ansari was riding high as one of America's most successful stand-up comics and writers when his reputation exploded in a ball of flames in early 2018. An American-born actor, writer, producer and director of Indian Tamil descent, Ansari had just won a Golden Globe as the creator of his own Netflix series, *Master of None*, the first Asian American to win such an honour.

Ansari was widely celebrated for satirical comedy that could plumb the depths—and uproarious heights—of issues like racism, migration, sexism and dating in the modern world. He'd even written a book about sex in the digital age, *Modern Romance*. Ansari had won critics' awards, people's choice awards, jury awards and he also happened to be a public champion of women's rights and the need to explore LGBTQI stories. He'd once told American television host David Letterman he was a feminist.

Then, on 13 January 2018, the American website *babe.net*, which prides itself on being an information space for 'girls who don't give a fuck', published a story with the headline: I WENT ON A DATE WITH AZIZ ANSARI. IT TURNED INTO THE WORST NIGHT OF MY LIFE.

The story was written by 22-year-old Katie Way, and it recounted a night in September 2017 when a 23-year-old Brooklyn-based photographer 'Grace' (the pseudonym given to her to protect her identity) went out for dinner with Ansari. It was eight days after the two had met at an Emmy Awards after-party in Los Angeles. Grace had approached Ansari that evening and, as she admitted to *babe*, flirted with the 35-year-old actor, even though she was there with another man. By the time she left the gala event, she'd given Ansari her phone number, at Ansari's suggestion.

When her plane landed in New York the following day there was a message from Ansari, and over the following week the pair exchanged playful texts. A date was set up for the night of Monday, 25 September.

'After arriving at his apartment in Manhattan on Monday evening, they exchanged small talk and drank wine,' *babe* reported. '"It was white," [Grace] said. "I didn't get to choose and I prefer red, but it was white wine." Then Ansari walked her to Grand Banks, an Oyster bar onboard a historic wooden schooner on the Hudson River just a few blocks away.'

It was a beautiful, balmy night and the two discussed college, comedy and a yet-to-be disclosed project Ansari was working on. According to Grace, Ansari did most of the talking and was the first to suggest they leave the restaurant, even though there was still wine in Grace's glass, plus a lot left in the bottle. The abruptness surprised her. 'Like, he got the check and then it was bada-boom, bada-bing, we're out of there.'

The couple walked back to Ansari's TriBeCa apartment, where Grace immediately complimented the marble counter-tops, a gesture which Ansari turned into an invitation. 'He said something along the lines of, "How about you hop up and take a seat?"' Within moments, Ansari was kissing Grace, putting his hand on her breast and trying to undress her.

Ansari then allegedly told Grace he was going to grab a condom. 'I said something like, "Whoa, let's relax for a sec, let's chill,"' but, according to Grace, Ansari resumed kissing her, briefly performing oral sex on her, then asking her to do the same to him. She did, but not for long.

In Grace's account, Ansari then began making a move on her that he repeated throughout the evening. 'The move he kept doing was taking his two fingers in a V-shape and putting them in my mouth, in my throat to wet his fingers, because the moment he'd stick his fingers in my throat he'd go straight for my vagina and try to finger me.'

Grace said Ansari also pulled her hand towards his penis a number of times throughout the night, even after she'd moved away. 'But the main thing,' *babe* reported, 'was that he wouldn't let *her* move away from him. She compared the path they cut across his apartment to a football play. "It was thirty minutes of me getting up and moving and him following and sticking his fingers down my throat again. It was really repetitive. It felt like a fucking game."'

Grace insisted that she repeatedly used 'verbal and non-verbal cues' to indicate her discomfort and distress. She kept pulling away, pursed her lips, felt herself becoming immobilised. Did Ansari notice? Who can say for sure.

Grace remembered Ansari asking repeatedly, '"Where do you want me to fuck you?" . . . "I wasn't really even thinking of that," she said. "I didn't want to be engaged in that with him. But he kept asking, so I said, "Next time." And he goes, "Oh, you mean second date?" and I go, "Oh, yeah, sure," and he goes, "Well, if I poured you another glass of wine now, would it count as our second date?"'

Ansari poured her a glass, but Grace excused herself so she could go to the bathroom to collect herself. She splashed water on her face, then went back to Ansari. Ansari asked Grace whether she was okay. Grace replied that she didn't want to feel forced, otherwise she'd end up hating him.

"'Oh, of course,' Ansari replied. "It's only fun if we're both having fun. Let's just chill over here on the couch.'"

This moment was particularly significant for Grace. She assumed this was the end of their sexual encounter. She believed her comment about not wanting to feel 'forced' had added a verbal component to the cues she was trying to give Ansari. She sat down on the floor next to Ansari, hoping he might rub her back, or play with her hair—something, *anything*, to calm her down.

But according to Grace, Ansari instructed her to turn around and then he sat back in the couch and pointed to his penis, gesturing to Grace to perform oral sex on him. "'And I did,' Grace recalled. "I think I just felt really pressured. It was literally the most unexpected thing I thought would happen at that moment because I told him I wasn't comfortable.'"

Ansari then pulled Grace back onto the couch and the foreplay continued. 'Doesn't look like you hate me,' Ansari said.

Midway through the encounter, Ansari said he had something to show Grace in another part of the apartment. He brought her to a large mirror, bent her over, and asked again, 'Where do you want me to fuck you? Do you want me to fuck you right here?'

"'I just remember looking in the mirror and seeing him behind me. He was very much caught up in the moment and I obviously very much wasn't. After he bent me over is when I stood up and said no, I don't think I'm ready to do this, I really don't think I'm going to do this. And he said, "How about we just chill, but this time with our clothes on?"'"

The two got dressed, sat on the couch, and watched an episode of *Seinfeld*. That's when reality kicked in for Grace. 'It really hit me that I was violated. I felt really emotional all at once when we sat down there.'

While *Seinfeld* played in the background, Ansari kissed Grace again, stuck his fingers down her throat once more, and tried to undo her pants. 'You guys are all the same, you guys are all the fucking same,' Grace finally told him.

Ansari asked her what she meant, and when she turned to answer he gave her 'gross, forceful kisses'.

That was it. Grace stood up and announced she was leaving. Ansari called an Uber and Grace cried all the way back to Brooklyn.

The following evening, she received a text from Ansari: 'It was fun meeting you last night.'

'Last night might've been fun for you,' Grace replied, 'but it wasn't for me. You ignored clear non-verbal cues; you kept going with advances. I want to make sure you're aware so maybe the next girl doesn't have to cry on the ride home.'

Ansari responded. 'I'm so sad to hear this. Clearly, I misread things in the moment and I'm truly sorry.'

That was the last exchange the two had. Nearly four months later, on 8 January 2018, Grace saw Ansari win his Golden Globe award on television. He was wearing a Time's Up pin on his jacket in support of the movement against sexual harassment.

In the weeks and months since that uncomfortable September night, Grace had sought counsel from a number of friends in an attempt to clarify in her own mind what had happened with Ansari. Had she had an 'awkward sexual experience', or had she been sexually assaulted? She decided she'd been sexually assaulted, and watching Ansari win his award only confirmed her profound feeling of distaste.

'It was actually painful to watch him win and accept an award,' she said. 'And absolutely cringeworthy that he was wearing the Time's Up pin. I think that started a new fire, and it kind of made it more real. I believe that I was taken advantage of by Aziz. I was not listened to and ignored. It was by far the worst experience with a man I've ever had.'

Five days after the Golden Globe awards—on 13 January—*babe* published its devastating lesson on modern dating. The following day Ansari issued a statement:

In September of last year, I met a woman at a party. We exchanged numbers. We texted back and forth and eventually went on a date. We went out to dinner, and afterwards we ended up engaging in sexual activity, which by all indications was completely consensual.

The next day, I got a text from her saying that although 'it may have seemed okay,' upon further reflection, she felt uncomfortable. It was true that everything did seem okay to me, so when I heard that it was not the case for her, I was surprised and concerned. I took her words to heart and responded privately after taking the time to process what she had said. I continue to support the movement that is happening in our culture. It is necessary and long overdue.

It didn't take long for the next commotion to erupt.

Writing in *The Atlantic*, Caitlin Flanagan accused Grace and *babe* writer Katie Way of teaming up to produce '3000 words of revenge porn'.

Then, on 15 January, Ashleigh Banfield, a respected broadcaster who was at the time the host of the legal and social issues TV program *Crime and Justice*, delivered a scathing open letter to Ansari's accuser on air:

Dear Grace (not your real name),

I'm sorry you had a bad date. I've had a few myself. They stink. I'm sure it must be really weighing on you. It's hard being a victim. Very painful. Just ask anyone who has been on that end of crime and justice. I cover them every day. It's no picnic.

But let's take a moment to reflect on what you claim was the 'worst night of your life.' You had a bad date. Your date got overly amorous. After protesting his moves, you did not get up and leave right away. You continued to engage in the sexual encounter. By your own clear description, this was not a rape, nor was it a sexual assault. By your description, your sexual encounter was unpleasant.

It did not send you to the police. It did not affect your workplace, or your ability to get a job. So I have to ask you what exactly was your beef? That you had a bad date with Aziz Ansari? Is that what victimised you to the point of seeking a public conviction and a career-ending sentence against him? Is that truly what you think he deserved for your night out?

She was just gathering steam.

Let me be clear. If you just had an unpleasant sexual experience, you should have gone home. Maybe tell the date himself that he's not the lover he thinks he is. And without doubt, certainly don't go on a second date with him, certainly do not marry a guy like that.

But what you have done in my opinion is appalling. You went to press with a story of a bad date and you have potentially destroyed this man's career over it, right after he received an award for which he was worthy.

Banfield then accused the two women—complainant and reporter—of undermining the feminist movement and its struggle for equality in the workplace, something she and her female colleagues and friends had been striving for, and dreaming about, for decades. Now, just as progress was being made to change 'an oversexed professional environment', Grace and her scribe had corroded a powerful movement with a vexatious public accusation.

'That is on *you*,' Banfield railed. All the gains that had been achieved on behalf of women were now being compromised, she said, by 'reckless and hollow' allegations made under cover of anonymity. Hardly the privilege she'd accorded Ansari. 'I hope the next time you go on a bad date,' she said, 'you stand up sooner, smooth out your dress, and bloody well leave. Because the only sentence that a guy like that deserves is a bad case of blue balls, not a Hollywood blackball.'

Babe reporter Katie Way was invited to appear on Ashleigh Banfield's program to discuss her story. She declined, sending an email to the network, HLN, instead.

'It's an unequivocal no from me,' she wrote.

The way your colleague Ashleigh (?), someone I'm certain no one under the age of forty-five has ever heard of, by the way, ripped into my source directly was one of the lowest, most despicable things I've ever seen in my entire life.

Shame on her. Shame on HLN. Ashleigh could have 'talked' to me. She could have 'talked' to my editor or my publication. But instead, she targeted a twenty-three-year-old woman in one of the most vulnerable moments of her life, someone she's never f**king met before, for a little attention.

I hope the ratings were worth it! I hope the ~500 RTs [real time strategies] on the single news write-up made that burgundy lipstick bad highlights second-wave feminist has-been feel really relevant for a little while. She DISGUSTS me, and I hope when she has more distance from the moment she has enough of a conscience left to feel remotely ashamed—doubt it, but still. Must be nice to piggyback off of the fact that another woman was brave enough to speak up and add another dimension to the societal conversation about sexual assault.

Grace wouldn't know how that feels, because she struck out into this alone, because she's the bravest person I've ever met. I would NEVER go on your network. I would never even watch your network. No woman my age would ever watch your network. I will remember this for the rest of my career—I'm twenty-two and so far, not too shabby! And I will laugh the day you fold. If you could let Ashleigh know I said this . . . it'd be a real treat for me.

Thanks,
Katie

This remarkable contretemps between older and younger feminists reminds us of what Zainab Salbi said earlier about our responses to the manifold ways in which men can express their sense of power and entitlement. With depraved men like Saddam Hussein, there is no debate. With men like Aziz Ansari, where licence is assumed but not explicitly granted, things are far more contentious.

That's why Salbi believes the Aziz Ansari story is, in many ways, more important than the Harvey Weinstein case. We can all agree on Weinstein, but with Aziz Ansari, that's where we enter the nightlands of doubt and ambiguity.

14

The grey zone

What matters in life is not what happens to you but what you remember and how you remember it.

GABRIEL GARCIA MARQUEZ, LIVING TO TELL THE TALE

The #MeToo movement began as an outing of men who had engaged in rape, assault, bullying and workplace discrimination, all of them unlawful acts. The Aziz Ansari story presented us with something else, an exposed raw nerve that most women have carried all their lives.

A night of not saying no, or saying no and not being heeded; a night of having been pressed too far, of a man not having read the cues, of *not knowing* the cues. A morning-after filled with self-recrimination, blame, guilt and regret.

When Zainab Salbi began her five-part series for PBS in February 2018, she gave little credence to what had happened between Grace and Aziz Ansari. Her priority was the predator. By the time the series ended, however, she was convinced the Ansari story was the one that needed deconstructing, more than Harvey Weinstein's predations.

'Weinstein reflects, let's say, 20 per cent of power,' she tells me. 'But the 80 per cent of the story is in the Aziz Ansari case. Most women go through that, and the only difference between a woman who holds her line and says "don't do that" and a woman who doesn't [is her age and experience].

'The only difference between me today at 48 years old and me when I was 23 years old is I have thicker skin. I have more confidence. I don't give a fuck anymore. And it's not that what I face is less from men. It's not that the attempts [from men] are less—not at all.

'It's that I have changed and become more gutsy. I don't care if he thinks I'm a bitch. I changed, not the behaviour changed. But when I was 23 years old, it was really hard for me to [draw] a line and walk out. It's still hard for me, it's just that I have the confidence to walk out now.

'But I still go through hesitation and doubt . . . and so that case, because it reflects such normalised behaviour of men lacking awareness, and women lacking the confidence to walk out—that *is* the case, in my opinion. That is the grey that is touching the larger majority. Obviously not all men are predators, by no means, but a lot of men push the envelope and are not aware, are not sensitive about a woman's feelings.'

Helen Garner takes a different view, as we might expect from the author of *The First Stone*, a book that stirred passions and created blazing headlines around Australia nearly quarter of a century ago.

Based on the most celebrated sexual harassment case since the 1950s, *The First Stone* was—as its subtitle made clear—an exploration of *Questions about Sex and Power*. It caused heated debate everywhere and, certainly in the circles I ran in, there was barely a social occasion that wasn't riven by arguments about the book's merits.

The First Stone was an examination of the case of Alan Gregory, the master of Melbourne University's elite Ormond College, who was accused of indecent assault by two female students at a valedictory dinner in 1991. One student claimed that while she was dancing with Gregory, he'd placed his right hand on her left breast and squeezed it. She'd walked away shaken.

Later that night, a second student struck up a conversation with Gregory—one that, according to the student, led to Gregory inviting her into his nearby office. Once inside, Gregory allegedly lowered the lights, cupped her breasts in his hands, squeezed them and asked for a kiss, while expressing 'indecent thoughts'.

Gregory denied both accounts, but was dismissed from his job and charged with four (later reduced to two) counts of indecent assault.

Four months after he was charged, Helen Garner picked up her copy of the Melbourne *Age* and read that the Ormond College master would soon be appearing before a magistrate, accused of putting his hand on a student's breast while dancing.

Garner was horror-struck. Like many of her feminist friends born in the 1940s, Garner regarded uninvited sexual advances as simply part of the human design. Why go to the police? As a friend of hers commented at the time: 'If every bastard who's ever laid a hand on us was dragged into court, the judicial system would be clogged for months.'

In her disenchantment, Garner wrote Gregory a letter. (She might as well have thrown a flaming torch into a dried-out eucalypt forest.)

I read in today's paper about your troubles and I'm writing to say how upset I am and how terribly sorry about what has happened to you. I don't know you, or the young women; I've heard no rumours and I have no line to run. What I want to say is that it's heartbreaking for a feminist of nearly fifty like me, to see our ideals of so many years distorted into this ghastly punitiveness.

I expect I will never know what really happened, but I certainly know that if there was an incident, as alleged, this has been the most appallingly destructive, priggish and pitiless way of dealing with it. I want you to know there are plenty of women out here who step back in dismay from the kind of treatment you have received, and who still hope that men and women, for all our foolishness and mistakes, can behave towards each other with kindness, rather than being engaged in this kind of warfare.

Throughout the 1960s and 1970s, Helen Garner's feminist credentials had never been in question. She'd helped change abortion laws and arrange safe terminations for pregnant women. She'd become involved with women's consciousness-raising groups, facilitated the establishment of communal households with other single women, and written for feminist newspapers like *Vashti's Voice*. She'd been an integral part of Australia's second wave of feminism, but now, as a result of her solicitousness towards Gregory, she was being cast as a traitor. In some quarters her book was boycotted and the author herself subjected to unprecedented levels of hatred and hostility, particularly from more radical feminist quarters.

I remember the period well, because I was assigned to write a cover story for *Good Weekend* about Garner and the furore *The First Stone* was almost certain to cause. We'd met for the first time a few months before publication, and it was clear to see how the charged intricacies of gender relations had drawn their roadmap of worry across her face—and this even before the shells had started to land.

So when we meet now at a Japanese restaurant in North Melbourne, 25 years into our friendship, it is not simply because I want to learn from her what she thinks about the #MeToo movement. It is also because I want her advice on how I might write this book. Where should I place myself in the narrative, if at all? Should a man write this and, if not, why not? How, with a subject so bewilderingly complex, could one possibly frame this in the right way? With more than seven billion people in the world, who should I speak to? Why them, not others?

Garner suggests I keep a diary. Write down at the end of each day everything that has happened, whether it seems relevant or not. Make jottings about the writerly process, how it's often a road to nowhere. Talk to myself. Record it on the page. Chart the misery and uncertainty. Why did *he* do this? How could *she* have thought that?

'Just humbly approach the mountain and go up it,' she tells me. 'One step at a time. Left foot, right foot. In the morning this happened . . . and in the afternoon this.' She offers a line from Homer: '*And the sun set and the roads of the world grew dark.*'

Garner knows I'm in that darkened world, but her mere presence gives me heart, the fact that she's still writing exquisite prose, revelling in the life of the mind and her family and friends, the fact that she's even more predisposed towards men than she's ever been, principally because she's not in a relationship—hasn't been for twenty years—so there's no longer any requirement, she says, to make herself smaller in order to be loved.

Besides which, her world didn't crumble when she was pounded by those waves of censure 25 years ago. In the long run, they made her stronger, better able to speak her mind, as she does now when describing her initial excitement over the #MeToo movement, particularly that thrilling moment in the beginning when women began throwing off their 'shackles of silence, modesty and fear'.

'The trouble is,' she says, 'that, as with most movements, there's a wonderful pure stage at the beginning, like someone has sunk a bore into an underground spring and it just comes surging up, this water, and it's pure and everybody rushes to it. But then after a while it starts to get a bit of grit in it . . . nothing can stay pure in this world.'

For Garner, the Aziz Ansari story is the paradigm for this. 'I had a very complex reaction to that. I started worrying about due process and people who were just taken down and given both barrels. Obviously a person like Harvey Weinstein deserved both barrels and he's copped it. But there are people whose offences are of much lesser magnitude who are mowed down by armoured vehicles and tanks.

'When that woman called "Grace" told the story of her nightmare with Aziz Ansari, I read it with a sort of squirmy feeling. The thing is with most of these stories, when they're told in detail, the complexities of the power relationship become manifest and things come up from one's own past and you think about how did I handle that back then? Did I feel this outraged? Should I have felt this outraged?

'So it all becomes more historical—in that personal referencing way—and then I'm always attuned to when a whiny note appears in these stories and a note of entitlement, which is a note that is inclined to be sounded by women that are much younger than me—one or two generations younger than me.'

Garner sees these younger women feeling a sense of entitlement that women of her own generation never had. It's not the entitlement to express outrage when outrage is warranted; rather, it's the entitlement to have the world go the way you think it should, or the way you want it to.

'Some young people tend to think of themselves as a bubble of rights moving around the world and they're in this little shining enclosure and that's their rights,' she says. 'It's like someone with road rage: anyone bumps against them and they go berko . . .

'But I do feel that when people discuss these matters—like who can do what, what can you do in an intimate relationship, or an erotic situation—when people fall back onto "Well I've got the right to . . .", that's when the whole thing ends for me.

'[There] are some situations in which, if you go into them with your rights banner flying, what could possibly happen, what new thing could happen? I don't just mean some new sexual position, but some engagement with another human being that is not covered by your bill of rights. It's as if everything has to be mapped out in advance like one of those terrible lists of "Can I do this? Can I put my hand on your breast? Is everything I've done okay so far?"'

Not surprisingly, when Garner first read the Aziz Ansari story, she began asking questions she knew she was not supposed to ask as a feminist. Questions like: 'What were you doing in his apartment? You hardly knew this guy and you went to his apartment expecting what? You wanted romance and you wanted sex and you went with him, and then the sex turned out to be not the kind of sex you wanted.

'And somehow this caused, not just alarm, because you weren't enjoying it, but kind of a feeling of outrage—as if sex has become a field where there is no surprise and no adventure and no shock.

'There's a moment in the story where she gets up and says, "I'm not liking this," and he says, "Well let's put our clothes on and sit on the couch," and she says, "I was expecting him to be sweet to me and I sat on the floor and I thought he might stroke my hair." And I thought: "This is not your father, this man is not your father. This is a man with whom you've willingly gone into a situation of high erotic exchange and you can't just expect him to suddenly turn into this benevolent figure." That's not what sex is about.

'And that's why, when Catherine Deneuve and those French women weighed in with rather heavy boots, I thought I saw what they were saying and I sympathised with it—that you don't know what's going to happen, and you don't go in there thinking, "Oh, he's going to fuck just the way I want him to fuck. It's going to be the way I want it to be."

'I'm not talking about violence and I'm not talking about rape and people being somehow forced into doing things they hate and really don't want to do. I would endorse any complaint or screaming about that. But the idea that he said, "Let's do this, I want to do this" . . . instead of her saying, "Wait a minute, whoa"—and this thing comes up that people call "the freeze". That's a very interesting area to go into. Why do women freeze?'

Before we address 'the freeze', let's first go to the contentiousness of Garner's comments, particularly as seen through the eyes of younger women, because when I send my younger daughter Hannah a transcript of Garner's comments she is predictably incensed. (Sorry, Helen.)

'My whole issue with the Garner rhetoric is that it continues to imply that men can use and objectify our bodies in any way they want,' she tells me in an email from Europe.

Why should we accept that that's just the way it is?

Women like Helen Garner fought for the rights of women in the workplace and home, so why is it not okay for young feminists today to continue to fight for differing aspects of equality? Why does that make us 'entitled'—because we demand that we don't want to live in a world where men can think it's acceptable to just grab our breast, or grab our arse, as they cycle down the road? Because that's exactly what happened the other day on the streets of Berlin.

And furthermore, she continues, 'what's so "entitled" about wanting to "have the world go the way you think it should go, or the way you want it to go"? Isn't that exactly what Garner and her second-wave feminist sisters were pushing for—a world that reflected better standards and higher aspirations?'

Hannah wanted me to know she was in total accord with Zainab Salbi's view that 80 per cent of the cases have nothing to do with Harvey Weinstein, and everything to do with issues of intimacy, connection, consent and power raised by the Aziz Ansari story.

'When I was thirteen,' she reminds me,

I got drunk with this guy I had been kissing, we went to bed and he hopped on top of me and took my virginity. There was no conversation. No consent. And I guess I only realised what was happening after it started. He didn't use protection. He didn't talk to me afterwards, and the next time I saw him was a couple of weeks later at a party at our house and he was making out with a friend.

It's only since the MeToo campaign that I've really reflected on all this. It's the first time I've actually been able to say out loud that I was taken advantage of. That event has stayed with me and probably will forever, because it affected my self-worth and my relationship to men.

Hannah didn't know then—and doesn't know now—whether to call what happened twelve years ago 'sexual assault' or 'sexual indecency'; perhaps neither, perhaps both. What she does know is that even if a woman visits a man in his apartment—as 'Grace' did with Aziz Ansari—there is still such a thing as common decency and respect around what is okay and what isn't.

'That actually takes an ability to read someone,' she writes, 'to listen to someone, to ask questions, to recognise that these experiences are supposed to be fun and pleasurable for *both* parties. Is that too much to ask?'

Okay, so that's the view of my redoubtable younger daughter. My daughter Jordan is 29, nearly five years older than her sister. While they are both millennials, Hannah is closer to Generation Z than Jordan and, in keeping with the descriptors for each generation, that makes Hannah arguably more political than Jordan.

When I show Jordan the transcript of my discussion with Garner about Aziz Ansari, she responds: 'If you don't want to give a guy a blow job, don't do it. And if you do, because you feel *that* pressured to please, well then that's a bigger conversation to have about your sense of self-worth and the lengths to which you'll go to feel desired by men.'

That was point number one. Point number two had to do with the importance of women telling men what they liked and didn't like.

'What's our obsession with non-verbal cues all of a sudden?' she asks me. 'Why can't you just say, "No, I don't like that," or, "Please stop"? I know it's scary to communicate this stuff "verbally", but it's also scary going home with someone you don't know very well with the anticipation of having sex with them.

'The whole thing is scary, but I think that if you're a big enough girl to make the decision to go back to his house, then you're a big enough girl to say, "I'm not feeling this," when you get there and then leave when you want to.'

The biggest issue for Jordan, however, was the public shaming of Aziz Ansari. Why couldn't Ansari have learnt his lesson behind closed doors, she wanted to know, rather than be held up to ridicule before the world?

'If he'd verbally abused Grace, or forced himself onto her after she'd said no, or stop, then it would be a completely different story, and I'd be on her team in a heartbeat. In fact, I'd probably want to warn the sisterhood by making it public, too.

'But that's not the case with this story. When he came on heavy she responded with, "Let's relax for a sec and chill," and then when he said, "Where do you want me to fuck you?", she said, "Next time." And when she finally felt too overwhelmed and actually said no, he stopped.

'It sounded like a disgusting one-night stand and he sounded like a really insensitive, selfish lover who'd watched too much porn and still has a lot to learn. But sexual assault? No. I've woken up a number of times over the years feeling miserable and used as a result of being intimate with someone who wasn't very respectful or sensitive. But did I ever think they deserved to have their life and reputation ruined as a result of it? No, I didn't.'

#

In December 2017, two months after the #MeToo movement proclaimed itself, the *New Yorker* published a 7000-word story about a date that had turned into a deep-freeze night of dreadful sex . . . for the woman.

'Cat Person' was written by Kristen Roupenian, a 36-year-old teacher and Harvard University PhD student who'd spent much of her twenties working for the Peace Corps. The story was a fictional reworking of an unpleasant night Roupenian had endured twelve months earlier with a man she'd met on a dating app. It became the *New Yorker*'s most widely read online fictional story of all time—2.6 million visits in a matter of months—and resulted in a seven-figure US book deal for its author, along with sale of the film rights.

Just as Helen Garner's *The First Stone* had polarised readers in Australia nearly 25 years earlier, so did Roupenian's 'Cat Person'. *The Times* in London praised the story for its probing 'questions about consent, gender roles, porn and patriarchal conditioning in sex'. For millennials in particular, it seemed a perfect encapsulation of the red-flag disenchantments that often accompany modern dating.

'Cat Person' revolves around twenty-year-old college graduate Margot, who meets 34-year-old Robert while working behind a theatre concession stand. Weeks of teasing, frisky text messages follow, then another brief meeting before the two go on a movie date, followed by drinks at an underground speakeasy.

It was outside the speakeasy that Robert kissed Margot for the first time. 'He came for her in a kind of lunging motion and practically poured his tongue down her throat. It was a terrible kiss, shockingly bad; Margot had trouble believing that a grown man could possibly be so bad at kissing.'

The kiss behind her, the drinks before her, she then relaxed. They talked about the film. They joked and laughed. Margot peppered Robert with questions. She warmed to his sensitivity.

After her third drink, Margot began speculating on what it would be like to have sex with Robert. Perhaps it would be as maladroit as that first kiss, but, at the same time, she imagined how turned on he would be to see her, how eager to impress. She felt the ache of desire.

Margot suggested they leave. They kissed again in the car and, once more, Robert's tongue came darting, snake-like, down her gullet. She encouraged him to kiss more gently. That seemed to work. They drove back to his house where she was relieved to see his choice of art, books and vinyl records. That offered confirmation of sorts that her decision to enter his territory was not unreasonable. Her only other sexual experiences had been with men her own age, sneaking around in shared accommodation.

Robert began kissing Margot, tossing her bag and their coats on the couch and leading her into the bedroom, all the while fondling and fumbling at her chest and bottom. It was that awkward kiss all over again.

Margot sat on the bed as Robert took off his shirt and unbuckled his pants. He then bent over to untie his shoes. That's when Margot noticed his thick, soft, hairy belly. She recoiled. How to get out of this now? Could she find a sensitive and discreet way to leave, given that she'd initiated the whole thing? How would she get home?

Robert fell on top of Margot with those loose, moist kisses of his. His hands moved routinely across her breasts and down to her crutch. She could hardly breathe. Robert tried to unfasten her bra. *Damn it, how does this thing work?* He commanded she take it off.

At the same time, Margot couldn't help but notice the look on Robert's face. It was similar to that of all the other guys she'd been naked with. 'He looked stunned and stupid with pleasure, like a milk-drunk baby,' she wrote. Maybe, that's what she loved most about sex—a man revealing his open desire, his *openness*.

As they kissed, Margot found herself transported into a fantasia of ego-filled delight where she imagined him drinking in her perfect body and unblemished skin, wanting her so desperately that he thought he might expire from excitement. The more she imagined his arousal, the more excited Margot became. They got into a rhythmic groove, until Robert let out a 'high-pitched feminine whine'. *Jesus.* She wished he hadn't done that. Her ardour was now dimming, her revulsion growing. He was shoving his finger into her—'a fat old man's finger'—and the revulsion was morphing into self-disgust.

Then, when he was on top of her, he began to slap her thigh, telling her how much *she* liked what he was doing. She couldn't tell whether it was a question, an observation or an instruction. 'Yeah, yeah, you like that.' Then he turned her over and growled in her ear that he always wanted to 'fuck a girl with nice tits'. Margot had to smother her face in the pillow to keep from laughing.

But he kept losing his erection, and every time he did he would say aggressively, '"You make my dick so hard," as though lying about it could make it true. At last, after a frantic rabbity burst, he shuddered, came, and collapsed on her like a tree falling, and, crushed beneath him, she thought, brightly, "This is the worst life decision I have ever made!"'

Yes, it's good writing, but there was more. At 3 am Margot asked Robert to drive her home. She was relieved she hadn't been murdered, and that Robert was agreeably taking her back to her dorm. She never wanted to see him again. Only trouble, Robert was smitten. He kept sending text messages and Margot didn't know how to respond to them.

Margot's roommate Tamara told her to just tell him she was no longer interested. 'I have to say more than that,' Margot replied. 'We had *sex.*'

Tamara snatched Margot's phone from her and dashed off a message, telling Robert she was not interested and to stop texting her. Margot reeled in horror. Too late. Robert's reply came in shortly after—a sweet, wistful message of understanding and hope that he hadn't upset her, together with a plea to let him know if she ever changed her mind.

A month later, she saw him in a bar alone, slouched over a beer. She avoided him but, later that night, the messages began lighting up her screen. He told her he missed her. He asked her what he'd done wrong. He said he thought there'd been a connection. Was he wrong? Was he too old for her? Was there someone else? Maybe that guy she was with in that bar tonight?

Margot didn't answer. More texts from Robert arrived.

'???'

'Or is he just some guy you are fucking'

'Sorry'

'When u laguehd [sic] when I asked if you were a virgin was it because youd [sic] fucked so many guys'

Robert wanted to know if she was fucking that guy now.

'Are you'

No answer

'Are you'

No answer

'Answer me'

No answer

'Whore.'

#

Sometimes the best thing you can offer up is your own doubt and confusion, although there is no doubt or confusion on my part about Robert's last comment. Here's more of mine. At the same time, I feel for the fictitious Robert and the all-too-real Aziz Ansari, for their haplessness and humiliation. On the other hand, I also feel for how Grace and Margot got themselves into the situations they did, why they recoiled from each man's touch.

The telling of their stories is important for a number of reasons. In the first instance, they seem to recount a near-universal experience for most women, in their legitimate fears of being injured, of humiliating a man through their rejection of him, of simply not being able to find the right words to verbalise what they want and don't want.

These stories also ask us to weigh the relative value—in the case of Grace and Ansari—of Grace's public revelations against Ansari's professional annihilation (although Ansari's career seems not to have imploded). They invite us to wrestle with gradations of offence—including blundering ignorance, if that is an act of wrongdoing.

Was the Aziz Ansari story one of sexual assault or merely soulless sex? Was Grace permanently scarred by her experience, or just bitterly disappointed? (And who but Grace can really answer that?) Why did she perform oral sex on Ansari? Did he have a gun to her head? Obviously not. Was Ansari's constant badgering a subtle, or not so subtle, misuse of his celebrity power, or was it just another case of male entitlement? Or was it ineptness? Or a particular modus operandi which had served him well up until this point?

Did Grace undermine the #MeToo movement—as her detractors claimed—or add substantially to the much-needed discourse on sex and dating, and the perils that lie in wait for us? Or did the fact that Ansari publicly championed the Time's Up movement make him fair game?

And if men related more to Ansari and women to Grace—which is possibly the case, notwithstanding the differences I've shared between my two daughters—what should that tell us about what women are wanting in their sexual encounters, and what men are so often failing to read?

#

(Another flight, this time from Auckland to Sydney—what is it about being 35,000 feet up in the air?) *A businesswoman is staring into the middle distance, probably contemplating her next meeting. A male passenger on the other side of the cabin is within her line of sight. He's convinced she's staring at him, but she's staring right through him. He gets up and walks across the aisle.*

'So how about it?' *he says. (And, yes, that's his way of introduction.)*

'What do you mean?' *she replies, shocked.*

'Well, you've been looking at me for the past ten minutes. I thought you might be up for it.' He mentions something about the toilet. The two of them. A quickie.*

She gives him a look, like: Are you completely mad? But she says aloud, 'I think there's been a misunderstanding.'

#

Getting back to Margot and Robert's encounter in 'Cat Person', was that consensual, even though she loathed practically every minute of it? (Certainly, it didn't meet the new standard of 'affirmative' or 'enthusiastic' consent which, according to one definition from 'Project Respect', on Canadian website Yesmeansyes.com, means 'mutual verbal, physical and emotional agreement that happens without manipulation, threats, or head games.') Should Robert have been able to intuit what Margot was feeling and, if not, what should Margot have said to him? 'Please put your pants back on and drive me home'? Or, 'Look, I'm realising I don't really want to do this and I appreciate that might make you feel bad. I'm sorry if I've led you on, but could we just chat instead because I think you're a good person?' Would Robert, though disappointed, have accepted her change of heart with equanimity, or might he have exploded?

Who was the bigger creep—Robert for his boofheadedness, or Margot for her narcissistic fantasies? Although Margot's friend sent the text to him, did she need to dump Robert with such gracelessness, and, even if she did, could that ever justify his final response? No, it couldn't. Who was the pursuer, the seducer, in this situation, and whose fault is it that it went so horribly wrong?

Obviously, the 'consent' part of this is crucial, but what should consent look like? There are many interpretations of this in different legal jurisdictions, but I like the one created by a blogger known as RockStarDinosaurPiratePrincess and promoted online by the British Crown Prosecution Service. It's simplistic, and it fails to deal with the ambiguity of relationships, the mysterious combination of chemistry, physiology and emotion that forms our connections. It doesn't deal with the perceived obligations that some women feel towards the men in their lives to grant them sex at whatever time of day or night they demand it, or the unwelcome attention, neglect and lack of consideration men so often display towards their partners. (Or, as Germaine Greer calls it in her new slim and, inevitably, controversial volume *On Rape*, the 'empty heartscape of dreary daily domestic rape'.) But it's useful nonetheless:

> If you're still struggling with consent just imagine that instead of initiating sex you're making them a cup of tea. You say, 'Hey, would you like a cup of tea?' And they go, 'Oh my god, I would love a cup of tea. Thank you.' Then you know they want a cup of tea.
>
> If you say, 'Hey would you like a cup of tea?' And they're like, 'Ah, I'm not really sure,' then you could make them a cup of tea or not, but be aware they might not drink it. And if they don't drink it—and this is the important part—don't make them drink it. Just because you made it doesn't mean you're entitled to watch them drink it.

And if they say, 'No thank you,' then don't make them tea. At all. Just don't make them tea. Don't make them drink tea. Don't get annoyed at them for not wanting tea. They just don't want tea. They might say, 'Yes please, that's kind of you,' and then when the tea arrives they actually don't want the tea at all. Sure, that's kind of annoying as you've gone to all the effort of making the tea, but they remain under no obligation to drink the tea. They did want tea. Now they don't.

Some people change their mind in the time it takes to boil the kettle, brew the tea and add the milk. And it's okay for people to change their mind. And you're still not entitled to watch them drink it. And if they're unconscious don't make them tea. Unconscious people don't want tea. And they can't answer the question: 'Do you want tea?' Because they're unconscious.

Maybe they were conscious when you asked them if they wanted tea, and they said yes. But in the time it took you to boil the kettle, brew the tea and add the milk, they're now unconscious. You should just put the tea down. Make sure the unconscious person is safe. And—this is the important part again—don't make them drink the tea.

If someone said yes to tea around your house last Saturday, that doesn't mean they want you to make them tea all the time. They don't want you to come around to their place unexpectedly and make them tea and force them to drink it, going, 'But you wanted tea last week.'

If you can understand how completely ludicrous it is to force people to have tea when they don't want tea, and you're able to understand when people don't want tea, then how hard is it to understand it when it comes to sex? Whether it's tea or sex consent is everything.

15

Tabula rasa

One can choose what to do, but not what to want.

ARTHUR SCHOPENHAUER, *ON THE FREEDOM OF THE WILL*

Everywhere we look today—online, offline, in cities and towns—there is flagrant 'hotness'. From omnipresent billboards displaying semi-naked models to little girls with crop tops and false eyelashes; hypersexualised music videos of women's thrusting breasts and gyrating bottoms, and men swaggering, strutting, preening; 'Peekaboo pole-dancing kits'—enabling you to erect your own pole at home and learn 'the Booty Shake' and 'Thighs the Limit'; ads for tingle-free arse colouring and anal fissure treatments. There are the billion-dollar advertising, porn and video game industries that characterise women as sexual objects. In the case of porn, women are invariably shaved and steaming and ready to take it from any entry point. And then there's sex robots—and the world's first sex robot brothel in Barcelona, 'for plastic-loving fun seekers'—allowing purchasers to customise nipple and vulva size, all in the name of artificial intelligence-driven intimacy. In California, there's currently a proposal to establish a robot brothel where the robot grants the customer consent *with the swivel of its head.*

Confused? Who wouldn't be. Heterosexual men have been hearing the siren's song, dreaming of the temptress, the endless wonder and diversity of the female form all their lives. She's been inhabiting our imagination—our films, songs, books, myths, legends, stories and conversations—ever since our balls headed south. She was placed on this earth, so the myth goes, to fulfil our desires; to provide us with children (that's the 'good' girl), or offer us her sexual favours (that's the less *good*).

And after centuries of having their sexuality disavowed, women are now urged to act like porn stars and literally gag for it; to have their breasts enlarged and to achieve the perfect 'designer vagina' through gynaecological rejuvenation.

'A woman gains self-esteem when she knows that her skin is soft, her figure pleasing and her countenance alluring,' says one website devoted to the surgical procedure known as labiaplasty. (Type the word into your internet search engine and you'll see more than half a billion entries. You can even watch the procedure on YouTube if you have the stomach for it.) 'These features can help a woman attract a man. Once in bed with a man, a woman can lose her self-esteem if she has unusually large or misshapen labia.' This is not a medieval pre-Islamic desert society we're talking about; this is the affluent west encouraging and promoting the severing of part of the clitoris so as to address female insecurity and women's desirability to men.

Everywhere a nod—or swipe right—to carnality, one that taps into our animal appetite for physical connection. But who among us—men or women—have been taught to talk about sex properly? Who's been given the manual for courting, for respect, for consent? Where's the educational guide on how to relate and connect in order to develop a healthy sexuality, let alone true intimacy with another person? Little wonder the everyday miscues:

Man: All this talk of consent is demoralising and confusing.

Woman: Why on earth is it demoralising? Just ask her what she wants.

Man: I can't.

Woman: Why not?

Man: Because asking isn't erotic, it takes the mystery out of things.

Woman: That's because you've never checked in with a woman on what she wants.

Man: 'This whole thing is just exhausting for men. It's not what sex is about.

Woman: Not as exhausting as it is for women.

Man: You can't legislate about these things. I had a female colleague in my office the other day and she was showing me her new dress. She was literally twirling in front of me and she had the skimpiest knickers on. She was having the time of her life.

Woman: That doesn't mean she wanted to fuck you.

Man: No, but it wasn't helpful. I don't know whether she was flirting with me or just being absolutely confident that I wouldn't take it the wrong way.

Woman: I'd go with the latter.

Man: Okay, but if it was the latter, that's a pretty high hurdle, and women should understand that, because at the end of the day we're all human.

Woman: Yes, but we all want respect and a woman will let you know if she wants to go beyond flirting.

Man: I wanted to respect her by bending her over my desk and fucking her.

Woman: Well, it's quite likely she didn't want that.

Man: Yeah, but maybe part of her did. Sex is often about two things at the same time, about wanting it and not wanting it. You know the mind tells you one thing, and the body screams for another.

Woman: It still doesn't mean she wanted to fuck you.

Man: Why did she dress like that?

Woman: Maybe she dressed like that for herself, or for other women, not you.

Man: Except she appeared in my office with that short skirt and her boobs hanging out when I was just minding my own business.

Woman: Well, just because your face is out doesn't mean she's got a right to punch you.

Man: What about if I'm in a bar and drinking with a woman who I've just met and we're getting on well. Can I touch her on the leg?

Woman: Maybe, but if you put your hand on her inner thigh you've crossed the line.

Man: Where is the line?

Woman: You should know.

American cultural critic and essayist Laura Kipnis, author of *Unwanted Advances: Sexual Paranoia Comes to Campus*, tried to do the calibrations on this last question in an opinion piece published in *The Guardian* in January 2018.

> A pat on the knee can be sexually benign, but maybe it's not? Move a few inches up and all bets are off. Measure the distance from kneecap to crotch, divide it in half, breach that line, and you've entered the zone of the upper thigh [and] I suspect every woman knows precisely where that line on her body is, and what trespassing it means.

A hand placed above that line requires one to make a deci-sion, in a way that flirting does not. Our bodies are zoned: there are public areas and private ones; parts you can touch without permission, such as my hand, and parts you're trespassing if you encroach on them without my permission.

#

(European actress to author in Cannes 2018): *For me it feels like the #MeToo movement hasn't even happened. Two days ago at a party I was wearing a red dress, nothing super provocative, and one guy was all over my knees and kissing my hands, and I was saying, 'Please don't.' Another guy touched my boobs, not accidentally . . . and there was a third guy touching my back.*

The next day I saw the guy who'd been all over my knees and I told him he'd been totally inappropriate and he started becoming really aggressive, saying, 'I respect women and there are women who are inappropriate with me.' And I said, 'But you were touching me and I never gave you permission to do that, I never gave you signs.' And that's my message to all men: 'Don't touch women unless they give you the sign.'

#

There are now consent apps setting out new rules for intimacy. One of them—uConsent—works like this: Person A meets Person B. When together in the same room, Person A types into the app what he or she is requesting, while also relaying that request verbally to Person B. Person B then types into his or her phone what he or she is agreeing to. A barcode is then generated, thus enabling Person A and Person B to hold their phones together so that the app captures the issued barcode. If Person A's request matches Person B's acceptance then that information is encoded and stored securely on a database in the cloud.

There are inevitable problems with this new mood-setting technology, as Elizabeth Bernstein pointed out in *The Australian* in May 2018. She quoted Helen Fisher, a biological anthropologist with special expertise in brain research and love, asking some obvious questions, like What happens if you agree to sex at 8 pm, but by 8.30 or 10 you've changed your mind? Can you go back onto the app and withdraw consent, or are you committed?

'You might say yes to the overall interest in sex with somebody,' Fisher said, 'but then you get with them and they don't smell good or they act strange or they get aggressive and you are frightened. We are constantly adding up the pros and cons of the situation at hand and changing our mind.'

And another thing: does the law recognise an app consent as a legally binding contract? Probably not. Think of it more as a digital handshake. All right, but what about engaging in one particular kind of sexual activity, as opposed to another, one that you never anticipated? Would the digital agreement help you if you felt forced into unexpected behaviour? Again, probably not.

Another app, LegalFling, claims to have overcome this problem by indicating at the beginning the do's and don'ts in the bedroom. You're into bondage, sadomasochism, fetishes, or you're not. You have an STD or you've got a clean bill of health. You're using a condom, or you've forgotten to bring one. Discuss, then swipe.

Most of these apps—if not all—are aimed at the tech-savvy young, particularly college students in the United States, where, according to a Department of Justice-funded Campus Sexual Assault Study, one in five women claim to have been assaulted. For men, the figure is one in sixteen.

In Australia, many universities have introduced a compulsory online course on sexual consent for new students. Designed by London-based company Epigeum, Consent Matters spells out the circumstances under which consent may or may not be granted.

It follows a landmark 2017 report published by the Australian Human Rights Commission which revealed that, of the more than 30,000 students surveyed, more than half had been sexually harassed on at least one occasion the previous year. Women were twice as likely as men to have been harassed, and four times more likely to have been assaulted in a university residence.

On the University of Sydney's website, students are told that consent needs to be communicated 'openly and clearly' every step of the way. No assumptions should be made:

'It needs to be given for each and every sexual activity, every time, with every person. It should never be assumed based on past sexual activity and can be taken away at any time. Everyone has the right to change their mind, and if this happens, you no longer have consent and should stop.'

This includes kissing or touching. 'Whenever you participate in any sexual activity, everyone involved needs to give their full consent. This means that everyone is entirely comfortable with the situation and freely able to agree, give permission or say "yes" to participating in a sexual activity.'

Consent, therefore, can never be ambiguous.

If someone is not able to offer an enthusiastic 'yes' to questions about sexual activity, you do not have consent. Consent is verbal and physical. Body language may indicate that a person is not certain about the sexual activity.

If someone indicates in a non-verbal way that they are unsure, for example they pull away, cover their body or eyes, push you away, you do not have consent and you should stop and talk to them. If you are unsure, then you do not have consent.

Critics have claimed no single program can combat sexual assault or harassment, that a one-off course will always be less effective than face-to-face training. How, for example, could these protocols deal with cases like the student who told the Human Rights Commission she'd been raped by a student leader during orientation week camp? The young woman later learnt that this same student leader had raped other students in previous years, with no action having been taken by university management. In the five years up to 2017, universities had only expelled six students, despite more than 500 official complaints, 145 of them specifically for rape.

And what of the kissing rule? Does that mean no stolen kisses under the Moreton Bay figs at University of Sydney? No touching on the arm on the South Lawn at University of Melbourne? How do you ask for an 'enthusiastic' yes? What *is* an enthusiastic yes, and how might you get that spelt out?

In 'How to Tell the Bad Men From the Good Men', an article for *New York* magazine's online publication *The Cut*, British author and broadcaster Caitlin Moran tried to make a distinction between illegal acts and the kind of bad experience that 'Cat Person' and the Aziz Ansari story zeroed in on: the bad sexual experience which often boils down to a stunning lack of education, dearth of positive male role models and a sexual culture that has left men operating mostly from a blank slate.

'Every problem I had as a teenage girl,' Moran wrote, 'noncriminal men also have. There are no manuals about being a man who wishes to have swashbuckling sex adventures with his peers. There are no templates for how to approach a woman in a jolly and uplifting manner, discover her sexual preferences, get feedback while you're rolling around naked, and learn from her without feeling oddly, horribly emasculated.'

Many Australian women in the 1970's and 80s grew up reading magazines like *Cleo* and *Cosmopolitan*, whereas Moran's knowledge of the opposite sex came mainly from MGM musicals and nineteenth-century literature. Men's 'knowledge', on the other hand, has come from an increasingly porn-driven culture where sex is outcome driven and all about 'winning'.

'There are definitely men who discover a way to be with women that doesn't inspire their former sexual partners to form a whole sociopolitical movement testifying to their awfulness, but I genuinely wonder how they're managing this,' Moran wrote. 'Given how dolorous their sexual role models are, men essentially are having to invent sex from scratch. There are no men blogging honestly about sex.'

Where are the men's movements, she asked, that are constructively analysing the politics of sex to everyone's advantage, as opposed to men's rights activists and 'incels' furiously railing at women's lack of sexual largesse? Where can a man express his vulnerability and uncertainty? Where can he ask the scared questions in this 'scrappy cargo cult of sexual information' that has been foisted on us, and is having such detrimental consequences.

Moran recounted an alarming story related by British writer Laura Bates from the Everyday Sexism Project. A sixteen-year-old boy has arrived home absolutely distraught. Eventually he tells his mother why.

He and his girlfriend tried to have sex for the first time and, at one point, he started strangling her. She started crying.
'Please don't, I don't like it!' she said.

'I don't like it either!' he said, also bursting into tears. 'I hate it! I just thought that was what you wanted! That's what they do in porn!'

'This is 21st-century male/female sexuality in a nutshell,' Moran wrote of Bates's observations.

Despite living in a world of every kind of niche pornography, strip clubs, Brazilians, sex toys, *Fifty Shades of Grey*, blow-job tips, sex education, contraception, anal-bleaching, designer vaginas, Viagra, pussy-grabbing scandals, and #MeToo; despite there being 6,500 spoken languages in the world allowed the infinite space of the internet; despite sex happening *all the time, everywhere,* we still—*still!* —haven't found a way to talk about it that is truthful, open, informative, and not scaring the living daylights out of our young people. We seem not to have told them, at any point, how *lovely* it all should be. We've somehow managed to screw this up. Our *tabula* is still *rasa*.

#

(Australian woman to author): *I asked him to stop. I told him, 'You're hurting me' and 'You're really hurting me.' He ignored me and held me down by my legs when I tried to get up. I tried to stop him but the penetration became harder and faster. He kept going until he had ejaculated. It was only then that he released his grip and allowed me to get up. I was pissed off and said to him: 'Why did you keep going? I told you that you were hurting me!' He said: 'I was almost there . . . I was just about to cum.'*

#

As I mentioned in chapter nine, my own *tabula* was pretty *rasa* until I went to Andrew Barnes's female orgasm workshop in

Byron Bay fifteen years ago. The truth is, I'm still uncovering new information, mainly because the research and writing of this book has revealed the depths of my own ignorance, taken me to places I might never have ventured—like Naomi Wolf's *Vagina: A New Biography*, which both my daughters urged me to read.

In a chapter titled 'Meet your incredible pelvic nerve', Wolf explained how a woman's pelvic nerves branch out to the base of the spinal cord, some of these nerves originating in the clitoris, some in the vagina, others in the cervix. Depending on their origin, they might extend to the larger pudendal nerve or the larger pelvic nerve.

'All of this complexity,' Wolf wrote, 'gives women several different areas in their pelvises from which orgasms can be produced, and all of these connect to the spinal cord and then up to the brain.'

Wolf didn't bother to hide her own astonishment at these findings. 'I almost fell off the edge of the exam table,' she exclaimed after being presented with these new facts by Dr Jeffrey Cole, an American expert on pelvic floor dysfunction.

'[So] that's what explained vaginal versus clitoral orgasms? *Neural wiring?* Not culture, not upbringing, not patriarchy, not feminism, not Freud. Do you realise,' she said to Dr Cole, 'you've just given the answer to a question that Freudians and feminists and sexologists have been arguing about for decades?'

All these people have assumed the differences in vaginal versus clitoral orgasms had to do with how women were raised . . . or what social role was expected of them . . . or whether they were free to explore their own bodies or not . . . or free or not to adapt their lovemaking to external expectations. And you are saying that the reason is simply that all women's *wiring* is different? That some are neurally wired more for vaginal orgasms, some more for clitoral? That some are wired to feel a G-spot more, others won't feel it so much?

Dr Cole confirmed this was the case. 'That's the reason women respond so differently from one another sexually. The pelvic nerve branches in very individual ways for every woman. These differences are physical.'

Wolf's book is shot through with other details worth pondering—or, perhaps better still, placed on the compulsory reading list for every teenage boy and girl in the world. She writes about the biology of female arousal and how activation of the autonomic nervous system paves the way for neural impulses to travel from the vagina, clitoris and labia, through an elaborate circulatory path to the brain: respiration, lubrication, flushing skin, dilating pupils and heart rate all influencing vaginal engorgement, muscular contraction and orgasm.

She explores, further, how the unconscious nervous system responds to a sense of safety or danger by sending signals to the brain; how female orgasm boosts levels of testosterone in a woman, observing:

That is one more reason that great sex makes women hard to push around easily. Sex raises women's testosterone, which in turn raises their libido further, which in turn makes them more assertive and more interested in having even more sex. So the fear that patriarchy always had—that if you let women have sex and know how to like it, it will make them both increasingly libidinous and increasingly ungovernable—is actually biologically true!

This is not to suggest the pornographic model for intercourse would do it for most women. What woman wants to be choked and gagged, have every orifice penetrated and her face drenched in semen? Okay, maybe some, but research has revealed alarming results about the way pornography has shaped young people's ideas of pleasure, power and intimacy.

A recent British study from the National Society for the Prevention of Cruelty to Children, together with the Office of the Children's Commissioner and Middlesex University, found that 65 per cent of fifteen- to sixteen-year-olds had viewed pornography. The vast majority had done so by the time they were fourteen. Those findings were particularly disturbing in light of a University of Nebraska study that showed the younger a man when he first viewed pornography, the more likely he would be to want to exert power over a woman when he was older. The older he was, the more probability of him wanting to act like a 'playboy'.

A third study conducted by the University of North Carolina found that early exposure to pornography increased the likelihood of perpetrating sexual harassment two years later, while a fourth study in the peer-reviewed *Journal of Communication* concluded that pornography consumption contributed to acts of verbal and physical sexual aggression.

This is all the more sobering given that there are porn sites currently attracting more hits every month than Netflix, Amazon and Twitter combined; Pornhub alone received 21.2 billion visits in 2015.

'The problem for contemporary men,' Wolf wrote, 'is that . . . the male brain evolved in a context in which the sight of a naked or copulating woman was extremely rare, and typically arrived at arduously—thus making it very, very exciting. This arousal and dopamine response was keyed to having actual sex with an actual woman.'

Wolf examined the way pornography acted neurologically as a 'woman's destructive rival', how it rewired the male brain, desensitising them through chronic masturbation and fostering a trend towards often violent anal penetration. She quoted psychiatrist Norman Doidge, who found that adults had little understanding of the extent to which pornography had rewired their brains, with male patients variously reporting difficulty being turned on by their real sexual partners, girlfriends and spouses, despite the fact they still considered them sexually attractive.

'They try to persuade their lovers to act like porn stars, and they are increasingly interested in "fucking" as opposed to "making love",' Doidge said. 'Humanity is running a massive, uncontrolled experiment, and we don't yet know the results. However, there's increasing evidence that there's no free lunch.'

Wolf suggested that modern men—hoodwinked into addictive behaviour by massive industries—deserved empathy rather than hostility. No one warned them of the problems they would have with their virility—or free will—once their brains had been bombarded with a relentless stream of highly sexualised images.

'The men who wrote to me about their porn addiction and potency problems were not monsters; they were suffering men who were loving husbands and boyfriends, who hated the pain they were causing their partners, and who were ashamed of what they now felt to be their sexual inadequacy,' she noted. 'Porn is leading men to become poorer lovers to women, and more specifically, training young men to mishandle or ignore the vagina.'

In Wolf's view, this helped to explain the epidemic of female unhappiness, citing as proof the American Psychiatric Association's 2007 symposium, Sex, Sexuality and Serotonin, which revealed up to 34 per cent of women—more than double that of men—reporting low sexual desire. She also quoted a 2010 Indiana University report that found only 64 per cent of female participants had experienced orgasm the last time they had sex.

Wolf's conclusions dovetail neatly with Australian sex therapist Bettina Arndt's findings in her 2009 book *The Sex Diaries*, and its raw and intimate documentation of the bedroom behaviour of 98 couples. Arndt claimed to discover deep seams of male anguish and frustration at being sexually rejected by their female partners because their libidos were far more 'distractable and fragile'.

'Here were these men,' she said, 'who would ask again and again, and try and plead and grovel and cook the dinner, whatever they thought was going to work to get the green light, and they got knocked back again and again and again.'

Arndt's advice—to both men and women, but particularly women—was for them to surmount 'that ideological roadblock of assumptions about desire "and just do it", [because] once the canoe is in the water, everyone starts happily paddling.'

Naomi Wolf suggested a different view, arguing that when circumstances were supportive, virtually every woman could reach orgasm.

What if so many women are suffering from low levels of desire, from frustration, and from sexual withdrawal, because—there is no way to say this but honestly—*many men are taught about women in such a way that they don't really know what they are doing.*

[And] even in this post-sexual revolution era, many women don't know how to identify, and then ask for what they need and want.

#

Sydney sex therapist Jacqueline Hellyer has seen thousands of couples and individuals over the course of her career. She believes, like Naomi Wolf, that men are often trapped by their own predictability.

'Most women out there are just bored,' she tells me during an interview in her clinic in Sydney's inner west. 'The reason they're not enjoying sex is because it's bloody awful. So many women come to me and say, "I don't like sex or I don't orgasm, what's wrong with me?" And then they describe the sex they're having, and I think, well, I'm not surprised. It's like being fed gruel every night and then saying you're not really that fond of food.'

Hellyer describes our inherited model of sexuality as a 'male masturbatory' one that's evolved over thousands of years of female sexual suppression. Unlike boys, girls have been raised to think they shouldn't be sexual.

'Essentially the model has been a lot of genital friction until he ejaculates. That's masturbation. But it became our model of sex because that's all anyone knew. No one knew anything about what women wanted. It was very much stuck in this immature sex—the kind that suits young men—where they're horny all the time and need relief.'

The problem with this restricted view of sex was that it became all about ejaculation and orgasm. 'It's like a KPI index,' she says. 'You've got to perform. Everyone is so driven by getting it right, instead of two people coming together and feeling lovely through physical pleasure and emotional connection.'

Add to this all the certitudes we've grown up with to explain the world; that is, until those certitudes get turned on their head. Bats were never blind; the forbidden fruit was never an apple (more likely it was a grape); and female libido—which Sigmund Freud barely studied—was always as high as men's, even if Charles

Darwin concluded that 'the female . . . with the rarest exception' was 'less eager than the male'.

In ancient Greek mythology, Tiresias was asked by Zeus and Hera, the first couple of the Greek pantheon, to arbitrate on the question of who enjoyed sex more—men or women. Zeus was certain it was women, his wife Hera equally confident it was men. Tiresias had lived as both—man and woman—and was in no doubt it was woman: nine times more, in fact. 'Of ten parts, a man enjoys only one,' he said, after which Hera struck him blind. (The ancient Indian epic, the Mahabharata, offered the same conclusion: women experience more pleasure than men.)

In 2006, Canadian sexologist and psychology professor Meredith Chivers conducted a landmark experiment to measure the responses of heterosexual men and women to a variety of 90-second sexual video clips, both straight and gay. The videos spanned the range of erotic possibilities—man with woman, woman with woman, man alone masturbating, woman alone masturbating, well-built man walking naked on the beach, willowy woman doing nude calisthenics and, finally, a short film of bonobos ('pygmy chimpanzees') fornicating furiously.

Each of Chivers's subjects was given a keypad to indicate his or her response to the video clips, while also wired up to a plethysmograph, a device that measures changes to blood flow, particularly in the genital region. Chivers was looking for two types of results—the first self-reported, the second physiological.

With gay and straight men, the results were unsurprising. Straight men were aroused when the films featured women— women alone, women with men and, above all, women with other women. Gay men's readings soared when men masturbated or had sex with other men, but dipped towards oblivion when women dominated the screen. Neither straight nor gay man demonstrated a reaction to animal sex, either on the keypad or the plethysmograph.

By contrast, the needle measuring 'vaginal pulse amplitude' moved with everything women saw on the screen, including copulating apes. Blood flow soared and capillaries pulsed arbitrarily, even when it came to bonobos humping. Women's pulsings were, in fact, higher with copulating bonobos than for a naked man alone on the beach.

Crucially, many of the women's keypad responses directly contradicted what researchers were seeing on the plethysmograph, suggesting that women's minds would tell them one thing, their bodies another. Men's subjective and objective responses were almost identical.

In *Sex at Dawn*, Christopher Ryan and Cacilda Jethá wrote that this research suggested strong differences in the 'erotic plasticity' of males and females.

> The human female's sexual behaviour is typically far more malleable than the male's. Greater erotic plasticity leads most women to experience more variation in their sexuality than men typically do, and women's sexual behaviour is far more responsive to social pressure.

> This disconnect between what these women experienced on a physical level and what they consciously registered is precisely what the theory of differential erotic plasticity predicts. It could well be that the price of women's greater erotic flexibility is more difficulty in knowing and—depending on what cultural restrictions may be involved—in accepting what they're feeling.

> This is worth keeping in mind when considering why so many women report lack of interest in sex or difficulties in reaching orgasm.

American journalist Daniel Bergner took up these ideas in his 2013 book *What do Women Want: Adventures in the Science of Female Desire*, where he argued that female libido is 'an underestimated and constrained force' that has been largely unexamined and overlooked for centuries.

'The history of sexuality, and perhaps above all the history of women's sexuality,' he offered, 'is a discipline of shards. And it is men, with rare exceptions, whose recorded words form the fragments we have of ancient and medieval and early modern ideas about female eros.'

Start with the subordinate role of women commanded by a patriarchal God, combine that with the 'beautiful evil' of Pandora, the original woman of Greek mythology, whose 'shameless mind and deceitful nature' made her as dangerous as Eve, the first sinner in Genesis. Pour into the mixing bowl a history of demonising, pathologising, silencing and commodifying female sexuality. Stir liberally with the 'lust-drunk' witches of the Middle Ages and the renunciations of the Victorian era. Then pepper all this with male entitlement and scientific indifference to the female body, along with evolutionary psychology's faith in male lustfulness and female restraint. And what have we got?

According to Bergner, we've got a fairy tale, one that speaks less to the absolutes of biology and our 'erotic hardwiring' than it does 'to the world's span of male-dominated cultures and historic suspicion and fear of female sexuality'.

#

'Dad, do you know OMGYes?'

'Never heard of it.'

'You should take a look.'

'Do you want to show me?'

'You've got to be kidding—it's a website for female sexual pleasure. Just sign up when I'm gone and you can see for yourself.'

I visit the website after Hannah leaves, and what I find is a revolutionary sex education platform offering viewers the 'latest science about what makes women feel good, and why'. It is based on research by Indiana University's School of Public Health and interviews with over 2000 women between the ages of eighteen and 95.

Scientific interest compels me to pay for a 'Season One' subscription. It is the most taboo-busting, eye-popping educational resource I've ever come across. There are various women explaining what turns them on, and when I say 'explaining', I mean demonstrating through a video tutorial how they like to be pleasured.

Some want to be surprised, some want consistency, some want it faster, slower, harder, lighter, further, closer, higher, lower. There are techniques I've never heard of, or can only speculate on: 'edging', 'framing', 'accenting', 'layering', 'orbiting', 'staging', 'hinting', 'signalling'.

It's an interactive website. I'll leave the rest to you, although I'll just add one more thing for your consideration. For centuries, Newtonian physics informed our scientific assumptions about how the physical world behaved—the world was orderly, determined and predictable; and the rational mind could make sense of it through the powers of logic and reason. If you understood the parts, you understood the whole. Then along came quantum physics, the body of scientific laws that describe the erratic, often bizarre behaviour of atoms, electrons and molecules—one minute behaving as particles, the next minute as waves. From this, an entirely new world view was born—scientifically, philosophically, spiritually. It was like an Escher print stairway which suddenly stopped leading from one place to another; and instead climbed everywhere and nowhere at once.

Perhaps it's the same with female sexuality. We've been stuck in an outdated mechanistic world for centuries, and we're only just beginning to glimpse the vast mysteries of female sexuality and its universe of untapped potential. This clearly holds great possibilities for women, but also for men if we're willing to face up to our own limitations.

16

Vigilante justice

The danger with hatred is once you start in on it you get a hundred times more than you bargained for. Once you start, you can't stop.

PHILIP ROTH, THE HUMAN STAIN

Every revolution has its purges, and in the chaos that ensues, there is usually blood.

A quick glance at history confirms this: the Reign of Terror during the French Revolution, the Great Terror of Stalin's Soviet Union, the murder of political rivals during China's Cultural Revolution, Saddam Hussein's execution of senior Ba'ath Party members, the Argentinian military junta and the thousands who disappeared under the generals' brutal diktat, the Iranian mullahs and their eradication of western influence, the Arab Spring.

The list is long and there are many who fall by the wayside; never mind their guilt, it's the accusation that affirms their guilt.

'Such things are always done in the name of ushering in a better world,' wrote acclaimed author Margaret Atwood in 'Am I a Bad Feminist?' published in the *Globe and Mail* in January 2018. 'Sometimes they do usher one in, for a time anyway. Sometimes they are used as an excuse for new forms of oppression.' Take 'vigilante justice'—or condemnation without due legal process—for example. It starts, often, as an understandable reaction to an absence of fairness and justness, because, either the system is crooked—as in eighteenth century pre-revolutionary France when the *ancien régime* was overthrown; or there is no system of justice at all—as in the American frontier days of outlaw gangs and gunslingers. Without recourse to the law, people assume the role of judge and executioner.

That's when extrajudicial punishment can transmute into a 'culturally solidified lynch-mob habit', Atwood wrote, where natural justice, a principle fundamental to democratic legal systems, is abandoned in favour of non-authorised power structures. A good example: La Cosa Nostra, the notorious Italian mafia, which emerged in early nineteenth-century Sicily as a resistance to central authority.

According to Atwood, the #MeToo movement has become a symptom of such a broken system, where women have all too frequently failed to get a fair hearing, not just through the law courts, but through institutions and corporate structures that should have protected them.

#

(Rape survivor to author): *How do you prove to the rest of the world that you didn't consent if no one else was there to see it? What can you do when someone turns on you and rapes you, but then claims everything that took place was consensual? There's no witnesses to my rape, so it will all come down to who the jury believes. But it's not simply a matter of being believed, it's a matter of being believed beyond a reasonable doubt.*

And, shockingly, it's the defence lawyer's job to attack my credibility and look for any inconsistencies in what I say; to plant that seed of doubt in the jury's mind, so that the person they are defending won't be found guilty.

#

The internet has become the new justice-seeking tool, just as the late Canadian professor Marshall McLuhan predicted 25 years before the invention of the internet. 'The medium is the message,' he said.

'But what next?' Margaret Atwood then asked. The legal system could be overhauled, or our society could jettison it. Corporations, institutions and places of employment could liberate themselves from oppressive, hidebound cultures, or more men—the powerful and the not so powerful—will be judged and tried without a fair hearing.

What then will replace the law? Who, then, will be the new kingmakers and friends at court? It won't be 'bad feminists' like Atwood, she argued, because women like her are tolerated neither by the right nor the left. 'In times of extremes, extremists win,' she said, and anyone who fails to emulate the views of the ideologue will be cast as traitor to the cause. In that event, the middle ground—where all the moderates prefer to stand—will simply collapse. Fiction writers, such as herself, will be particularly at risk because they write about the 'morally ambiguous' universe of the human condition, and the whole point of ideology is to eradicate ambiguity.

There is nothing ambiguous, of course, about women being assaulted, abused, fearing for their lives; equally, there's nothing hazy about the global fury demanding this behaviour stop.

But there is something ambiguous—make that deeply troubling—about accusations issued through the megaphone of social media, where discourse is energised and limited at the same time. Inner screams brought to our little screens. Pot shots fired from dancing, staccato fingers. Public demonstrations of toxic, partisan outrage, particularly on Twitter, the 'anger video game'—as the *New York Times*' Maggie Haberman put it—where people 'feel free to say things they'd never say to someone's face'.

Sometimes, though, they do say it to someone's face—directly, publicly, dramatically—as American writer Zinzi Clemmons demonstrated at the 2018 Sydney Writers' Festival when she accused Junot Díaz, the Dominican-American Pulitzer Prize-winning author, of sexual harassment.

It happened towards the end of a panel session when, by all accounts, Díaz was in good humour. Clemmons, a fellow guest of the festival, stood up to ask Díaz about a recent essay he'd written for the *New Yorker*—an excruciatingly honest and heartbreaking piece about how, at eight years old, he'd been raped by an adult he'd previously trusted. The experience had plunged him into crippling depression and, at times, uncontrollable rage. In high school he had tried to kill himself. By the time he was in college he'd locked himself behind a brilliant mask, although he was never able to escape the nightmares, self-blame and suicide ideation. He moved through life, formed relationships, but blew them apart with his lying and cheating, with his use of sex to fill an unquenchable, gaping hole. He hurt women. Deeply, consistently, a 'bursting-at-the-seams club of hurt souls', as one would later describe his treatment of her.

And here he was now on a public stage in Sydney—less than three weeks after his act of literary purification in the *New Yorker*—being confronted by a fellow writer who had presumably picked this moment for maximum effect. Why, she wanted to know, had he treated her the way he had six years earlier when she was a graduate student at Columbia University? Those in the room who could hear what Zinzi Clemmons was saying were stunned. (There were many in the room who couldn't hear her.)

A few hours after the panel session, Clemmons repeated her accusation, this time to a much larger audience. 'As a grad student,' she tweeted, 'I invited Junot Díaz to speak to a workshop on issues of representation in literature. I was an unknown wide-eyed 26 yo, and he used it as an opportunity to corner and forcibly kiss me. I'm far from the only one he's done this 2, I refuse to be silent anymore.'

Clemmons also stated her belief that Díaz had written the *New Yorker* essay in a cynical attempt to pre-empt allegations like hers.

That same evening, two other writers addressed the issue publicly. The first, Carmen Maria Machado, an American author, also a guest of the festival, fired off a tweet claiming Díaz had turned on her angrily when she'd once questioned his 'pathological' attitude to women in one of his fictional characters. She then raised the stakes with a flurry of tweets accusing Díaz of being an 'utterly beloved misogynist' whose books were 'regressive and sexist'.

Monica Byrne, an American playwright and author, added her voice to the uproar that night, in a tweet claiming that, five years earlier, she'd sat next to Díaz at a dinner and, after a disagreement about a 'minor point', Díaz had shouted the word 'rape' in her face, then subjected her to the most 'virulent misogyny' she'd ever experienced.

By the following morning, Junot Díaz had cancelled his remaining sessions at the festival—including one on the Politics of Empathy—and left the country. As he was on his way to the airport, the Sydney Writers' Festival issued the following statement:

> Following the allegations of inappropriate and aggressive behaviour towards Zinzi Clemmons and other women, Mr Díaz has withdrawn from his remaining sessions at Sydney Writers' Festival. In his recent *New Yorker* essay, Mr Díaz wrote, 'Eventually the past finds you.' As for so many in positions of power, the moment to reckon with the consequences of past behaviour has arrived. We remain committed to ensuring that [the sharing of stories] occurs in a supportive and safe environment for our authors and audiences alike.

Coming from what is arguably the country's premier literary festival, many in the world of books and writing found this a troubling response.

'Did it not occur to anyone at the festival that this statement had defamed Díaz?' asked Margot Saville in an article published on the Australian news website *Crikey*. 'It's a very poor precedent for the festival to allow Díaz to flee the country and metaphorically kick him in the arse on the way out.

'After this incident, what male writer would fly around the world to come to Australia? Why not put Díaz in front of an audience to take questions—aren't argument and debate the whole point of a literary festival?'

In a statement provided soon after to the *New York Times* through his literary agent, Díaz said: 'I take responsibility for my past. That is the reason I made the decision to tell the truth of my rape and its damaging aftermath. This conversation is important and must continue. I am listening to and learning from women's stories in this essential and overdue cultural movement. We must continue to teach all men about consent and boundaries.'

Two months later, in an interview with the *Boston Globe*—his first since the Sydney showdown—Díaz appeared to disavow those comments, while also denying the allegations, including having 'forcibly kissed' Clemmons. He said he was 'distressed', 'confused' and 'panicked' at the time the accusations were made in Sydney, but vowed he had not bullied the women or acted in a sexually inappropriate way.

'I've written a lot of crap in my life,' Díaz told the *Globe*, his Boston lawyer by his side. 'One does when one's a writer. But, definitely, that statement is the worst thing I've written, the worst thing I've put my name to. Boy, I wish I'd had the presence of mind to rewrite the damn thing. I did not kiss anyone. I did not forcibly kiss Zinzi Clemmons. I did not kiss Zinzi Clemmons. It didn't happen.'

Díaz provided evidence of a friendly email he'd received from Clemmons the day after the Columbia workshop. It made no mention of a kiss. A Columbia professor also recalled to the *Globe* seeing Clemmons after Díaz had left the event. He described her as 'delighted, not shaken'.

When contacted by the newspaper, Clemmons insisted Díaz had kissed her as she'd walked him out of the building, 'positioning her against a wall in an enclosed stairwell'. Asked to characterise the kiss, Clemmons declined to specify whether it had been on the mouth or not.

In the clap of social media thunder after Díaz's return to the United States, the literary world was both divided and riveted. Díaz's work abounded with men behaving badly towards women.

Did that mean distinctions couldn't—and shouldn't—be made between an artist and his art, between sexual transgressions and relationships of mutual consent that happened to unravel?

'There is a line between being a bad boyfriend and having a lot of regret, and predatory behavior,' Díaz told the *Globe*.

Amid all the sound and fury of who said what—and who *meant* what—Carmen Maria Machado clarified later that, in accusing Díaz of displaying 'a pathological attitude with women' through one of his characters, she was not inferring that she had experienced a #MeToo moment with the author. Yes, Díaz had become 'enraged' and had veered towards 'bullying' and 'misogyny' in his response to her, but: 'I never characterized it as harassment. The reporting that happened after I tweeted was so irresponsible, it was actually sort of astonishing to me.'

What was also astonishing was the official recording of the event at the University of Iowa in which Díaz was alleged to have bullied Machado. Perhaps my bullying barometer is seriously defective, but when I listened to the recording (which surfaced in June 2018), I could hear defensiveness in Díaz's words, but certainly not bullying—though who am I to argue with how Machado felt?

There is a similar disconnect between Díaz's and Monica Byrne's recollections of the discussion that led to her accusing him of 'virulent misogyny'. In a conversation about the statistical disparity between male and female authors appearing in the pages of the *New Yorker*, Byrne suggested to Díaz—a regular contributor to the magazine—that this disparity was surely evidence of gender bias. Byrne said she considered Díaz's comments in response 'completely bizarre, disproportionate and violent', while Díaz recalled them as part of a 'messy conversation'.

Messy is right, and attempts to clean up the mess have possibly been as messy as the mess itself, although in June 2018, four weeks after the allegations first aired against Díaz, the Massachusetts Institute of Technology (MIT) where Díaz is a faculty member, cleared Díaz of sexual misconduct or verbal abuse. That same month, the *Boston Review* decided to continue employing Díaz as its fiction editor, while in November 2018, the Pulitzer Prize board concluded a five month investigation, finding no evidence requiring Díaz's removal as chairman. Díaz had joined the board in 2010 and had stepped down as chairman after the allegations first surfaced in Sydney.

#

It is increasingly difficult now for institutions to ignore claims of objectionable behaviour. In the wake of the Matt Lauer sexual harassment allegations, for example, the American television network NBC reportedly introduced new behavioural guidelines that include rules on how to hug. (Hug quickly, but then release immediately before stepping away from further body contact.) According to the London *Telegraph*, guidelines around NBC's staff socialising also prohibit sharing taxis home and 'taking vegans to steakhouses'.

Following the Kevin Spacey convulsions on *House of Cards*, Netflix is also reported to have established new strictures on eye contact between production staff. Time limit: five seconds. Anything longer and that might be taking things into the 'creepy' realm. No lingering hugs either. Or flirting. Or asking for a colleague's phone number.

On Wall Street, according to a recent Bloomberg report, a number of bankers, investors and lawyers have adopted new personal codes to deal with the #MeToo movement, including no more dinners with female colleagues, no more sitting next to them on flights, ensuring hotel rooms are booked on separate floors and no one-on-one meetings. It's been dubbed 'the Pence effect', owing to US vice-president Mike Pence having forsworn dining alone with any woman other than his wife Karen.

Such is the charged atmosphere in some American universities that words, ideas and subjects which might possibly cause discomfort have been removed, and this began applying well before the #MeToo movement erupted in late 2017. In December 2014, for example, Harvard law professor Jeannie Suk Gersen described in an article in the *New Yorker*—'The Trouble With Teaching Rape Law'—the growing anxiety among students about discussing in class laws governing sexual violence:

Student organizations representing women's interests now routinely advise students that they should not feel pressured to attend or participate in class sessions that focus on the law of sexual violence, and which might therefore be traumatic. These organizations also ask criminal-law teachers to warn their classes that the rape-law unit might 'trigger' traumatic memories. Individual students often ask teachers not to include the law of rape on exams for fear that the material would cause them to perform less well. One teacher I know was recently asked by a student not to use the word 'violate' in class—as in 'Does this conduct violate the law?'—because the word was triggering. Some students have even suggested that rape law should not be taught because of its potential to cause distress.

At Columbia and Brown Universities women have scrawled warnings about men on campus bathroom walls. At one college, a liberal-minded academic admitted to being terrified of his liberal students, for fear of saying the wrong thing. Irony—to the extent that irony ever existed in America—has been snuffed out. Jokes have been pathologised to such an extent that comedians like Jerry

Seinfeld and Chris Rock have vowed never to perform again on American campuses.

Students have reported feeling 'disempowered' for falling short of an A for their final grade. One eighteen-year-old student from a major university was effectively expelled for two years for 'emotional and verbal coercion' of his then nineteen-year-old girlfriend. He'd asked her for oral sex. She'd baulked at the request, then complied. Her 'blow job' had, therefore, been 'ambivalent'.

The couple had had sex before, but on this occasion, when the young man realised his girlfriend was less than enthusiastic, he'd stopped. Nonetheless, he was accused of coercion months later, following their break-up.

'The ruling [from the university],' wrote Laura Kipnis in her book *Unwanted Advances: Sexual Paranoia Comes to Campus*, 'was that he should have known that consent had to be "voluntary, present and ongoing".' (And possibly retrospective, too.) 'For campus officials to find this kid responsible for "emotional coercion" not only means prosecuting students for the awkwardness of college sex, it also brands an eighteen-year-old a lifelong sex criminal [as] all college applications now ask if a student has been found responsible for "behavioural misconduct" at a previous institution.'

Laura Kipnis is a professor of filmmaking at Northwestern University in Illinois and a self-described 'left-wing feminist'. In 2015 she wrote an essay for the *Chronicle of Higher Education*, 'Sexual Paranoia Strikes Academe', about the implementation of new codes in American universities prohibiting consensual professor–student relationships. Kipnis knew many women— herself included—who had had 'a teacher or two in their past'. Most of those relationships, she said, were remembered with great fondness. Her argument against these new codes was that it infantilised students and heightened an atmosphere of censure on campus. In response, students staged a protest march against her carrying mattresses and pillows. They claimed to feel a 'visceral reaction' to what she'd written and demanded that authorities protect them from her 'terrifying ideas'. (Proof, perhaps, of the soundness of her arguments in the first place.)

A 72-day investigation by the university followed under Title IX, the federal civil rights law initially proposed by feminist advocates to prevent sexual assault, harassment and discrimination in federally funded educational institutions.

Kipnis was flabbergasted. For one thing, mattresses had become the symbol of student-on-student sexual assault since 2014, when Emma Sulkowicz, a Columbia University student, had carried a blue mattress around campus to protest the university's ruling on a sexual assault complaint. (The university had rejected a ruling of rape against Sulkowicz's former boyfriend, and Sulkowicz's one-woman demonstration had become a piece of performance art, resulting in her being dubbed 'Mattress Girl'.)

What disturbed Kipnis most, however, was that the noble principle of universities being a 'refuge for complexity, a setting for the free exchange of ideas' was now getting buried 'under an avalanche of platitudes and fears'.

'It turns out,' she wrote in her 2018 book *Unwanted Advances*, 'that rampant accusation is the new norm on today's campus; the place is a secret cornucopia of accusation, especially when it comes to sex. Including merely *speaking* about sex.'

Kipnis was at pains to acknowledge that sexual assault was a reality in colleges and universities, and had probably *always* been a reality. What was new was the conflicting stories about sex that students were now receiving from the cultural zeitgeist. One story was all about hooking up, binge-drinking and watching porn; the other was that sex was dangerous and could traumatise you for life.

'It's contaminating,' she wrote.

> You can catch trauma, which, like a virus, never goes away. Shifting the stress from pleasure to danger and vulnerability not only changes the prevailing narrative, it changes the way sex is experienced.
>
> If the prevailing story is that sex is dangerous, sex is going to feel threatening more of the time, and anything associated with sex, no matter how innocuous (a risqué remark, a dumb joke) will feel threatening. [And] teaching under these conditions can feel like a tightrope walk.

Furthermore, in a sexual culture that 'emphasises female violation, endangerment and perpetual vulnerability ("rape culture"), men's power is taken as a given instead of interrogated: men need to be policed, women need to be protected'.

#

In chapter twelve, I described how in August 2018 Michael Kimmel, the pro-feminist sociologist and gender studies professor, was himself accused of sexual harassment. In the aftermath of the allegation levelled at him anonymously, a number of other unattributed allegations were made via social media, before a select few began nailing their colours firmly to the mast. A reputation for publicly championing women's rights over three decades was now in ruins.

In an article for the online publishing platform *Medium*, Robert Jensen, professor in the School of Journalism at the University of Texas, called on pro-feminist men—like himself, presumably—to believe and support women in their complaints against Kimmel.

Silence would otherwise be construed as negligence. Jensen said he had not spoken up earlier because the pro-feminist men's movement had enough problems already reaching out to men—as well as earning the trust of women. The last thing the movement needed, he said, was for the most prominent male feminist writer in America to be accused of misconduct.

Jensen's second expressed reason for not speaking earlier was his previous experience with Kimmel. This had led him to believe Kimmel would come out fighting against his critics, and he—Jensen—was loath to get involved. On further reflection, he decided this was both unsustainable and cowardly.

Jensen then quoted Kimmel's own words to drive home the importance of being courageous—and who could fail to see the stunning irony here?

'We are in a new moment,' Kimmel wrote for the *Harvard Business Review* in January 2018,

> For many of us, particularly men, it is scary and uncomfortable. Men are feeling vulnerable and afraid of false accusations (or perhaps true ones). They fear that things they did a long time ago will be re-evaluated under new rules. They tell me they're walking on eggshells.
>
> Because of this, many men are staying silent rather than taking part in the conversation. And yet inaction isn't necessarily the right approach; there are important things men can do and say to support the women in their lives.

Jensen claimed to have no 'insider knowledge' of the accusations against Kimmel, and this prevented him from reaching any 'definitive judgement' as to Kimmel's guilt. Nonetheless, he was prepared to recount one of the anonymous accusations for his readers' consideration:

[Kimmel's] treatment of me negatively impacted me for a very long time. Reading his assertion that he has been 'professional and respectful in . . . relationships with women' is painful, and reveals the extent of his denial and misunderstanding, to say the least, of the harm he has caused.

I have not experienced professional, respectful treatment, though I know other women he has worked with who have. However, I am not alone in being subjected to his worst treatment, and sadly, it goes beyond simply being sexually propositioned and objectified.

In a separate article for Medium, M.J. Murphy, an associate professor of gender studies at Illinois University, wrote of 'the two Kimmels'—the first being the public 'feminist' who has called on men to display humility, the second a man with 'an ego the size of Alaska' and an explosive temper to match.

Four days later, Bethany M. Coston, one of Kimmel's former graduate students and now an assistant professor of women's, gender and sexuality studies at Virginia Commonwealth University added their (Coston's preferred gender pronoun) weight to those of the unnamed accusers.

Coston said Kimmel had been guilty of favouritism, was biased against non-binary and LGBTQI people, resisted the use of preferred pronouns (such as 'they' and 'them'), exploited graduates' work, displayed homophobia, transphobia, lack of respect for non-cisgender heterosexuals and engaged in sexist talk. An example of this sexism, Coston said, was allegedly telling one student that he couldn't help looking at another student's low-cut shirt and large breasts. Apparently, Kimmel had also indulged in a 'power trip' by replaying to a few of his graduate students a phone call from actor Jane Fonda.

Kimmel's perspectives, Coston said, were 'securely rooted in a benevolent sexist, second-wave feminist, trans-exclusionary frame of reference, which relies so heavily on stereotypical understandings of the gender binary that it also necessitates a homophobic understanding of sexuality'.

To translate from gender studies parlance, Bethany Coston seemed to be saying Michael Kimmel had it coming.

Kimmel didn't only get skewered by feminist academics and anonymous complainants. Men's rights proponents were only too happy to oblige with some schadenfreude of their own.

Writing in A Voice for Men (AVFM)—an online platform designed to lift boys and men 'above the din of misandry'—AVFM founder Paul Elam described Kimmel as 'a long-time feminist "scholar", liar and purveyor of all manner of anti-male ideology'. Elam then borrowed from 'the standard feminist demand' by calling on Kimmel to acknowledge what he'd done and believe the survivor. This was 'feminist codespeak', Elam explained, for, '"Admit you did it, you slimy bastard."' Whether Kimmel was guilty or not was beside the point, Elam observed. 'He's been accused [and] in the world Michael Kimmel worked feverishly to create, that is no different than a guilty verdict in a court of law. This is the moment that destroys him.'

Elam noted correctly that charges against Kimmel had not yet been proven (nor have they been at the time of writing) and that the problems of false accusation—which Kimmel had tried to 'minimise' over a professional lifetime—had not gone away. It was appropriate, Elam suggested, to question whether asking another adult to sleep with you constitutes sexual harassment. (It certainly can if there's a power differential.) But he reserved his best shot for last, revelling in the professor's fall from grace: 'We know of no one else who deserves the unfair disgrace, the stigma of accusation and its ruinous effects on their lives than this lowlife academic fraud,' Elam wrote. 'Enjoy the level of public attention you've always craved, Michael. It's finally here and it looks damned good on you.'

#

Let's flip this story now and examine the case of Avital Ronell, the internationally renowned professor of German and comparative literature at New York University. At first and second glance, it looks like day to Michael Kimmel's night.

In September 2017, Nimrod Reitman, an Israeli-born, former graduate student at NYU, filed a complaint against Professor Ronell, the daughter of Israeli diplomats and a pre-eminent figure in the world of academia, for sexual harassment, sexual assault, retaliation and stalking over a three-year period. Professor Ronell was, at the time, a 65-year-old lesbian, Nimrod Reitman a 33-year-old married gay man.

According to the *New York Times*, the problems for Reitman had begun five years earlier in Paris, in the spring of 2012, a few months before Reitman officially commenced his studies at New York University. (Reitman is now a visiting fellow at Harvard University.) Professor Ronell invited Reitman to stay with her in Paris for a few days and, on the day of his arrival, asked him to read poetry to her as she took an afternoon nap. In documents obtained by the *Times*, Reitman said, 'That was already a red flag to me. But I also thought, O.K., you're here. Better not make a scene.' Then Professor Ronell pulled Reitman towards her in bed.

'She put my hands onto her breasts, and was pressing herself— her buttocks—onto my crotch,' he said. 'She was kissing me, kissing my hands, kissing my torso.'

Reitman said he told Ronell her behaviour was not acceptable because she was his adviser, but, after arriving in New York, the behaviour continued, particularly after Hurricane Sandy slammed into the city in late October 2012.

According to Reitman, Professor Ronell arrived at his apartment one evening because the power had cut out in hers and, despite his objections, persuaded Reitman to let her sleep in his bed. She then reportedly groped and kissed him every night for nearly a week.

Through her lawyer, Professor Ronell denied allegations of sexual contact, insisting her client had only stayed at Reitman's apartment for two nights after the hurricane.

In dozens of emails provided to the *Times* by Reitman, Professor Ronell referred to Reitman variously as 'my most adored one', 'Sweet cuddly Baby', 'cock-er spaniel,' and 'my astounding and beautiful Nimrod'.

In a 16 June email following their Paris sojourn, Ronell wrote: 'I woke up with a slight fever and sore throat. I will try very hard not to kiss you—until the throat situation receives security clearance. This is not an easy deferral!'

The following month she sent this message: 'Time for your midday kiss. my image during meditation: we're on the sofa, your head on my lap, stroking you [sic] forehead, playing softly with yr [sic] hair, soothing you, headache gone. Yes?'

Two years after earning his PhD, Reitman filed his complaint under Title IX, the US federal statute that addresses gender discrimination. In the context of the #MeToo movement, Reitman's and Ronell's accounts were all too familiar for their furious claims and counterclaims. Reitman maintained he was afraid of the power his professor wielded over him, and that he'd only complied with her wishes because of that power. He felt violated.

Ronell insisted that Reitman was desperately in need of her attention and guidance and she had no idea of his discomfort.

In March 2018, Ronell complained that Reitman had compared her to 'the most egregious example of predatory behaviors ascribable to Hollywood moguls who habitually go after starlets'. In a statement to the *New York Times* a few months later, she said, 'Our communications—which Reitman now claims constituted sexual harassment—were between two adults, a gay man and a queer woman, who share an Israeli heritage, as well as a penchant for florid and campy communications arising from our common academic backgrounds and sensibilities. These communications were repeatedly invited, responded to and encouraged by him over a period of three years.'

Following an eleven-month investigation, New York University suspended Professor Ronell for one year after finding her guilty of sexual harassment. The university found that her behaviour was 'sufficiently pervasive to alter the terms and conditions of Mr. Reitman's learning environment'. There was insufficient evidence, however, to find her guilty of sexual assault.

Shortly after NYU completed its confidential investigation, a group of more than 50 international scholars—including prominent feminist academics and authors—wrote to the university defending Professor Ronell and accusing Reitman of wishing to do their colleague and friend harm. Their letter was strikingly similar to the defence often mounted on behalf of powerful men: namely, that the accusations were false, the accuser motivated by malice, and the charges hardly sufficient to qualify as legal evidence. Moreover, as a woman of enormous stature in the academic world, Professor Ronell was entitled to a fair hearing and the preservation of her dignity.

'Although we have no access to the confidential dossier,' the letter stated,

> . . . We have all seen her relationship with students and some of us know the individual who has waged this malicious campaign against her. We wish to communicate first in the clearest terms our profound and enduring admiration for Professor Ronell whose mentorship of students has been no less than remarkable over many years. We deplore the damage that this legal proceeding causes her and seek to register in clear terms our objection to any judgment against her. We hold that the allegations against her do not constitute actual evidence, but rather support the view that malicious intention has animated and sustained this legal nightmare.
>
> We testify to the grace, the keen wit, and the intellectual commitment of Professor Ronell and ask that she be accorded the dignity rightly deserved by someone of her international standing and reputation.

A few weeks after he made this letter public, Professor Brian Leiter from the University of Chicago's Law School condemned Ronell's defenders in one of his regular *Philosophy Blog* posts, under the title 'Blaming the victim is apparently OK when the accused in a Title IX proceeding is a feminist literary theorist'.

> Apparently in the view of these 'theory' illuminati, dignity . . . is to be doled out according to one's 'international standing and reputation.' So while Professor Ronell 'deserves a fair hearing, one that expresses respect, dignity, and human solicitude,' other 'lesser' accused can be subject, without international outcry, to whatever star chamber proceedings the university wants.
>
> Moreover, only one outcome of the process is acceptable, regardless of the findings: acquittal. Any other result 'would

be widely recognized and opposed,' I guess because grace, wit and intellectual commitment are a defense against sexual misconduct and harassment.

I'm not sure I buy this argument. Yes, Professor Ronell was supported by a legion of feminist colleagues, unlike Michael Kimmel whose colleagues seemed to desert him. But regardless of Ronell's transgressions—and this is not to condone them—I would have thought the bigger picture here was the rule not the exception: infinitely more women suffer from harassment, abuse and violence from men than vice versa.

In the United States, nearly eighteen million women have been raped, and one in four will be sexually assaulted in their lifetime. In Egypt, according to the United Nations, 99 per cent of women surveyed across seven regions have experienced sexual harassment. In Denmark—yes freewheeling, progressive Denmark—52 per cent of women have experienced physical and/or sexual violence. In the United Kingdom and France it's 44 per cent. In Brazil, 84 per cent of women have reported being sexually harassed by police. In South Africa a woman is raped every 26 seconds . . .

There is no way, of course, to absorb these numbers because, as American writer Paul Brodeur once observed, 'Statistics are human beings with the tears wiped off.'

17

Voyage around my father

Do I contradict myself? Very well then I contradict myself.
I am large, I contain multitudes.

WALT WHITMAN, 'SONG OF MYSELF'

If only the world were tidier. If only all men were toxic bastards and women morally unsullied, things would be a lot easier.

We'd have clear, straight lines, rather than blurred horizons, and there'd be no need to point out—as critics of the #MeToo movement are often wont to do—that women can also be violent, manipulative, hurtful and abusive (as if we didn't know); that they can misuse their power, make false accusations and/or embellish the truth (yes, we know that too); that they can refuse to own their share in the destruction and mess of relationships; that they can shatter men's lives and scorn their tears and raise entitled sons who then grow up without a shred of respect for women; that female bosses can terrorise their employees, or enable male bosses to do likewise; that some older feminists are deeply uncomfortable at the sight of their younger sisters moving through the world with their rights flags held aloft; that some women love to invite male attention (have you seen the latest episode of *The Bachelor*?), and—in the case of 'raunch culture' in all its 'twerking' provocation—proudly flaunt their sexuality for male appreciation; that other women will cheerily deflect approaches from the occasional frog in the hopes of attracting the hovering prince (and they might even miss the day when that no longer occurs); that in some circumstances, *the right circumstances*, they don't mind being looked at, approached, propositioned, claimed; that they enjoy a zipless fuck and a one-night stand as much as a man might; that they love the primal dance between a man and a woman and look back on their own struggle for equality and lament the fact that minor infractions by men are not calibrated in more nuanced ways; that they don't feel the same sense of indignation or, worse, outrage, for these minor lapses; that they believe it's important to make distinctions between aggressive sexual behaviour and bog-standard bungling, or a decent man's out-of-character moments; that they understand the horror and confusion most men feel at being cast as potential rapists and abusers of women and children; that they see all the conspicuous flaws in men, and forever roll their eyes at their failings, but actually love men for their purpose, clarity, decisiveness and, yes, tenderness, and want them as their friends and lovers; that, although they would never countenance sexual predation, they know that there are grades of offence and that good people can behave badly at times because the human heart is often riven by complex and often contradictory needs and motivations.

So, yes, we know all this because we know not all men are bad and not all women good, and to be human is often an endless tangle of invisible forces and confounding paradoxes, of being many things all at the same time.

And yet, as Grayson Perry wrote in *The Descent of Man*, 'most men are nice, reasonable fellows. But most violent people, rapists, criminals, killers, tax avoiders, corrupt politicians, planet despoilers, sex abusers and dinner-party bores do tend to be, well . . . men.'

So we know historically that way more men than women do bad things, and that every time women demand that we reset the rules of life, so that they are treated equally and as more than just the decorative objects of the male imagination, there is a predictable counterattack, subtle or overt.

At the Seneca Falls Convention in 1848—the first ever in the United States to publicly discuss women's role in society—the mere idea of female equality was dismissed by its critics as 'excessively silly' and 'amusing'.

'This bolt is the most shocking and unnatural incident ever recorded in the history of womanity,' lamented one New York newspaper at the time. 'If our ladies will insist on voting and legislating, where, gentlemen, will be our dinners and our elbows? Where our domestic firesides and the holes in our stockings?'

It's been a variation on this theme ever since—nearly every advance met with a retrograde response. In America (and Australia, too) women were fired en masse from their jobs after World War II so that returning veterans might be re-employed. During the Reagan years of the 1980s, many of the advances that American women had gained a decade earlier in terms of equal employment and reproductive rights were undermined—just as today reproductive rights are under sustained attack by the Trump administration.

As Susan Faludi pointed out in *Backlash* more than 25 years ago, the arguments mounted against women's empowerment have always run to a familiar soundtrack. Women are unhappy because they are free. Being a working mother is incompatible with being a good mother and wife. Concentrating on your career can render you manless and childless. And here is the implicit—or explicit—corollary: pushing for economic parity threatens a man's sense of himself.

'What exactly is it about women's equality,' Faludi asked, 'that even its slightest shadow threatens to erase male identity? What is it about the way we frame manhood that, even today, it still depends so much on "feminine" dependence for its survival?'

Faludi found part of the answer in the Yankelovich Monitor survey which tracked social attitudes and, for twenty years, shone a spotlight on male definitions of masculinity. 'It isn't being a leader, athlete, Lothario, decision-maker, or even just being "born male",' Faludi wrote. 'It is simply this: being a "good provider for his family."'

I can relate to this sentiment because, all through my 23-year marriage, I internalised that requirement. Whenever the discussion arose about the possibility of my working part-time or becoming a househusband, I was seized with the same inchoate sense of emasculation. Beyond the achievements and status I craved, beyond the need to live up to the brief of being the son of a powerful, successful father, there was also this primitive instinct: How could I ever hold my head up high if I forfeited the role of breadwinner? What would my colleagues say, my friends (a definite 'bravo' from the female ones, that's for sure), my daughters, my mother and, most particularly, my father? As Faludi observed, masculinity is such 'a fragile flower—a hothouse orchid in constant need of trellising and nourishment', that even small 'losses' for a man—(read equal opportunities and advantages for a woman)—could be interpreted as large threats.

I was not like my old friend John, who had willingly given up full-time work to look after his young children, so that his wife Trish could advance through the corporate world. Their arrangement had become so normalised that on one rare occasion, when Trish arrived at the daycare centre to pick up their toddler daughter Ruby, one of Ruby's friends turned to another child and said, 'There's Ruby's mum,' and the other toddler replied, 'No, Ruby's mum got a beard.'

I was not that bearded househusband and never would be. And I can see clearly now how my own barely examined preoccupations and assumptions contributed to my wife's unhappiness.

In retrospect, my understanding of gender roles was already an artefact of the past, but as a baby boomer I was still stranded in the mythical golden age of male performance and (professional) power.

There was also something else that didn't help, although I can only see this now in hindsight. (As the nineteenth-century Danish philosopher Søren Kierkegaard observed, while life is lived forwards, it can only ever be understood backwards.) In my rear-view mirror I can see today the various ways in which my view of women was shaped growing up. As I mentioned in chapter nine, my father Bernard Leser launched Australian *Vogue* in 1959. With the support and guidance of his female colleagues through the 1960s and 70s, he turned it into the country's premier fashion magazine before going on to run Condé Nast Publications (publishers also of *Tatler, Brides, Glamour, Vanity Fair* and the *New Yorker*) first in Britain, then in America, for the better part of twenty years, up until 1994.

I drank this in as a young boy without comprehending it—the regular presence of female editors, fashion designers, photographers and models at our family dinner table; *Vogue* posters adorning the walls, tear sheets laid out across the carpet; the latest skincare products and fragrances from Estée Lauder and Chanel in my parents' bathroom cabinets, their seasonal wardrobes arranged precisely . . . all this telling a story, suggesting a currency system, that reinforced the exquisite masquerade that beauty imposes, while also feeding my lurid imagination. I was reared on what Naomi Wolf called 'the beauty myth', an impossible fable for any woman to live up to, but one which satisfied men in all their animal cravings. It was only in adulthood—with the help of my women friends and, later, my wife—that I began to critique this narrative.

My father admired strong, beautiful women, but as far as I can recall, he never gave much thought to how the fashion and cosmetics industries fuelled women's anxieties and insecurities. The right body (often undernourished), the right face (perfect bone structure), a phantasm of loveliness on every glossy page . . . he simply couldn't see the enormous weight this placed on a woman's shoulders to conform to whatever the male verdict of 'beautiful' was. Then again, neither could many women.

#

(Female friend to author): *I used to go out always wearing little crushed velvet shorts—I remember them particularly—they practically fell off me I wore them so much. Fishnets, high-heeled boots, really tiny little tops. I made sure there was a lot of skin showing. Lots and lots of make-up. I never left the house without make-up. It was just unthinkable to me that I wouldn't have a full face. It was like your game face. I'd walk out of the house like that. That was, I think, all the pressure to fulfil my purpose of being a woman and being desired. Because I really didn't know who I was without that. If men weren't looking at me I would have such low self-worth.*

#

In my father's defence, I suspect his preoccupations with beauty derived, in part, from his early days in Nazi Germany, where everything had been drained of colour, and he'd seen the rage of a nation turn inexorably on its own (Jewish) people. Perhaps he could hardly believe his miraculous good fortune in having escaped all this, only to then find himself in a remote, sun-kissed corner of the world as an arbiter of trends and styles.

Given the nature of the magazine he published, it is hardly surprising he employed so many women, and yet he still surpassed himself during his years at the helm as an unrivalled equal opportunity employer. It was a legacy that Jonathan Newhouse, today's chairman and chief executive of Condé Nast International, noted when he first visited Australia in 1990, and then remarked upon 25 years later at my father's memorial service in New York.

'The Australian company at that time had 95 staff, and 94 were women,' Newhouse said. 'The only man was a chain-smoking driver named Tony. Everyone else—executives, sales people, editors, journalists, accountants, and of course the president [Eve Harman] and editorial director [June McCallum], were women.

'This was truly remarkable. Remember, this was the close of the eighties. A thriving publishing enterprise composed entirely of females. In those days, it was customary for top editors to be women but nearly all executive positions were filled by men. Thus, Bernie was kind of a revolutionary. And I think not because he was driven consciously to champion the female cause, but because he deeply respected women and selected them for their ability to do the job.'

So this was the background I came from and I'd like to think if my father were alive today he'd be a supporter of the #MeToo movement, although he'd probably qualify this support with arguments for an old-world courtliness consistent with his generation. He'd also be cautious about judging people's pasts by the standards of today. Consistent with these sentiments, he'd be mystified by the idea that a man might no longer feel free to flirt with a woman at work, kiss her on the cheek, touch her hand, pay her a compliment. He would probably also resist the idea that a woman didn't bear some responsibility for how she dressed or the effect she might have on men—primarily, I think, because he'd see all forms of power, including sexual power, as requiring its own special kind of wisdom, the kind that probably only comes with age. I dare say he'd also want to talk about treating people kindly, avoiding acts of malice or the pursuit of revenge, and he'd argue for a world in which we were able to make distinctions between minor and major offences.

Part of me would argue for that world too, and in so doing I have to admit to a sometimes crippling confusion in this time of ceaseless upheaval. On the one hand, I see a continuum between the worst and least depredations against women—the common denominator being that for centuries men have regarded women as there for the taking. On the other hand, I don't think shaming and humiliating anyone, be they man or woman, has ever been the best way to achieve results. Nor do I think that when men lose their jobs for making slight sexual innuendos, or trying it on, that the punishment of public shaming fits the crime. We need to live in a world of moral proportion and, right now, we don't.

There is also something to be said here about all the beautiful, brave men who disappear into cave systems to rescue boys they've never met, who rush into burning homes to save strangers, who paddle out into the wild surf to bring the drowning back to shore, who risk their lives for something bigger than themselves, whose natures are kind and gentle. It's easy to forget these things in times of churning division, but those men are everywhere and, hopefully, anyone reading this book can readily attest to that.

At the same time, we also know that, in times of revolution, the world tips out of alignment before balance is restored. People take the fall—usually unwillingly—for the larger cause, although I wonder, again, what have the consequences been for many of those accused?

Many have lost their jobs, of course, but others, like Aziz Ansari and Louis C.K., have returned recently to stand-up comedy. And wasn't there talk of a Charlie Rose comeback on television, hosting a program on which he would interview *other disgraced men*? Who's actually been run out of town, instead of just forced to sit quietly at home for a while and reflect? I don't know the answer to that, although Roxane Gay, writing in the *New York Times* in August 2018, certainly has a strong view on the matter:

> In each instance it has been less than a year since the allegations against these men surfaced, and in each instance, the men have done little in the way of public contrition. When they have apologised, they have done so with carefully worded, legally vetted statements.
>
> They have deflected responsibility. They have demonstrated that they don't really think they've done anything wrong. And worse, people have asked for the #MeToo movement to provide a path to redemption for these men, as if it is the primary

responsibility of the victimised to help their victimisers find redemption.

In November, 2017, Louis C.K. released a statement saying that stories about him taking out his penis and masturbating in front of women were true:

At the time, I said to myself that what I did was okay because I never showed a woman my dick without asking first, which is also true. But what I learned later in life, too late, is that when you have power over another person, asking them to look at your dick isn't a question. It's a predicament for them.

The power I had over these women is that they admired me. And I wielded that power irresponsibly. I have been remorseful of my actions. And I've tried to learn from them. And run from them. Now I'm aware of the extent of the impact of my actions.

The hardest regret to live with is what you've done to hurt someone else. And I can hardly wrap my head around the scope of hurt I brought on them. I have spent my long and lucky career talking and saying anything I want. I will now step back and take a long time to listen. Thank you for reading.

For Roxane Gay, the apology fell way short of meaningful redress. Nine months after issuing that mea culpa, Gay asked how long a man like Louis C.K. should pay for what he had done. Should it be as long as he'd tried to silence the women he'd assaulted? As long as he'd allowed them to doubt themselves and suffer in the wake of his misconduct? Or as long as the comedy world had shielded him, despite having heard the 'very loud whispers' about his behaviour for decades? What should the calculation be?

Perhaps, she argued, Louis C.K.'s debt should last until he truly comprehended what he had done wrong, and the extent of the damage he'd caused. Perhaps he should financially compensate his victims for all the work they'd missed out on through his efforts to silence them.

'He should finance their mental health care as long as they may need it,' she wrote. 'He should donate to non-profit organisations that work with sexual harassment and assault victims. He should publicly admit what he did and why it was wrong without excuses and legalese and deflection. Every perpetrator of sexual harassment and violence should follow suit.'

Women are finally saying: 'Enough.' Enough of being fearful for life and limb, enough of being viewed as a sexual object, an object of possession, a medium of exchange. ('How many camels do you want for your daughters?' the carpet salesman asked me in Istanbul.) Enough of being jealously controlled, coerced, taunted, demeaned, ignored. And enough of the rot at the centre of power structures that seems to regard everyone and everything as part of Man's sphere of influence.

#

I know many men—as you do too, probably—who would never dream of making unwanted comments to a woman, touching her inappropriately, or trying to force her into non-consensual sex. And yet here we have Michael Kimmel, a renowned male feminist, accused of sexual harassment.

Here we have Eric Schneiderman—former attorney general of New York, darling of the liberal establishment, a man known for his widespread support of women, indeed his support for the #MeToo movement—accused of assaulting four women with whom he'd been sexually involved.

Here we have Sogyal Rinpoche, the Tibetan Buddhist teacher (my own teacher for a few years!) and author of the 1992 international bestseller *The Tibetan Book of Living and Dying*, found guilty by an international law firm of years of violent and abusive behaviour, of using his position as an international spiritual figure to coerce, intimidate and manipulate young women into granting him sexual favours. ('He roughly put his hand up my long dress, groped my privates, unzipped himself and lay on top of me, literally grunting for the minute or two until he released,' one of his former students told me.)

Here we have every active bishop in Chile resigning over their collective failure to deal with sexual abuse, along with the thousands of other cardinals, bishops and priests around the world who have been found guilty of sex crimes over the past several decades.

And then there's all the artists we've celebrated for their genius. (What was it Picasso said? 'For me there are only two kinds of women, goddesses and doormats'.) All the books we've read. All the disturbing, disdainful, objectifying songs we've sung (The Police's 'Every Breath You Take', for example, which only now, 35 years after it was recorded, have I come to realise is about—*was always about*—a stalker.) All the films we've watched that were a reflection of the desires of the men writing, financing, producing and directing them. Everything we've ever assumed, the values and tastes we've acquired, the beliefs and standards we've adopted, the lens through which we've viewed the world . . . so much of it manufactured by men, for men, about men.

Is it any surprise then, that the global 'forces of dark and furious energy' inside women—as Australian writer Charlotte Wood put it in *The Guardian* in December 2017—have burst forth so spectacularly, particularly when the most powerful man in the world doesn't even bother to hide his vile and instinctive contempt for women?

Little wonder, too, the temptation for some women to direct their fury at all men, to lump them into one toxic bundle, rather than deconstruct the suffocating models of masculinity that have wrought this damage in the first place; models which, at their deepest level, have disconnected men from their hearts, stripped language of its full range of emotions, and prevented men from expressing their terror, grief or sadness, let alone allowed them to see women in all their humanity.

That is not to ignore individual responsibility, but more to probe the systems and structures that brought us to this historic tipping point.

'Are we going to fire every man?' Eve Ensler asked me rhetorically when we spoke via Skype. 'Are we going to put every man in prison? Are we going to punish every man? What is going to be the process by which we transform patriarchy?

'I've always said that men are . . . equally tyrannised by the patriarchy, sometimes more damaged by it, because at least women got to keep their hearts intact. Men have been removed from their tenderness, their tears; the centre of their own beings.

'So this is a really critical question for men. What are men going to do to help themselves break out of patriarchy and come into a new system where they get to be tender, loving, caring, heart-opened, feeling beings?'

18

India's daughter

*The human face has limited space. If you fill it with
laughter there will be no room for crying.*

ROHINTON MISTRY, *A FINE BALANCE*

Leslee Udwin never set out to spark a global movement, nor to
be showered with prestigious awards. She simply wanted to direct
her own film after years of working as an actress and producer.

The documentary she chose to direct—*India's Daughter*—
would prove her first and last. Not because the film was banned
in India (which it was), or because it failed to resonate around
the world (which it did, garnering numerous awards, including
Amnesty International's best documentary of the year and the
Peabody Award), but because Udwin was utterly transformed
by her experience making the film. What had previously been
a comfortable life was now supplanted by a higher purpose: to
revolutionise global education.

You may have seen *India's Daughter*, but even if you haven't you are probably aware of the gang rape, torture and murder of 23-year-old medical student Jyoti Singh in Delhi on the night of 16 December 2012.

Singh had boarded a bus in the south of the Indian capital that night with her friend Awindra Pandey after going to an evening screening of *Life of Pi*. It was 9.30 pm and they were met on the bus by six drunken men on a 'joyride' demanding to know why a woman was out so late with someone who was neither her husband nor brother.

An argument ensued and Pandey was beaten, gagged and knocked unconscious. Singh was dragged to the back of the bus, gang-raped, penetrated with a rusted iron rod and disembowelled. Along with Pandey's body, she was then dumped, half naked, from the moving bus and found at about 11 pm by a passer-by.

For two weeks, Jyoti Singh clung to life in a Delhi hospital, before being transferred to the Mount Elizabeth Hospital in Singapore on 26 December. Two days later she succumbed to her catastrophic injuries. Her last words to her mother were: 'Sorry, Mummy, I gave you so much trouble.'

When news broke of this appalling crime, India erupted in the largest and most sustained protests against gender-based violence ever seen in the country. Thousands of demonstrators clashed with police in Delhi, while tens of thousands more—women (and men too) of every creed, class, caste, community, religion and age group—took to the streets in Kolkata, Mumbai, Bengaluru, Chennai and other major urban centres, braving physical injury from police, arrest and the biting cold of winter.

'India has always had a dubious fame for being a place where women are harassed, threatened, groped, violated, abused, raped, stabbed, burnt, hanged and melted by acid,' wrote Delhi-based

Mitali Saran in *Walking Towards Ourselves*, a collection of essays written by Indian women writers and edited by Australian Catriona Mitchell. 'But somehow we never got a national conversation going about it until December 2012.'

The protesters' example was then taken up in neighbouring Nepal, Sri Lanka, Pakistan and Bangladesh, where violence against women had also long been a fact of daily life.

Leslee Udwin was at home in England when she heard the reports from Delhi. She left almost immediately for India, determined to fund the film on her own coin, although the BBC would later provide her with 40 per cent of the financing.

Like anyone who read those reports from India, the Israeli-born, South African-raised filmmaker was horrified. What drew her to the Subcontinent, however, was not the brutality of the attack itself, as shocking as it was, but the wave of furious protest that had begun to grip the largest democracy in the world.

'I just thought—very naively, looking back—that this was the beginning of the end of violence against women,' she tells me when we meet in Melbourne in November 2018. 'I thought this would spark a world movement because of the passion and commitment to change, and because these protests went on for over a month.'

A woman of warmth and irrepressible energy, Leslee Udwin had long understood activism. At the age of twelve, she'd mounted a one-girl protest at her Jewish religious school in Johannesburg after discovering on her first day of school that the Jewish morning prayer—Shacharit—invited boys and men to praise God for not having made them female. (Yes, the same prayer I might have recited as a boy.) Udwin was so enraged she stormed into her rabbi's office and said, 'You know what, Rabbi? You can take your Jewish Torah and shove it up your arse.' She was expelled immediately.

Udwin was brought up to be strong. As a child, her father had treated her as a boy for the simple reason that that was what he'd wanted: a son. Instead, he was given two daughters, and on the day Leslee, his second daughter, was born he'd danced a jig of happiness in the hospital ward after being told—mistakenly—that his wife had just given birth to a boy. (Udwin says this story might be apocryphal, but that it speaks, nonetheless, to her father's strong biases.)

Six years later, Udwin came to know first-hand the multifaceted trauma of sexual assault. At eighteen she was raped by an acquaintance, but never considered reporting the incident. 'At that time,' she says, 'in terms of maturity, confidence and self-esteem, I was what I would want every young girl to be—empowered and confident. And yet I didn't tell anybody about that rape for twenty years.

'It wasn't because dishonour and shame would have been heaped upon my family. It was because I was absolutely convinced that everyone would say, "You idiot. What did you think you were doing? You went to a guy's place who told you he was having a barbecue party and then you got there and no one else was there. Why didn't you turn on your heels and leave?" I didn't because he told me that everyone was coming to the party later. Then he dragged me into the house and raped me. I thought he was going to kill me.'

That was in 1975. Thirty-seven years after this event, Udwin flew to India with permission to interview Jyoti Singh's rapists in Delhi's Tihar Jail. Before her meeting with them, she wanted first to interview other men convicted of rape. 'I didn't want to find myself physically assaulting [Jyoti Singh's attackers],' she tells me now. 'That's what I feared I would do when I saw them, because I'd suppressed my own rape for twenty years.'

One of her first interviews was with a man named Gaurav, convicted of forcing himself on a five-year-old girl. 'He took me through what he did to this girl,' Udwin says. 'How he took her from both sides, held his hand over her mouth, but left her nose free so she could breathe. He told me everything he'd done to this little girl. Described her in such detail that I could see her.

'Then, at a certain point, I said—and this is the most chilling moment I've ever experienced in my entire life—I said, "Gaurav, I really need you to help me now. I need you to explain to me how you go from thinking these thoughts and looking at this tiny, fragile girl [to] actually acting on it." And he looked at me like he'd never seen such a fucking idiot in his entire life and he said, "She was a beggar girl, her life was of no value."'

That was the insight—in all its violent eloquence—that Udwin took with her into her 31 hours of interviews with Jyoti Singh's rapists: that Indian men—just like men around the world—are programmed from the earliest age to view females with disdain and derision, no matter what the law has to say about it.

'It would have been easier to process this heinous crime if they had been deranged monsters, rotten apples in a barrel,' Udwin says. 'But the truth couldn't be further from this. These rapists were ordinary, apparently normal men. It is society itself and our shared culture when it comes to attitudes to women that is responsible for these men and for their actions. It is the barrel that is rotten, and the barrel rots the apples.'

Read the words of the uneducated Mukesh, one of Jyoti Singh's rapists, and it is all here—the deep-seated misogyny, the lack of remorse, the self-justification: 'A decent girl won't roam around at nine o'clock at night. A girl is far more responsible for rape than a boy . . . When being raped, she shouldn't fight back. She should just be silent and allow the rape. Then they'd have dropped her off after "doing her", and only hit the boy.'

Read the words of the educated M.L. Sharma, one of the rapists' defence lawyers: 'That girl was with some unknown boy who took her on a date. In our society, we never allow our girls to come out from the house after . . . 8.30 in the evening with any unknown person. You are talking about man and woman as friends. Sorry, that doesn't have any place in our society. We have the best culture. In our culture, there is no place for a woman.'

Read the words, too, of another defence lawyer, A.P. Singh: 'If my daughter or sister engaged in pre-marital activities and disgraced herself and allowed herself to lose face and character by doing such things, I would most certainly take this sort of sister or daughter to my farmhouse, and in front of my entire family, I would put petrol on her and set her alight.'

#

India is the birthplace of four world religions (Hinduism, Buddhism, Jainism and Sikhism), home to several hundred languages, seat of the old Mughal Empire, staging post for the British East India Company, and dwelling place for a multitude of deities, including formidable, bare-breasted goddesses who were once able to create and destroy the universe. And yet for all its diverse wonders and ancient wisdoms, India is also one of the most dangerous countries in the world for women.

'India is at war with its girls and women,' wrote Dr Deepa Narayan, the eminent Indian writer and one of *Foreign Policy* magazine's 100 Leading Global Thinkers, in an opinion piece for *The Guardian* published in April 2018.

[The country] can arguably be accused of the largest-scale human rights violation on Earth: the persistent degradation of the vast majority of its 650 million girls and women. Our oppression starts innocuously: it occurs in private life, within families, with girls being locked up in their own homes. This everyday violence is the product of a culture that bestows all power on men, and that does not even want women to exist. This is evident in the unbalanced sex ratios at birth, even in wealthy families.

According to the National Crime Records Bureau, nearly 340,000 crimes against women were committed in 2016, more than 10 per cent of them rape.

In the aftermath of the outcry over Jyoti Singh's death, the Indian government established a three-member committee—headed by Justice J.S. Verma, a former Chief Justice of the Supreme Court—to recommend amendments to the Indian criminal code. The committee found that although equal rights and dignity for women had been enshrined in the Indian constitution, the constitution was being violated daily. Yes, women were now an integral part of the new economy. They were finding levels of independence undreamt of by their mothers and grand-mothers—working as auto-rickshaw and taxi drivers, judges and lawyers, actors and singers, entrepreneurs and reporters; reading Shakespeare and Milton, and graduating in huge numbers from colleges and universities; starting women's magazines, writing poems, forming protest movements, agitating for new legislation.

But they were also being groped and harassed and threatened on the streets, in buses and trains, at night-time and in broad daylight. They were being raped at home and in public, and, when they reported it—which most were too terrified to do—they were often subjected to demeaning two-finger medical examinations and humiliating cross-examinations in court: a double trauma that almost always resulted in social ostracism and disgrace. (Survivors of rape in India are known as *zinda laash*—living corpses.)

Despite the practice being outlawed, widows were still self-immolating on their husbands' funeral pyres, such was the stigma—and poverty—attached to women whose husbands had died. Female foetuses were still being aborted or dumped; girls were still being married off to older widowed men; women were still being regularly stalked and, often, disfigured in acid attacks for spurning suitors, rejecting marriage proposals or denying dowries—because, as the committee reported: 'The attacker cannot bear the fact that he has been rejected and [so] seeks to destroy the body of the woman who has dared to stand up to him.'

The crimes against children were no less monstrous, with 44,000 children going missing each year, many of them girls abducted by organised crime syndicates and forced into paedo-phile, sex trafficking and organ transplant networks.

According to the Association for Democratic Reforms, there were also—as of 2013—at least 48 members of parliament across India with cases against them relating to crimes against women, one-quarter of whom were members of the ruling Bharatiya Janata Party (BJP).

Between 2008 and 2013, political parties preselected for state elections at least 27 political candidates previously charged with rape. Hundreds more faced other criminal charges, including assault, causing 'miscarriage without consent', 'wrongful confine-ment', 'procuration of a minor girl', 'importation of girl from foreign country' and 'kidnapping or abducting child under ten years of age'.

This was obviously not what Mahatma Gandhi, the leader of India's independence movement, envisaged for his country. 'Woman is the companion of man, gifted with equal mental capacities,' he proclaimed in one of his many stirring speeches before the country was freed from British rule.

> She has the right to participate in the minutest details in the activities of man, and she has an equal right of freedom and liberty with him.
>
> She is entitled to a supreme place in her own sphere of activity as man is in his. This ought to be the natural condition of things and not as a result only of learning to read and write. By sheer force of a vicious custom, even the most ignorant and worthless men have been enjoying a superiority over woman which they do not deserve and ought not to have.

This is where Leslee Udwin comes in. After making *India's Daughter*, Udwin decided to launch Think Equal, a global initiative aimed at introducing into every school in the world a program designed to transform mindsets through social and emotional learning in children from three to six years old. (By January 2017, the program had been piloted in 147 schools in fifteen countries.) Skills like empathy, critical thinking, self-regulation, collaboration, appreciation of diversity and emotional intelligence are all being taught at the very time the young brain is still forming neural pathways.

This has become Udwin's life's purpose: nothing less than changing the world.

'The [educational] program is incredibly simple,' she explains. 'It's so simple that one wonders how in God's name we haven't done this until now. It takes as its premise that the education system we have is not fit for purpose. It was designed in—and for—the Industrial Revolution, and it hasn't really been revised in more than 200 years.

'The first question I ask an education minister when I sit down with them is, "How can you, who has a duty of care to the children in your country, say that it's compulsory for your children to learn mathematics when we have computers and artificial intelligence coming, and yet it's optional for your children to learn how to have healthy relationships?"

'It's a no-brainer, right? So what we're saying is that there's a missing subject, especially in the early years, that bolsters a child and gives a child the tools and life skills so that they don't grow up to rape, bully, become addicted to substances or commit suicide.'

It's no use believing parents can address these problems, Udwin says, because, all too often, they've been subjected to the same cultural programming as their children. 'We're saying as a world that is the parents' job, but what a naive, negligent thing to think. Parents are often grossly incapable of doing it because they're mired in discrimination too, so all they can do is pass that discrimination on down the line.'

Who taught Gaurav that a five-year-old beggar girl had no value? Who led Jyoti Singh's rapists and murderers to believe that this young woman could be discarded like scrap metal? Obviously the culture in which these men had grown up; the same culture that celebrated the birth of a male child over a female, and then entrenched that attitude inexorably throughout a person's life.

As the Verma Committee observed: 'Boys are conditioned to believe that power and violence reside unchallenged in their bodies, [while] girls are brought up to uphold notions of traditional values and virtues to protect family honour. Boys are also expected to protect that honour and control girls and women.'

The committee found that 'touching, harassment and forced intercourse' were all regarded as 'normal to masculinity' across the country, and that the use of force was not only 'normal' but also 'essential and ideal'.

'All these are constructs of patriarchy, which men use to negotiate power or dishonour somebody else,' the committee said.

This is not just true of India, or Indian culture, of course. This is the mindset that has prevailed around the world, whether you happen to have been raised in India or in the Middle East or the affluent west, still steeped as it is in centuries of Judaeo-Christian moral thinking. It is the alphabet soup of patriarchy that gets served to us every day, whether we know it or not.

'Almost every culture is programmed against the value of girls,' Udwin says. 'That is common to every single culture in the word. If it weren't, we wouldn't have Kavanaugh and Trump. They're just another expression of those rapists, another form of the same thing.

'So in order for me to see you as an equal, I need to be taught various values, competencies and skills. I need to be able to see things from your point of view, and empathy is the glue that sticks it altogether. So I need to practise empathy. I need to be inclusive. I need to be able to problem-solve because I need to be able to see the differences between us and not see these as a problem. It's the right of every child to have this foundation, this nurturing, this learning.'

#

Jyoti Singh was quite possibly the perfect daughter, before her death helped alter the course of Indian history. (She would become known as Nirbhaya, 'the fearless one'.)

Nirbhaya was born into a desperately poor family and from the time she was a little girl her ambition was to become a doctor.

'Papa, whatever money you've saved for my wedding,' she once told her father, 'use that to educate me.'

That's precisely what he did, selling the family's ancestral lands to pay for her university fees.

Nirbhaya not only wanted to be a doctor, she wanted to build a hospital on those ancestral lands, and in pursuit of those goals she studied all day, then worked from 8 pm to 4 am at an international call centre, before snatching a few hours' sleep. 'A girl can do anything,' she often told her parents.

At the time of her death, Nirbhaya had six months of her internship to complete before qualifying as a doctor. As her mother recounted in *India's Daughter*, 'She said, "Mum, Dad, now you don't have to worry anymore. Your little girl is a doctor. Now everything will be fine. It seems that God didn't like this. He ended everything there."'

Certainly, for Nirbhaya, that was the case—but not for the hundreds of millions of Indian girls and women who are now witnessing the eruption of the #MeToo movement in their country.

In September 2018, almost a year after the movement ignited in Hollywood, Tanushree Dutta, an Indian actress and former Femina Miss India Universe, accused celebrated Indian actor, writer, filmmaker and philanthropist Nana Patekar of groping her on the set of the film *Horn 'Ok' Pleassss* in 2008. Then, after she'd objected to his behaviour, he mobilised a group of men to prevent her driving out of a car park. Dutta was so shaken by the incident that she abandoned the film, then the industry, then the country, emigrating to the United States and into a life of relative obscurity.

Her allegations against Patekar, which she made public a decade later, provided the spark and kindling for India's #MeToo movement. It was no accident that Dutta's allegations against Patekar coincided with the incendiary US Senate Judiciary Committee hearings into Brett Kavanaugh's confirmation, where the testimony of a woman was once again overwhelmed by the denials of a man.

'Of course, everyone was discussing that,' said Rituparna Chatterjee, the Indian journalist who decided to compile and document a list of accusations against prominent Indian men. 'The thing in my mind was, I know this guy. I've met this guy. I've met this guy over and over again . . . We've faced violence, including verbal violence, all our lives. Somewhere, I think, we've snapped.'

No sooner had Dutta revealed her experience with Patekar than Indian Twitter erupted with accusations of alleged sexual misconduct: first against a stand-up comic—he was accused of masturbating on a colleague—then prominent journalists, actors, directors, advertising executives. (And, yes, India now has a 'shitty media men' list like America.)

On 8 October 2018, the allegations reached the highest echelons of the Indian government when journalist Priya Ramani accused M.J. Akbar, the country's junior foreign minister and a former confidante of the late Indian prime minister Rajiv Gandhi, of having harassed her when he was a newspaper editor and she a 23-year-old reporter.

'You were as talented a predator as you were a writer,' she said, before twenty other women came forward to accuse Akbar of sexual harassment and misconduct during his newspaper career.

If every sexual predator had his modus operandi, then M.J. Akbar's looked as though it might have come directly from Harvey Weinstein's playbook: purported invitations to women to discuss work in hotel rooms, arriving at the door in his underpants or bathrobe, followed by propositions and groping.

A few days after resigning his position in Narendra Modi's government, M.J. Akbar launched criminal defamation proceedings against his principle accuser, claiming she had 'wilfully, deliberately, intentionally and maliciously' defamed him. Akbar retained no fewer than 97 lawyers to fight his case.

Akbar's response couldn't have been more different from that of stand-up comedian Utsav Chakraborty, accused of sending unsolicited lewd pictures and messages to women and girls. After a flurry of denials, Chakraborty then issued a belated apology on Twitter.

'It's a little too late now,' he wrote, 'but I am sorry. I really am. The past 24 hours were a crucible. I faced a very scary personal truth. I can't think of myself as a victim anymore. Please tell me what to do now. How to make things right? I don't want anyone to be hurt anymore.'

19

Tenderly, gently

*And now we welcome the new year, full of things that
have never been.*

RAINER MARIA RILKE

My late friend Neil Roberts spent more time than any man I've
ever known exploring the boundaries of masculinity.

As an artist and human being he was a gentle giant among men,
a warm-hearted, brilliant and creative force who challenged the
way we thought and felt about everyday objects and the memories
they contained: a piece of wood, an old garden tool, a shard of
glass, a length of rope, a bicycle wheel—all of them grist for his
prodigious mill. Up until his sudden death in 2002, he was always
looking for the hidden meaning of things, fragments of history,
human traces that told us stories about ourselves.

In one of his exhibitions, Roberts unstitched footballs then
flattened them out and re-presented them as flower petals, so that

they would appear as both floral arrangements and a study of the masculine force and energy contained inside those once bloated, leathery bladders. In the late 1980s, amid the corporate madness of a Western Australian political scandal, he strung two words in neon across the Perth skyline: *Tenderly, gently.*

Although physically tall and imposing, Roberts was as tender and gentle a man as you could meet. In his company men dropped their guard and women could be intimate without ever feeling threatened.

He was the first man I ever knew who deliberately crossed the road at night to avoid walking behind or towards a woman on her own. Somewhere deep in his marrow, he understood women's fear, and wanted to shoulder some of the responsibility for it.

#

(Female friend to author): *When I was in my early twenties I had a job in a bookshop that didn't close until midnight. I couldn't afford a taxi so that meant getting the late bus home and then walking to my block of flats a few streets away.*

I was young and pretty fearless in the way that most young people are, but I did get spooked if a man got off at the same stop and walked behind me. My usual strategy for dealing with this was to pretend I lived somewhere close by and hide in a front garden or driveway until I felt confident the threat had passed.

One night it took me a bit longer to register the heavy footsteps behind me, but just before the panic set in a loud and kind voice said, 'I'm just letting you know that I'm going to pass you now.'

I have never forgotten the kindness of this particular stranger, nor ceased to marvel about his sensitivity and awareness of my feelings.

#

To observe Neil Roberts was to witness a man forever fascinated by what it meant to be a good son, a good husband, a good father, a good brother, a good friend. To observe his work was to witness—as Deborah Clark, former curator of the National Gallery of Australia, said—a man investigating the depths of 'masculinity, its culture, its rituals, its nonsense, and the fantastic possibilities of its transformation'.

Maybe this struggle between the sexes will never be put to rest. Maybe, in the unfathomable reaches of the male psyche, men have always been frightened of women—or at least frightened of the *feminine* qualities within themselves: those qualities that point inwards, to that place where our deepest feelings are lodged, but which centuries of masculine culture have repressed or removed.

Perhaps, this is the place where violence against women begins: in the shutting down of this inner world where relationships and connection truly reside, because the models we've been given for manhood fail to recognise a fundamental truth, which is that nothing meaningful in life ever happens without the ability to be vulnerable.

Nearly 25 years ago I interviewed Dr Peter O'Connor, a Melbourne-based family therapist, Jungian psychotherapist and expert on male anxieties, fantasies and fears, and his ideas feel as relevant today as they did then.

O'Connor had counselled thousands of men in his career and had written bestselling books like *Understanding the Mid-Life Crisis*, which explores how men are all too often at the mercy of their logic and reason. They operate almost always in the external world, where occupation remains a cornerstone of their identity, and where the compulsion to know, to be right, to be pragmatic and in control, especially of emotions, is their constant companion.

O'Connor believed this severed a man's internal life from his external life because the terror of being overwhelmed by feelings was simply too much. This was the heart of men's rage, whether expressed through murder, rape, domestic violence, suicide, alcoholism, reckless driving or simply sullen withdrawal from the world. If men attacked—or were in conflict with—women in the outer world, it was because there was a conflict within their own psyches towards their feminine qualities. They'd been raised to reject or scorn the feminine, so why should it be surprising that they would then grow into men who disrespected women, who saw them as less than fully human?

'Men are actually terrified of women because they're terrified of themselves,' O'Connor told me. 'They're terrified of being swallowed up by women. They're terrified that somehow they'll lose control, or that they'll actually get in touch with some feelings when they're with women.

'So for men to be liberated from their own oppression, which manifests itself in the oppression of women, they must turn in, not out. Male liberation can only be born out of the integration and inner union of masculine and feminine.'

It is my strong belief that a lot of men, today, are desperate to transform, and/or be part of the process that transforms other men; to travel as far from their fathers and grandfathers as possible.

I'm thinking here of many of my daughters' male friends who've done just that—young men who rejoice at the fact that the women in their lives are empowered, and who see nothing unmanly about acknowledging their own feminine qualities.

I'm thinking of men like singer Jimmy Barnes, one time exemplar of the hell-raising, hard-drinking Australian male, who, through his confessional writings and one-man show, has sought to redefine a model of manhood based on the courage and strength it takes to be vulnerable. I had dinner with Barnes two years ago and all he could talk about was the liberation that came from being brave enough to go to the centre of his own anguish.

If we care to look—and I think we should—there are men everywhere trying to self-correct. Well-known men like British actor Benedict Cumberbatch, who now refuses to take roles if his female co-stars are paid less. Unknown men like Jakson Elfring, the young diesel mechanic from rural Victoria who published a four-and-a-half-minute video on Facebook in July 2018, decrying Australia's culture of violence towards women. He urged men to set an example of common decency for each other instead of hurling abuse at women who dared to call out gender violence for what it is.

'Someone needs to stand up and start saying something,' he said in a post that, at the time of writing, had been viewed by 2.4 million people. That might start, he suggested, by men showing respect for their mothers, and by adhering to three of the easiest words in the English language: No means no.

'If you can't live by that,' he said, 'there's something wrong with ya.'

> The rape culture here in Australia . . . is shocking. It starts with a joke at work or a text message, or it can be something you tag your mate in on Facebook. Or just as easy as little comments like, 'I saw this sheila on the weekend, she's a slut.'
>
> It's gotta stop. That's crap. If I ever hear my boys say something like that I will not be happy. Stand up to your mates. If you hear them saying this stuff, you need to tell them that that's not acceptable. And don't back down if they start getting cranky. Back yourself, and say something, otherwise this is never going to stop.

Models of self-correction can be found in men like Jakson Elfring, in the parched flats of rural Australia, and men as far from here as possible, in the frozen wastes of Iceland, where it is now illegal to pay women less than men, and where Canadian journalist Liz Plank travelled in April 2018 to meet arguably the most progressive men on the planet.

Plank: So you all want to smash the patriarchy?

First man: Yes.

Plank: Is it totally normal for men to be feminists?

Second man: It is now. It wasn't. It was a negative. But, now, if you're not a feminist, you're in the Stone Age.

Third man: I have no idea how I became a feminist. I have no idea where these ideas come from, but I suppose it's just a matter of being decent.

Plank: So what's your advice to men?

Fourth man: Don't be afraid to listen.

First man: Embrace it because it benefits everyone.

Fifth man: If you are not having half the population taking part in society, society will not grow as fast as you would like. Gender equality should be as normal as drinking water.

Despite the recent scandal gripping his government, this model for self-correction is embodied by men like Canadian prime minister Justin Trudeau, an unabashed feminist who introduced the first gender-balanced cabinet in his country's history, as well as the first 'gender trade agreement' with Chile, one that seeks to foster female participation in the economies of both nations, encourage female entrepreneurship, and remove gender-related barriers that limit or distort trade. Since assuming office in 2015,

Trudeau has regularly encouraged men to get behind equality, 'not just because it's the right thing to do, or the nice thing to do, but because it's the smart thing to do'.

It's in men like Ed Yong from *The Atlantic* and David Leonhardt of the *New York Times*, who in their stories try always to quote female experts in their field, be it foreign affairs, business, political science, neuroscience . . .

It's in men like British children's writer Ben Brooks, who wants to redefine masculinity for young boys; American young adult fiction writer Brendan Kiely, who believes the rise of Trump is a wake-up call for all male authors; and British writer and illustrator Ed Vere, whose latest picture book for three-to-seven-year-olds, *How to be a Lion*, employs the maxim that 'you don't have to roar to be heard'.

'We need to teach compassion, respect and empathy at an early, foundational age,' Vere told *The Guardian* in July 2018. 'If we can teach this to boys at around five, and demonstrate that being gentle, sensitive or emotionally engaged isn't a weakness, but part of being a fully rounded grown up man, then we're getting the message through to them before toxic attitudes have a chance to solidify.'

It's in men like the ones in North America—hundreds of them—who have signed an online petition organised by the website *Gender Avenger* vowing not to appear on all-male panels. It's in men in business like Robert Baker who, through his global human resources company Mercer, has been engaging corporate leaders for years on the moral and business case for gender equality, talking to them about the importance of listening and sharing and—here's a novel thought—giving up some power and privilege.

Another shining example of male improvement—despite the predictable outrage it caused—can be found in the ground-breaking new Gillette advertisement that challenges 'toxic masculinity'. It turns on its head the global company's old tagline, 'The Best a Man Can Get, with a campaign—and new tagline—tied to the #MeToo movement, 'We Believe: The Best Men Can Be.' Instead of excuses like 'boys will be boys', the ad says, 'we need to make a change . . . We need to hold other men accountable.'

It's there to be seen in men like Frenchman Michel Landel who, as chief executive of Sodexo, one of the world's largest multi-national corporations, arranged for 50,000 employees—men and women—to enrol in gender diversity training, encouraged paternity leave, and reconstituted his board and executive committee to achieve greater gender balance (38 per cent of Sodexo's board is now female and 43 per cent of the executive committee).

'I am a man, a husband, a father and a leader,' Landel says in Marie-Christine Mahéas's *Gender Balance: When Men Step Up*, explaining his commitment to gender equality.

All these facets foster a strong commitment towards the advancement of women . . . I am firmly convinced that gender balance issues go beyond a moral obligation and are more than just a 'women's issue'. A gender balanced workforce is a powerful driver of performance, innovation and operational effectiveness in organisations . . .

We need to fight all stereotypes and this starts with the words and phrases we use daily. The French language, for example, has the annoying habit of putting everything in the masculine form. I prefer the English practice of specifying 'he' or 'she'. Similarly, I prefer to systematically say 'women and men', rather than only 'men'.

These are details that shouldn't be taken lightly. If we don't change our behaviour, how can we move beyond the ingrained stereotypes that complicate our lives?

It's in men like the young fathers in rural Rwanda who, through a program called MenCare, have been learning over the past few years about birth control, maternal health, parenting and non-violent communication. It's mini-skirted men who've marched in Azerbaijan, Turkey and the Netherlands in solidarity with female victims of sexual violence, as well as men in Iran posting selfies in hijabs to express fealty to their veiled wives and female friends.

It's in a growing army of men who are allowing their little boys to cry when they're hurt, thereby encouraging the fullest expression of their softer sides.

It's in men who are now finally examining their behaviour, privately or in groups, and are in some instances—although not enough—apologising for how inappropriate they've been, how much they've tried to bolster their own self-esteem through sexual conquests, how little they've respected women, or looked out for them, or imagined themselves in their shoes, or remained bystanders to unacceptable behaviour. And in this new calculus of self-examination, they've begun to realise how far they are from where they'd like to be.

#

On 8 January 2018, Oprah Winfrey delivered a speech for the ages at the 75th Golden Globes in Los Angeles.

In accepting the Cecil B. DeMille award for outstanding contribution to entertainment, Winfrey managed to do three things at once. She captured perfectly the deep-rooted inequalities at the heart not just of the entertainment industry, but across all industries, blue collar and white. She sparked wild speculation regarding her own presidential ambitions. And, most importantly, she delivered a rousing message of hope to young women and girls everywhere in the face of sexual abuse and marauding male power.

'For too long, women have not been heard or believed if they dared to speak their truth to the power of those men. But their time is up. Their time is up,' she told her star-studded audience, most of whom were dressed in black to support the Time's Up campaign, aimed at ending sexual harassment and gender disparity.

She finished: 'So I want all the girls watching here and now to know that a new day is on the horizon. And when that new day finally dawns, it will be because of a lot of magnificent women . . . and some pretty phenomenal men, fighting hard to make sure that they become the leaders who take us to the time when nobody ever has to say "me too" again.'

Watching that speech from his Washington DC home was Steve Bannon, the right-wing ideologue who, five months earlier, had been forced out of Donald Trump's White House after playing an instrumental role in Trump's astounding election victory. Sitting next to Bannon was Josh Green, the national correspondent at *Bloomberg Businessweek* who was about to update his new book *Devil's Bargain: Steve Bannon, Donald Trump and the Nationalist Uprising.*

'It's a Cromwell moment,' Bannon, the so-called 'king of disorder', shouted at Green as he watched, red-faced, the parade of women in black dresses and listened to Oprah's speech. (Bannon was referring to the radical Puritans in the seventeenth century who overthrew the British monarchy.) 'It's even more powerful than populism,' he continued. 'It's deeper. It's primal. It's elemental. The long black dresses and all that—this is the Puritans. It's anti-patriarchy.'

For Steve Bannon, Oprah was the incarnation of this threat. 'You watch,' he said, 'the time has come. Women are gonna take charge of society. And they couldn't juxtapose a better villain than Trump. He is the patriarch. This is a definitional moment in the culture. It'll never be the same going forward . . . The anti-patriarchy movement is going to undo ten thousand years of recorded history.'

Steve Bannon might never have uttered a truer word. If patriarchy had a beginning, it might also have an end. If so, this might be the beginning of the end—a last stand at which, as Grayson Perry argued in *The Descent of Man*, there is a reframing of masculinity 'fit for a happy future [in which] perhaps we would be less likely to go to war, be more empathetic to the weak, be less bound up in the status of wealth and be more concerned about the reward of good relationships'.

This is a world for emancipated men, especially given that the ascent of women appears unstoppable. 'As men are falling, women are rising,' Maureen Dowd wrote in the *New York Times* on 16 December 2017. If that's true—and it might well be—it carries with it both terrifying and electrifying implications. Terrifying because there is nothing good about a broken man—not for himself, his children, his partner, his friends or his community. Terrifying also, because—as we have seen with Brexit and the election of Donald Trump—millions of working-class men (and women too) will blow up a system when they feel disempowered by forces beyond their control. Brokenness begets brokenness.

But it is beyond thrilling to imagine a new world in which the potential of female power, passion and ingenuity might be unleashed, as it has been to varying degrees in China, Rwanda, Botswana and Morocco over recent years, not to mention the recent American midterm elections when a record number of women were elected to Congress (thank you, Donald Trump).

In 1994, Rwanda lost nearly one million people during the genocide. A decade later, the country boasted one of the fastest-growing economies in the world—thanks in large part to female participation in the workforce and gender equality in political life. (At the time of writing, women hold 61 per cent of seats in the lower house of Rwanda's national legislature, compared to 29 per cent in Australia.)

Muhammad Yunus, the Bangladeshi social entrepreneur, Nobel Peace Prize-winner and father of microcredit, lends almost solely to impoverished women in the developing world, because he knows their families and communities will benefit more than if he extends loans to men.

Look for an image around the world today that inspires and delights, and cast your eye no further than New Zealand's prime minister, Jacinda Ardern: leading her country while pregnant; walking the halls of Buckingham Palace full-bellied and draped in a feathered Maori cloak; returning to work after giving birth while her partner, Clarke Gayford, remains at home to look after their baby girl; legislating paid leave for victims of domestic violence; pledging to get the country's homeless population off the streets and into shelters; offering refuge to the traumatised outcasts of Australia's deadly asylum seeker regime; smashing every conceivable glass ceiling, while showing in the process that there is a different way of exercising power—not by emulating the archetypal male values of domination, aggression and a win-at-all-costs approach, but through cooperation, connection, inclusion and sustainability. And all this well before her stunning display of leadership in the aftermath of the Christchurch terror attack.

Around the globe, the mighty force of female power is asserting itself, while at the same time women continue to be abused, commodified and dehumanised. The very week Donald Trump was heard bragging on the *Access Hollywood* tapes about grabbing women by the you-know-what, Regena Thomashauer's book *Pussy: A Reclamation* was hitting the *New York Times* bestseller list with its exhortation to reclaim true feminine power.

'Most women in the world are operating from a huge amount of scarcity and ignorance in our sensual lives—and our lives overall,' Thomashauser wrote. 'Women have been ignored for centuries. We were never the priority. Our hunger was never met.'

The #MeToo campaign is a symptom of this furious hunger, both ancient and contemporary and, as far as I can see, despite the fear and confusion roiling the sexes, the world is a far better place for its expression, especially if women can provide the moral leadership that has so sorely been missing from men.

When I spoke to Zainab Salbi in New York about her experience in Saddam Hussein's Iraq, about having been raped by her first husband, about the anger that fired her work among rape victims in war zones, she told me a story that demonstrated the kind of thinking that might inform this new moral governance.

Salbi had been working in a refugee camp in the border region between Afghanistan and Pakistan when two turbaned men approached her and her staff. 'They looked like the Taliban,' she says. 'The war was still going on and I thought, shit, these are Taliban members, they're coming to kill us, *to kill me*, because I'm a foreign woman.

'"We have to leave," she told one of her colleagues urgently, but her colleague replied that if they did that, they'd always be under suspicion and never be allowed back into the camp.

'So these men walked towards us and I was scared and my heart was palpitating . . . and they reached out and spread their arms and gave me their hands, and one man said, "I want to thank you. You're making our wives happy by helping them, something we haven't been able to do for a long time."'

Salbi had caught herself in her own act of prejudice. For all her adult life, she'd been joined to a lifelong struggle to help women, while avoiding casting women as victims. And yet, in her fight for dignity and equality, she'd come to regard all men as aggressors, including those she loved.

'Even my brother suffered from me,' she says, 'and my ex-husband [second husband] who was the kindest person . . . If he said something, I'd just lash out. "Oh, you men . . . the patriarchy." . . . And I realised at this moment that I'd become the oppressor myself, out of my own commitment to women's rights, out of my own self-righteous beliefs. I didn't even allow for the good man, or [the possibility] of seeing men in their complexities.'

Salbi began interviewing militia leaders in Congo, executioners in Iraq, rapists in Rwanda and soldiers in Bosnia, one of whom recounted to her his most painful experience of the war. It was not all the deaths he'd witnessed. It was not the burning. It was not the starvation. It was that he was unable to kill. He'd enlisted in the army, but he couldn't shoot another person, even when that other person was his enemy. 'And his own men laughed at his inability to kill,' Salbi recalls, 'and they made him the cook, which he was willing and happy to do. But the . . . trauma of his life came from his own friends making fun of him as the man who is not man enough.

'So what I discovered—and this is my call-out to women—is that we need to be aware that we don't, in this moment of rage and anger, lose our sight and become the oppressors. We've got to stay core to our values. We have the right to be angry, but how do we manage this anger and communicate this anger and process this anger to change the narrative and change the culture around us?'

Perhaps this is too much to ask right now, given all the injuries and rage, given all the confusion and hostility, given how far apart we all seem to be, and given the fact that the very exemplar for patriarchal aggression and arrogance bestrides the world from the White House.

I'd like to believe, though, that there's a legion of us men who know that our own liberation is joined to the liberation of women, who recognise that the triumphs and achievements of one cannot happen without the triumphs and achievements of the other, and that the next part of the women's movement is a men's movement that rejects so many of the old definitions of masculinity.

We've had the shake-up; now it's time for the wake-up. And I'd like to think there are enough of us men who are rousing from our slumber. By doing so, hopefully we will be helping a whole new generation of boys grow up in a more integrated way, where both their masculine and feminine qualities are celebrated, and where ideas around consent, mutuality, healthy communication and respect are first and second nature.

'Embrace sensitivity,' Clementine Ford beseeched her young son in Boys Will Be Boys. 'Don't let a world that's frightened of soft men succeed in breaking you. We have too many broken men. We need [future] men like you, men whose strength comes from being gentle.'

I'd like to believe, too, there are women who understand how the wellsprings of male anguish have brought us to this remarkable moment in time, who can see that most men want to be good and kind and honourable and that only jointly can we heal this collective wound of our conditioning.

As New Zealand prime minister Jacinda Ardern told the United Nations in September 2018, 'Me Too must become We Too [because] we are all in this together.'

We need new conversations and role models to light the way, and we need each other now, more than ever.

Acknowledgements

This book was researched and written over eight white-knuckle months in 2018: a race against time in what now seems like a timeless, ever-breaking global story.

What was a vast and complicated undertaking at the outset only grew more so by the day as the plot kept thickening and the dimensions kept expanding and intensifying.

Every writer says this—because it is true: there is no way you can face the isolation and fear of the blank page without the help of a number of people.

In my case, they are the ones who granted me interviews—on and off the record; who guided me towards the books, articles, research papers, podcasts, YouTube videos . . . that they thought I should be aware of; who offered me their homes in far-flung places (you know who you are); who cooked for me, brought me meals, sent me notes of encouragement, imbued me with their belief and, generally, raised my spirits, while also checking my levels of sanity.

So to Andrew Barnes, Eric Beecher, Steve Biddulph, Carolyn Biggs, Susan Bogle, Rachel Braunschweig, Tina Brown, Silvia Buhler, James Button, Jennifer Byrne, Rosalie Chapple, Paul and Jane Collings, Ian and Min Darling, Jeff and Genevieve David, Christopher Dean, Andrew Denton, Helen Garner, Ingrid Elenius, Jane Enter, Audette Exel, Jutka Freiman, Esther Gemsch, Vanessa Gorman, Melanie Greblo, Steve Gunther, Eleanor Hall, Jeremy Heimans, Jacqueline Hellyer, Rob Hirst, Libby Houston, Michael Kimmel, Natalie Lascelles, Andrew Lee, Jill Levy, Alan Lovell, Catharine Lumby, Jacqui McNamara, Marie-Christine Maheas, Monica Masero, Coleen MacKinnon, Robert Mercer, Catriona Mitchell, Monica Nakata, Josephine O'Brien, Cameron and Ilse O'Reilly, Lulu Pinkus, Michael Rennie, Joan Rolls, Arne Rubinstein, Jan Russell, Steve Sailah, Zainab Salbi, Marlène Schiappa, Tracey Spicer, Aimee Pedersen, Deborah Thomas, Chris Thomas, Marijcke and Peter Thomson, Leslee Udwin, David Williamson, Roxane Wilson, Alexandre Wilson and Avivah Wittenberg-Cox, my huge thanks for helping me more than you will ever know.

My special thanks also go to:

Susan Biggs and Miriam Hechtman for acting as my two principal (unpaid) researchers-at-large, and, by doing so, helping me cover enormous stretches of territory that I might never have stumbled across.

Richard Guilliatt and Paul Collings for all the whisky-soaked nights of challenging, deep and necessary conversation.

Anna Fienberg, Hall Greenland, Damien O'Brien and Fenella Souter for caring enough—and being devoted enough friends—to read the first draft, then provide the necessary feedback to save me from myself.

Jeremy Meltzer for all his inspiration, brotherly love and encouragement.

Katrina Strickland for setting this wild train ride in motion in the pages of *Good Weekend*.

Merran Morrison for all the things we learnt together over a lifetime.

My mother Barbara, sister Deborah and brother Daniel for their enduring love, support and belief.

My in-house editor at Allen & Unwin, Tom, and, particularly, structural editor Sarah Baker and copyeditor Ali Lavau (the two editors I always wanted) for all their editorial touches and insights.

My wonderful publisher Jane Palfreyman for believing that a man could—and should—write a book on this subject, and then for being brave enough to act on this belief.

My agent Jane Novak for being the best agent a writer could possibly hope for, for helping—at almost all times of the day—to lift my sometimes flagging spirits with her humour, clarity and confidence. And for helping to raise my head above the powerful currents of this story instead of drowning in the middle.

And, finally, my daughters Hannah and Jordan, whose intelligence, humour, compassion, integrity and love continue to inspire, nourish and delight me in countless ways.

References

Arndt, B., *The Sex Diaries*, Melbourne: Melbourne University Press, 2009

Atkinson, M., *Traumata*, Brisbane: University of Queensland Press, 2018

Atwood, M., *The Handmaid's Tale*, London: Jonathan Cape, 1986

Atwood, M., 'Am I a bad feminist?', *Globe and Mail*, 13 January 2018

Baldwin, J. & Peck, R., *I Am Not Your Negro*, New York: Vintage Books, 2017

Baird, J., ' Women are burning with a kind of cold fury', *Sydney Morning Herald*, 9 November 2018

Beard, M., *Women & Power: A Manifesto*, London: Profile Books, 2017

Bell, J., 'What Went Wrong With Men That 12 Million Women Said #MeToo?', *yes!*, 15 December 2017

Bergner, D., *What Do Women Want?*, Melbourne: Text, 2013

Bly, R., *Iron John: A Book About Men*, New York: Vintage Books, 1992

Biddulph, S., *Manhood: An Action Plan for Changing Men's Lives*, Sydney: Finch Publishing, 2002

Biddulph, S., *Raising Boys in the 21st Century*, Sydney: Finch Publishing, 2018

Biddulph, S., 'The trouble with men', *Sydney Morning Herald*, 4 April 2018

Bukowski, C., *On Love*, Edinburgh: Canongate Books, 2016

Chamorro-Premuzic, T., 'Why Do So Many Incompetent Men Become Leaders?', *Harvard Business Review*, 22 August 2013

De Beauvoir, S., *The Second Sex*, London: Vintage, 2011

Denton, A., 'Tim Winton', *Interview*, Channel 7, 27 June 2018

Despentes, V., *Fuck Me*, New York: Grove Press, 2003

Ensler, E., *The Vagina Monologues*, New York: Ballantine Books, 1998

Ensler, E., *Insecure At Last: A Political Memoir*, New York: Villard Books, 2006

Eugenides, J., *Middlesex*, London: Bloomsbury, 2003

Faludi, S., *Backlash: The Undeclared War Against Women*, London: Chatto & Windus, 1992

Faludi, S., *Stiffed: The Betrayal of the Modern Man*, London: Chatto & Windus, 1999

Farrell, W., *The Myth of Male Power*, New York: The Berkley Publishing Group, 1993

Farrell, W., *The Boy Crisis: Why Our Boys Are Struggling and What Can We Do About It*, Dallas, Texas: BenBella Books, 2018

Farrow, R., 'From Aggressive Overtures to Sexual Assault: Harvey Weinstein's Accusers Tell Their Stories', *New Yorker*, 10 October 2017

Fine, C., *Testosterone Rex: Unmaking the Myths of Our Gendered Minds*, London: Icon Books, 2017

Fisher, H., *Anatomy of Love: A Natural History of Mating, Marriage, and Why We Stray*, New York: W. W. Norton & Company, 2016

Ford, C., *Fight Like a Girl*, Sydney: Allen & Unwin, 2016

Ford, C., *Boys Will Be Boys*, Sydney: Allen & Unwin, 2018

Friedan, B., *The Feminine Mystique*, London: W. W. Norton & Company, 1974

Garner, H., *The First Stone*, Sydney: Picador, 1995

Gay, R., 'Louis C.K. and Men Who Think Justice Takes as Long as They Want It To', *New York Times*, 29 August 2018

Gerson, J., 'The Trouble with Teaching Rape Law', *New Yorker*, 15 December 2014

Graves, R., *The Greek Myths*, London: Penguin Random House, 2017

Greer, G., *The Female Eunuch*, London: MacGibbon & Kee, 1970

Greer, G., *The Whole Woman*, London: Doubleday, 1999

Greer, G., *On Rape*, Melbourne: Melbourne University Press, 2018

Hanson-Young, S., 'When Senator Leyonhjelm told me to "stop shagging men", I had to speak up', *The Guardian*, 29 June 2018

Harari, Y., *Sapiens: A Brief History of Humankind*, London: Penguin Random House, 2011

Heimans, J. & Timms, H., *New Power*, New York: Doubleday, 2018

Hirsi Ali, A., *Infidel*, New York: Free Press, 2007

Holland, J., *Misogyny: The World's Oldest Prejudice*, London: Constable & Robinson Ltd, 2006

Hussey, A., *Paris: The Secret History*, London: Viking, 2006

Jensen, R. 'What are the responsibilities of pro-feminist men in the Michael Kimmel case?', *Medium*, 7 August 2018

Jones, R. & Davies, E., *Under My Thumb: Songs That Hate Women and The Women Who Love Them*, London: Repeater Books, 2017

Kimmel, M., *Angry White Men: American Masculinity at the End of an Era*, New York: Nation Books, 2015

Kimmel, M., 'Getting men to speak up', *Harvard Business Review*, 30 January 2018

Kipnis, L., 'Has #MeToo gone too far, or not far enough? The answer is both', *The Guardian*, 13 January 2018

Kipnis, L., *Unwanted Advances: Sexual Paranoia Comes to Campus*, London: Verso, 2018

Kivel, P., *Men's Work: How to Stop the Violence That Tears Our Lives Apart*, Minnesota: Hazelden, 1992

Kristof, N. & WuDunn, S., *Half the Sky: How to Change the World*, London: Virago Press, 2010

Lee, B., *Eggshell Skull*, Sydney: Allen & Unwin, 2018

Leiter, B., 'Blaming the victim is apparently OK when the accused in a Title IX proceeding is a feminist literary theorist', *Leiter Reports*, 10 June 2018

Lerner, G., *The Creation of Patriarchy*, New York: Oxford University Press, 1986

Leser, D., *To Begin to Know: Walking in the Shadows of my Father*, Sydney: Allen & Unwin, 2014

Lloyd-Roberts, S. & Morris, S., *The War on Women: And the Brave Ones Who Fight Back*, London: Simon & Schuster, 2016

Mahéas, M. (ed), *Gender Balance: When Men Step Up*, Paris: Eyrolles, 2016

Mann, K., *Down Girl: The Logic of Misogyny*, New York: Oxford University Press, 2018

Marsden, J., *Secret Men's Business: Manhood, The Big Gig*, Sydney: Pan Macmillan Australia, 1998

Meltzer, J., 'Where is Men's Roar?', TEDx, December 2012

Miller, M., *Circe*, London: Bloomsbury, 2018

Mitchell, C. (ed), *Walking Towards Ourselves: Indian Women Tell Their Stories*, Melbourne: Hardie Grant, 2016

Montreynaud, F., *Love: A Century of Love and Passion*, Cologne: Benedikt Taschen Verlag, 1997

Moran, C., 'How To Tell The Bad Men From The Good Men', *The Cut*, 9 July 2018

Murakami, H., *Men Without Women*, London: Vintage, 2017

Narayan, D., 'India's abuse of women is the biggest human rights violation on Earth', *The Guardian*, 27 April 2018

O'Connor, P., *Understanding the Mid-Life Crisis*, Sydney: Pan Macmillan Australia, 1981

Palmieri, J., *Dear Madam President: An Open Letter to The Women Who Will Run the World*, London: Hodder & Stoughton, 2018

Perel, E., *Mating in Captivity: Sex, Lies and Domestic Bliss*, New York: HarperCollins Publishers, 2006

Perry, G., *The Descent of Man*, London: Penguin Random House, 2017

Peterson, J., *12 Rules for Life: An Antidote to Chaos*, Toronto: Penguin Random House, 2018

Porter T., 'A call to Men', TED, December 2010

Rees, L., *The Holocaust: A New History*, London: Penguin Random House, 2017

Roiphe, K., *The Morning After: Sex, Fear and Feminism*, New York: Little Brown & Company, 1993

Roth, P., *Portnoy's Complaint*, New York: Random House, 1969

Roth, P., *The Human Stain*, London: Jonathan Cape, 2000

Roupenian, K., `Cat Person', *New Yorker*, 11 December 2017

Rubinstein, A., *The Making of Men*, Sydney: Brio Books, 2013

Ryan, C. & Jethá, C., *Sex at Dawn*, New York: HarperCollins Publishers, 2010

Salbi, Z. & Becklund, L., *Between Two Worlds: Escape from Tyranny, Growing Up in the Shadow of Saddam*, New York: Gotham Books, 2006

Sennett, R., *The Corrosion of Character*, New York: W. W. Norton & Company, 1998.

Severson, K., 'Asia Argento, a #MeToo Leader, Made a Deal With Her Own Accuser', *New York Times*, 19 August 2018

Shannon, L., *A Thousand Sisters: My Journey into the Worst Place on Earth to Be a Woman*, Berkeley, CA: Seal Press, 2010

Slaughter, A-M., *Unfinished Business: Women, Men, Work and Family*, New York: Penguin Random House, 2015

Stone, M., *When God Was a Woman*, London: Virago Ltd in association with Quartet Books Ltd, 1976 (first published under the title *The Paradise Papers*)

Summers, A., *Damned Whores and God's Police*, Sydney: University of NSW Press, 2016

Thomashauer, R., *Pussy: A Reclamation*, Carlsbad, CA: Hay House, 2016

Watson, D., *The Bush: Travels in the Heart of Australia*, Melbourne: Penguin, 2014

Way, K., 'I went on a date with Aziz Ansari. It turned into the worst night of my life', *Babe*, 14 January 2018

Whipp, G., '38 women have come forward to accuse director James Toback of sexual harassment', *Los Angeles Times*, 22 October 2017

Whyte, D., *Consolations: The Solace, Nourishment and Underlying Meaning of Everyday Words*, Langley, WA: Many Rivers Press, 2014

Wilkinson, R. & Pickett, K., *The Spirit Level: Why Equality is Better for Everyone*, London, Penguin Books, 2009

Wittenberg-Cox, A., *How Women Mean Business*, Chichester: John Wiley & Sons, 2010

Wolf, N., *The Beauty Myth*, London: Chatto & Windus, 1990

Wolf, N., *Vagina: A New Biography*, London: Virago Press, 2012

Wood, C., 'We are told female anger is finding its moment. But I can't trust it', *The Guardian*, 18 December 2017

Index

David Leser is an Australian journalist, author and public interviewer. A former Middle East and North American correspondent he has been a journalist for 40 years and become widely known in Australia for his in-depth profiles and stories on social and political issues.

He has interviewed everyone from Meryl Streep, Germaine Greer and Ayaan Hirsi Ali to Gina Rinehart, Alan Jones and the Dalai Lama. David is the recipient of numerous awards for his journalism and his memoir *To Begin To Know: Walking in the Shadows of My Father*, was shortlisted for the National Biography Award in 2015.